Discovering
Lapidary Work
John Wainwright

Through the spirit of counsel
you do not hide away the talents
given to you by God, but, working
and teaching openly and with humility,
you faithfully reveal it to those who
desire to learn.
Theophilus
– Prologue to his Treatise on Divers Arts

MILLS & BOON LIMITED
London

First published in Great Britain 1971 by Mills & Boon Limited,
17–19 Foley Street, London WIA IDR

ISBN 0 263.51531.1

Filmset by Keyspools Ltd, Golborne, Lancs.
Made and printed by
C. Tinling & Co. Ltd, London and Prescot

Contents

Acknowledgements

I wish to acknowledge the assistance given by the many friends who have made this book possible.

First to Mr Kenneth Parkinson, F.G.A., without whose help I would never have cut my first stone and also for his kindness in loaning of photographs and specimens.

My thanks also to my headmaster, Mr A. J. Sinclair for making it possible for me to introduce a new craft into his school and also to my former pupils, David Prosser and Michael Pearman, who helped with the design and construction of the machines and are now themselves teachers of craftwork.
I am indebted to Mr George Witley who made the working drawings of our Mark I machine and to Mr R. Jones, F.G.A., not only for divulging his prospecting sites and much other valuable information, but also for the colour plate of fluorescent materials.

To my colleagues at school, members of the Kingston Lapidary Society, Messrs Gemstones of Hull for the loan of colour plates, and last but not least, to my publishers for their help and encouragement, I give my sincere thanks.

The extract from 'Theophilus, A Treatise on Divers Arts' is reproduced by courtesy of the University of Chicago Press.

Introduction

It has been apparent to me for some years that not all boys are attracted to either Metalwork or Woodwork as taught in schools, and this fact, together with the proposed raising of the school-leaving age, makes it essential that syllabuses be broadened. With these, and other considerations in mind, lapidary work was introduced into my Metalwork Room and has proved to be more than popular both during and outside teaching periods.

Although at present comparatively little practised in this country, it is a popular hobby in the U.S.A. where it has been estimated that "Rockhounds", as the devotees of the hobby are termed, are numbered in millions, subscribers to relevant periodicals by the hundreds of thousands, and clubs and societies by the hundred.

There is, however, a rapidly growing interest in home jewelry making arising in this country, and it can only be a short time before the hobby attains a widespread popularity. The first "Gem Club" in England, The Kingston Lapidary Society, was founded in 1964 in Hull by Mr Kenneth Parkinson, F.G.A., and within five years the club had a membership of 150, to which number it is now restricted. Similar clubs have been formed in various parts of the country, from North Yorkshire down to Hampshire. One has only to meet a member to become infected with the desire to learn more about this fascinating craft.

It is not only the desire for personal adornment, or the opportunity for the teenager to impress the opposite sex by presenting a piece of jewelry of his, or her, own making which stimulates their interest. There is the far greater thrill of finding out what a suitable piece of rock or mineral looks like when beautifully cut and polished.

The sense of achievement experienced by a child who cuts through a piece of rough agate, of uninteresting exterior, and releases its hidden beauty, imprisoned in the rock since the formation of the earth and now brought to view for the first time, millions of years after its formation, is only equalled by the satisfaction of the teacher who has made this possible.

As some measure of justification for writing this book, I would ask "What craft or hobby has so wide a range of appeal?" In my school workshop, boys and girls of 12 years and upwards derive as much satisfaction as do my Evening Class students, some of whom are over 65 years old.

The financial range is just as wide, the same basic processes being applicable to a piece of stone from the garden or an opal from

Australia. Whilst the more affluent or more mature workers may mount their opal in gold, the young people will use identical techniques when mounting their specimen in silver, nickel, copper, gilding metal or brass. In both cases, a thing of beauty has been produced which may be given away as a gift or worn with pride. It is not suggested that the making of pieces of jewelry is the sole end product of lapidary work. Many people derive great pleasure from polished collections of geological specimens or pebbles.

There can be few of us who have not walked along one of our beaches and admired, or collected, beautifully coloured pebbles, gleaming wet and shining, only to experience disappointment later when they have dried and become comparatively dull. The lapidary worker, with his skill and knowledge, can cut and polish them to a standard of perfection surpassing that of nature itself.

Present-day methods of producing plastics and synthetic materials are making an ever-increasing impact on life today. These materials undoubtedly have their place, but it is surely beneficial to encourage children to find out for themselves some of the hidden beauties of nature which cannot be surpassed by man's ingenuity or technology.

The present generation of young people will undoubtedly be faced with longer periods of leisure time than are their parents, owing to the trend towards shorter working hours and earlier retirement. In view of this recognised fact it is incumbent upon all teachers, whatever their subject, to ensure that the maximum benefit is derived from this free time. In introducing lapidary work the craft teacher is most assuredly educating for leisure.

Some of the equipment described in this book can be made without the facilities of a fully equipped Metalwork Room and all the operations can be carried out in the home workshop, garage or garden shed. I am certain that anyone who teaches the craft, or takes it up as a hobby, will derive as much satisfaction from it as I have done.

Prices quoted in the text were correct at the time of going to press but it may be advisable to check in manufacturers' catalogues beforehand.

All measurements in the text are in imperial units. The combination lapidary machine described in detail in Chapter 6 was made by some pupils in my school, so it seemed sensible to retain the actual measurements that were used. For those who will be working in metric units, however, there is a detailed conversion table in Appendix 2. Another strong reason for the retention of imperial units is that most lapidary manufacturers and suppliers will continue to use them because of the very important American market.

Identification of specimens

"Could I cut and polish a gemstone?" In asking themselves this question, many people may think that the creation of a gem from a piece of rough material is beyond either their capabilities or, possibly, their financial resources. I hope to prove that neither of these conditions applies to anyone who wishes to take up a hobby which, in addition to being enjoyable, can also be profitable to the amateur craftsman. The teacher who introduces the craft to children will find that it becomes the centre of an expanding circle of activities and interests.

Although lapidary work can be learned from books, undoubtedly the best method is to watch an expert, for, as I was once told by Ken Parkinson, "I can show you more in five minutes than I could describe in many pages of writing."

Fortunately, the craft is no longer regarded as highly secret; in fact the reverse is true, as members of lapidary societies all appear to be imbued with the sole idea of disseminating their knowledge and skills to any kindred spirit. Distance from the headquarters of a society is not an unsurmountable barrier. Naturally it is a great advantage to be able to attend their regular meetings, demonstrations and field trips, and to use the clubroom facilities, but the warmth of their welcome on the occasion of a holiday visit, together with the contacts made and subsequent correspondence, makes membership worth while. This has been my experience, for before joining the Kingston Lapidary Society, I explored many fruitless avenues in an effort to add this additional facet to the multi-faced craft of metalwork as taught in schools. It is intended that this book will save other people this trouble.

The first question which will arise in the teacher's mind is "Can the school afford it?" which is quite easily answered. This is a subject which any school would be well advised to consider, not only from the craft angle but also as an ideal basis for integrated studies. As lapidary work becomes established, the opportunities for correlation with other subjects become increasingly apparent; local studies, geography, geology, art, science and mathematics all becoming involved.

Once the initial outlay on equipment has been made, the subject becomes financially self-supporting, as both children and their parents are appreciative of the opportunity to purchase items of jewelry for a fraction of their value.

The amateur craftsman who takes up the craft as a hobby will appreciate the fact that a machine based on the one described in

Chapter 6 can be constructed for a very moderate cost, and will give him years of service.

Many varieties of gemstones bought in the rough are still comparatively cheap. Local sources of suitable native materials will be investigated in a subsequent chapter. Despite the fact that the price of silver has soared during recent years, the small amount used in the rings, brooches, pendants and other jewelry which beginners can make, still keeps the cost of the finished article to a very reasonable level.

The effects of working with a precious metal are soon reflected in the more traditional aspects of metalwork carried out by children. They soon realise the importance of working to very fine limits, for once they have completed their finished stone, they find that it is essential for the mount to fit exactly. The fact that they inevitably graduate to the use of silver, inculcates in them a feeling of importance which is soon translated into a sense of pride in their work; more and more care is taken, problems of design are studied, and their aesthetic appreciation is increased as each succeeding piece of jewelry is completed.

WHAT CONSTITUTES A GEMSTONE?

This is a difficult question to answer because so many considerations are involved. A wide range of different materials can be classified as precious or semi-precious stones, although some experts deprecate the use of the two terms and insist that all stones used in the making of jewelry should be termed gemstones. In identifying a specimen, it is sometimes necessary to repeat the question which opened so many editions of the Twenty Questions radio programme—"Is it animal, mineral or vegetable?" Rocks and minerals form the major portion of the lapidary's raw materials; amber, jet and the many beautiful fossilised and opalised woods are vegetable in origin. The animal kingdom provides us with pearls, shell, coral and ivory.

If asked to furnish a list of gemstones, the average person would probably commence with diamonds, rubies, emeralds, sapphires, pearls, before pausing, and then add perhaps a further six or seven before coming to a halt. A good gemmologist, however, could easily add another fifty names to the list and it has been truly stated that many people spend more money on gems and know less about them than on anything else which they buy.

In the early part of the last century, the secretary of the Geological Society of London compiled a list of some 250 known minerals. Today there are almost 2,000 different species but only about 5 per cent provide gem material. Gemstones may be either an individual or a composite of several minerals, usually termed rock, but two basic qualities are necessary for the constitution of a gem. These are beauty and hardness, two qualities which are natural, as opposed to what

most people would consider other essential requirements such as
rarity, scarcity or cost. This is a very common fallacy because both
scarcity and cost can be artificially created. On the other hand, there
are rare minerals which, lacking beauty, or being beautiful but too soft,
are never used as gems. The chief exception to this rule is, of course,
the precious opal, which is accepted as a gemstone despite its
comparative softness because of the exceptional beauty of its
colouring.

The colours of gems are synonymous with perfection of colour. We
speak of the blue of the sapphire, ruby red, the white fire of a diamond
and emerald green. This latter colour is frequently misunderstood, as
the emerald is the most valuable of all gems and many people do not
have the opportunity to examine closely an emerald of the finest water,
but once seen, it is a colour which is never forgotten.

These are, of course, the more exotic stones, renowned through the
ages for their beauty of colour. Equally beautiful, although in a
different way, is the chatoyancy of Labradorite and Tiger Eye, the
differing colours of the needles in Rutilated Quartz, the natural
pictures and patterns in agates, no two of which are ever similar, and
the fern-like inclusions in clear chalcedony, or moss agate as it is
commonly called, to mention but a few of the materials which are
cheap enough to use for the novice's first attempts.

All these possess the second quality of hardness in varying degrees,
and this is essential, because gems are created in order to be worn.
The late Ian Fleming chose as title for one of his James Bond adventures
Diamonds are for Ever and this is a true statement of fact, as diamonds
are virtually indestructible. Other gems, however, being of a lesser
degree of hardness, are liable to become scratched or chipped through
being rubbed or knocked whilst being worn. Hence, with the
exception of the opal, it is a fact that all the most expensive gems are
extremely hard.

DEGREES OF HARDNESS

When learning the properties of metals, students are told that the
definition of hardness is "resistance to scratching or abrasion", and
reference is made to the Brinell or Rockwell systems of degrees of
hardness. In consequence, they may find some difficulty at first in
understanding the accepted scale of hardness as applied to gemstones –
the Mohs's Scale.

Friedrich Mohs was a German mineralogist who lived from 1773 to
1839 and was the discoverer of the mineral named after him, Mohsite
(crystallised titanite of iron), but he is better known to the lapidary
worker for his scale of hardness in which he gave the hardest known
mineral, diamond, the value 10 and the softest mineral, talc, the
value 1.

Mohs's scale of hardness

Talc	1	Feldspar (Orthoclase)	6
Gypsum	2	Quartz	7
Calcite	3	Topaz	8
Fluorite	4	Corundum	9
Apatite	5	Diamond	10

This can easily be memorised by using the first letter of each mineral to form a simple mnemonic, *The Gem Class Finishes At Four. Question Time Clarifies Doubts.*

Unfortunately for the beginner, the numbers give no real indication of the hardness of the minerals, as the scale is purely arbitrary. Diamond (10) is not twice as hard as apatite (5), but thousands of times harder, and there is a greater degree of hardness between diamond and corundum than there is between corundum and talc.

The professional lapidarist, working as he most frequently does with specific gems, has rarely any need to identify specimens, as this is usually carried out by a gemmologist. Indeed, the identification of expensive gems is essentially a job for the expert in this field, as it calls for the use of expensive equipment by a highly skilled operator, and modern methods of creating synthetic gems have made testing extremely complex.

The gemmologist is virtually a combination of geologist, petrologist, crystallographer and chemist. The teacher who introduces lapidary work into school will soon find that he is inundated with queries, both from children and staff, as to the suitability for cutting and polishing of innumerable samples of pebbles and rocks.

By working with known gemstones, a superficial knowledge is soon acquired, and within a short time, the teacher will be able to recognise a considerable number of the more popular materials both in the rough and finished state, but it is advisable to know of some of the more simple methods of testing for identification.

ROCKS AND MINERALS

Lapidary materials consist mainly of rocks or minerals, and the aspiring lapidarist would be well advised to consult at least one of the many excellent books on elementary geology which are available, in order to acquire some background knowledge to assist in the identification of specimens.

Very briefly, a mineral is inorganic, and has a specific chemical composition with the constituent elements in a fixed proportion. Therefore, minerals can be represented by chemical symbols and these vary from the very simple, for example the letter C, the symbol for carbon, the element from which diamond is composed, SiO_2 (pure quartz) to some extremely complex formulae such as $3CaO.Al_2O_3.3SiO_2$, which represents one of the more common types of garnet.

CRYSTALS

When the word crystal is used by the layman in connection with jewelry, he is usually referring to colourless quartz or rock crystal, but the skilled lapidarist knows that most minerals occur in crystalline form.

Each of the molecules of a particular mineral are identical in shape, being held together by molecular attraction. Under favourable circumstances they may grow into perfect crystals, varying in weight from fractions of an ounce up to several tons, depending on the type of mineral and other considerations. These natural terminated crystals are identical in shape with their molecules and the natural faces have the appearance of a cut and polished stone. Unfortunately, perfectly formed crystals are comparatively rare, as interference with growth causes malformation or distortion. Tiny particles, examined under a powerful magnifying glass, will, however, reveal the basic shape.

Some knowledge of crystal structure assists the lapidary in deciding how to cut his material, as some minerals have strongly defined cleavage planes. The passage of light through the crystals of transparent gem material decides the best method of faceting the finished gem. As a basis for further study, it can be stated that there are six main crystal systems.

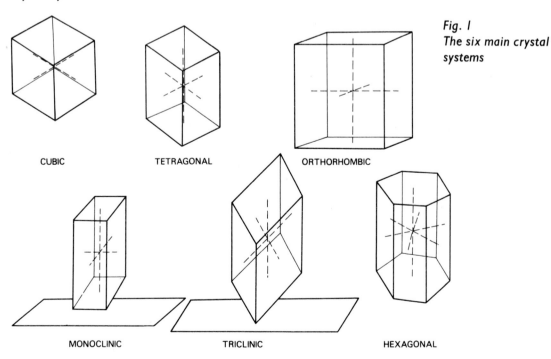

CUBIC   TETRAGONAL   ORTHORHOMBIC

MONOCLINIC   TRICLINIC   HEXAGONAL

Fig. I
The six main crystal
systems

Cubic
Has three axes of equal length which meet at right angles, thus forming a cube.

Tetragonal
The three axes meet in the centre at right angles but only two are equal in length, the third being either longer or shorter than the pair.

Hexagonal
Has four axes; three laterals of equal length which meet at angles of 60° in the centre and a fourth, at right angles to them, of a different length.

Orthorhombic
These crystals have three axes, all at right angles, and although they meet in the centre at right angles, each axis is of a different length.

Monoclinic
Crystals of this system have three unequal axes, two of which meet at an oblique angle whilst the third is at right angles to them.

Triclinic
Crystals have three unequal axes, all inclined to one another without forming a right angle.

Examples of gemstones with their appropriate crystal systems are as follows:

Cubic
Diamond, Fluorspar, Lapis Lazuli, Sodalite, Garnet, Spinel.

Tetragonal
Idocrase (Californian Jade), Rutile, Zircon, Scapolite, Scheelite.

Hexagonal
Apatite, Beryl, Corundum, Quartz, Rhodochrosite.

Orthorhombic
Barite, Chrysoberyl, Dumortierite, Iolite, Peridot, Topaz, Zoisite.

Monoclinic
Azurite, Diopside, Malachite, Orthoclase Feldspar, Epidote, Nephrite, Serpentine, Petalite.

Triclinic
Labradorite, Rhodonite, Turquoise, Kyanite, Plagioclase Feldspar.

TESTING FOR HARDNESS

The simplest way in which to test rough specimens is to scratch one
against another; the softer of the two will, of course, be marked by
the harder specimen. The human fingernail, approximately $2\frac{1}{2}$ Mohs,
will scratch Talc and Gypsum, but not Calcite (3), which can be
scratched by the edge of a penny (4). A good file is approximately 7
and will just mark some varieties of quartz, but for school work, it has
been found that most stones which will scratch window glass ($5\frac{1}{2}$) are
suitable for polishing.

With the growth of interest, more accurate methods of determining
the hardness of specimens may be thought desirable, and the best
method is to invest in a set, or part set, of hardness pencils. These are
minerals of specific hardnesses, mounted usually in a capped metal
holder, bearing the hardness number of the mineral, and may be
purchased in complete sets or individually. The pencil is drawn firmly
across the specimen under test, and if the specimen is marked, the
next lower numbered pencil is used and if this does not make an
impression, the number of the pencil gives the hardness. There are, of
course, exceptions to every rule and the most noteworthy in this
respect is Kyanite, a transparent mineral found in Kenya, Brazil, the
U.S.A. and Scotland, which varies from colourless to blues and greens
of varying intensity. The crystals of this mineral form themselves into
layers and the hardness is 5 Mohs along the layers but 7 across the
layers. Diamond also has a similar directional hardness but this is only
very slight.

It is, perhaps, advisable to insert a few words of caution regarding
hardness pencils, as it may not be apparent to the beginner that by
virtue of the manner in which they are used, they will soon be
damaged if tests are carried out indiscriminately. The points of the
lower grades, say 1 to 4, will be worn away quite quickly on many of
the specimens children will wish to test unless they remember to
start with the hardest pencil. In fact, for general use in schools, it is a
good idea for the children to make their own pencils in the most used
grades, 5, 6, 7, by the following method.

To make a hardness pencil
Chuck a piece of $\frac{3}{16}$ in. or $\frac{1}{4}$ in. diameter brass rod, say 5 in. long in the
lathe and after centring with a Slocombe drill, drill with a Letter B or
Number 17, respectively, to a depth of approximately $\frac{1}{4}$ in., thus
leaving a wall of some 6 thousandths of an inch thickness. The edge of
the hole is further reduced either by lightly filing the outside or
relieving the inside with a small scraper, after which the end of the
hole is annealed. A small wedge or conical piece of Apatite is then
inserted into the hole, leaving a sharp point projecting, after which
the wall of the hole is either burnished over or the hole filled with
solder to retain the stone in position. A flat can be filed on the rod,
stamped with figure 5 and after cleaning up, a No. 5 hardness pencil

has been made. A fragment of Feldspar will give No. 6 and a similar piece of Agate provides No. 7; these three will suffice to carry out most of the tests needed by the children in their searches for gem material. It must be emphasised to them that a sharp point or corner must be maintained on the pencils as even the hardest of materials if rounded off smoothly will not make a mark.

*Fig. 2
A hardness pencil
showing method of
construction*

SPECIFIC GRAVITY TESTING

The hardness test in itself cannot give a positive identification of any mineral, as there are many other considerations involved, and many minerals have similar hardness numbers. Consequently other tests must be applied and a simple test which can be carried out in any school is to ascertain the specific gravity of the mineral.

The specific gravity of a substance is its relative weight compared to the weight of an equal volume of water. A simple method is to weigh the specimen in grammes and calculate its volume by measuring the amount of water it displaces in either a measuring jar or a Eureka can. As one cubic centimetre of water weighs one gramme the specific gravity can then be calculated by dividing the weight of the stone by the weight of the water. For example, a purple stone weighing 8·72 grammes displaces 2·75 cubic centimetres of water which gives 3·17, the specific gravity of Fluorspar (Blue John).

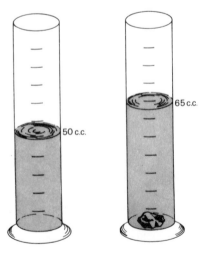

50 c.c.

65 c.c.

*Fig. 3
Ascertaining volume of
specimen by
displacement of water*

An alternative and more accurate method is to use Archimedes'
Principle, which states that a body immersed in a liquid is buoyed up
by a force which is equal to the weight of the liquid displaced. To
calculate the specific gravity of a specimen by this method, it must be
weighed on a chemical balance in order to ascertain its exact weight.
A beaker of water is next placed on a bridge which spans the pan of
the balance, without touching the pan or pan arms, and the specimen
is suspended by a thread from the arm and immersed in the water, any
air bubbles which may adhere to the stone being displaced by using a
small paint brush.

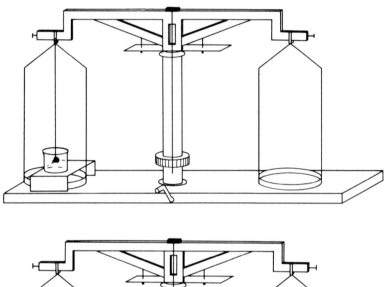

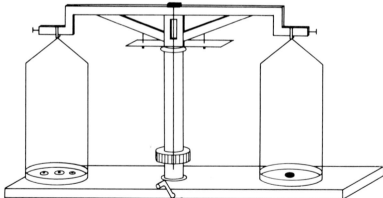

*Fig. 4
Ascertaining volume of
specimen by
Archimedes principle –
weighing in air and
water*

Upon weighing the stone again, there will be an apparent loss in
weight and the specific gravity is calculated by dividing the true
weight by the apparent loss in weight. For example, a black stone
which weighs 6 grammes in air weighs only 3·5 grammes in water. The
apparent loss in weight is therefore 2·5 grammes. Dividing 6 by 2·5
gives the answer 2·4, which is the specific gravity of obsidian.

There are, of course, other methods of calculating specific gravity, but
there may be occasions when weighing and calculating are inconvenient
and in such cases, a rapid and quite accurate result can be obtained by
the use of:

Heavy liquids

Whilst it does not fall within the province of this book to delve too deeply into this aspect of identification, it is a well-known fact that a substance floats on a liquid of higher density than itself and sinks if the density of the liquid is lower than that of the substance under test. Should the two densities be identical, the substance will neither float nor sink, but will remain suspended in the liquid.

A solution of common salt in the proportion of 1 level tablespoonful to 4 fluid ounces of water has a specific gravity of approximately 1·13. This is useful to differentiate between amber (1·08) which would float in the solution, and a synthetic resin of similar appearance but a specific gravity of 1·26 which would sink, as also would Perspex and most other plastics.

*Fig. 5
Specimen suspended in heavy liquid. The specific gravity of the specimen will therefore be the same as the specific gravity of the liquid*

This solution is not really a heavy liquid and although several of these are available, only two or three are needed for general testing purposes. These are Bromoform, Methylene Iodide and Clerici solution, the densities of which are 2·9, 3·33 and 4·15 respectively when in their pure state, but all may be diluted to give a wide range of definite density values.

Bromoform Colourless when fresh, but turns brown on exposure to sunlight. Its density of approximately 2·9 can be reduced by the addition of monobromonaphthalene, benzene or toluol.

Methylene Iodide Pale brown in colour but darkens almost to black on exposure to light. It can be diluted with bromoform and its diluting agents to reduce its density of 3·33.

Clerici Solution A saturated solution of thallium malonate and thallium formate in water, having a density of approximately 4·15. This can be reduced by the addition of distilled water or re-concentrated by gently heating. This solution should be treated with great care as it is corrosive and poisonous in addition to being rather expensive.

With all these liquids certain precautions should be taken and it is obviously advantageous to store them in dark-coloured bottles. All specimens tested and tweezers, tongs or rods used whilst testing, should be thoroughly washed after each immersion to prevent any contamination of the solutions, and wiped dry before placing into another solution. Clerici solution must never be mixed with either of the other two liquids mentioned.

Only small pieces of specimens, rather less than match-head size, are necessary for testing purposes and it is suggested that a suitable range of solutions of known densities be kept easily available.

A block of wood, bored to take the full length of a number of test tubes, securely corked, will form a suitable rack and the respective densities can be painted on the rack.

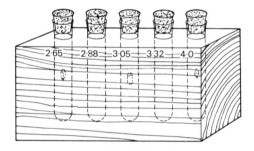

Fig. 6
A rack of five useful heavy liquids

For use in the school workshop, a suggested range of five liquids corresponding to density values 2·65, 2·88, 3·05, 3·32 and 4·00 will be found sufficient to assess the specific gravities of most of the stones used or brought for identification.

Making up solutions
No. I liquid   A small piece of quartz, say for example rock crystal, is placed in pure bromoform when it will float on the surface. Use a glass tube to add benzene or other diluting agent, drop by drop, stirring thoroughly with a glass rod until the stone will remain at whatever level it is placed. It must be emphasised that a very few drops of diluting agent will considerably reduce the specific gravity of an ounce of bromoform, some of which should be kept in reserve in case of too great a dilution.

The tiny piece of rock crystal should be kept in the test tube as a check against any variation in density of the solution due to evaporation or temperature change, when the necessary correction could be made to bring the density back to 2·65.

No. 2 liquid is, of course, pure bromoform.

No. 3 liquid is methylene iodide, diluted with bromoform until a piece of tourmaline will remain suspended.

No. 4 liquid is pure methylene iodide.

No. 5 liquid is Clerici solution diluted with distilled water to a density of 4·00 when corundum will remain suspended.

These are only suggestions, and some teachers may prefer to have a wider range of solutions, each with their own control specimens.

The specific gravities of some of the more common gemstones are:

Amber	1·08	Andalusite	3·15
Jet	1·20 to 1·30	Fluorspar	3·18
Fire Opal	2·00	Spodumene	3·18
Opal	2·10	Apatite	3·18
Obsidian	2·40	Jadeite	3·33
Serpentine	2·50	Peridot	3·34
Feldspar (varieties of)	2·54 to 2·72	Idocrase	3·38
Iolite	2·59	Sinhalite	3·48
Crypto Crystalline		Diamond	3·52
Quartz (varieties of)	2·60 to 2·65	Sphene	3·53
Crystalline Quartz		Topaz (varieties of)	3·53 to 3·56
(varieties of)	2·65	Spinel	3·60
Calcite	2·71	Garnet (varieties of)	3·41 to 4·20
Beryl (varieties of)	2·65 to 2·85	Chrysoberyl	3·71
Turquoise	2·60 to 2·84	Malachite	3·80
Beryl	2·63 to 2·80	Corundum	3·99
Lapis Lazuli	2·80	Zircon (varieties of)	4·00 to 4·69
Nephrite	3·00	Pyrites	4·90
Tourmaline	3·05	Hematite	5·10

More comprehensive lists are contained in many of the excellent books listed in the bibliography, but the above list should prove adequate for most purposes.

The steel yard

On field trips, specific gravity can be fairly accurately assessed by means of an adaptation of the old-fashioned steel-yard; a simple piece of apparatus which can be quickly made from a 30-centimetre steel rule, a darning needle and a piece of sheet brass approximately $3\frac{1}{2} \times \frac{1}{2}$ in. × 16's gauge

The brass is bent over a piece of $\frac{1}{2}$-in. thick bar to form a stirrup, $\frac{1}{2}$ in. wide by $1\frac{1}{2}$ in. long, and a diametrically opposite hole drilled in each leg about $\frac{1}{4}$ in. from the end. These holes should be of sufficient diameter to allow a small darning needle to pass through, a No. 56 drill will usually be adequate. The holes should then be made into

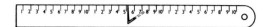

Fig. 7
*Apparatus for weighing
specimens for specific
gravity testing on field
trips*

elongated key holes by means of a coarse blade mounted in a piercing
saw, after which a ring or hook can be soldered onto the top. A hole
which will just take the needle is then drilled through the rule about
$6\frac{1}{2}$ inches from the end, to enable the needle, which forms the pivot, to
be soldered in. Before doing this, the needle should be heated to red
at the point and $\frac{3}{8}$ in. bent at 90°, the rest of the shank then being cut
down to $\frac{3}{4}$ in.

The needle is then soldered into the rule, with the point vertical and
$\frac{3}{8}$ in. projecting from each side and fixed into the stirrup. A 10-gramme
weight is then suspended from the rule by fine cotton at such a
distance from the pivot that the rule is exactly level when the pointer
will be in line with the key-hole slot. The distance from the pivot to
the point from which the weight is suspended must be carefully noted
and for convenience called distance A. If a specimen of rock is now
suspended from the rule on the opposite side of the pivot at a distance
B, the 10-gramme weight must now be moved until the rule is again
level (distance C from the pivot) and the weight of the rock can be
calculated from the formula

$$10 \times C - A = B \times \text{weight of rock}$$

The specimen can then be suspended in a small container of water and
the apparent loss of weight assessed enabling the specific gravity to be
calculated.

It must not be assumed that hardness and specific gravity tests on
gemstones are conclusive, as variations of specific gravity may occur
in varieties of the same species, for instance, colourless beryl
(Goshenite) has a specific gravity of 2·70 whilst that of pink beryl
(Morganite) is 2·80.

To ensure correct identification, the gemmologist carries out many other tests, using a refractometer to measure refractive index, a dichroscope to check for dichroism (two-colour effect) or pleochroism (multi-colour effect), the microscope and spectroscope in addition to many types of light filter and light sources.

BLOWPIPE TESTS

Although specimens subjected to this type of test will rarely be used as gem material, it is advantageous for the teacher of lapidary work to be conversant with them because of the links which can be created between the craft, science and geography departments. These tests will also prove to be of great interest to children, especially if they themselves are allowed to carry them out on specimens which they may have collected.

In the craft room, the standard gas/air brazing torch can be used, whilst in the laboratory, the tests can be carried out by means of a simple mouth blowpipe, used in conjunction with a bunsen burner, gas jet or spirit lamp. The mouth blowpipe is a tapered metal tube, bent to 90° in a gentle curve, and a steady flow of air is blown through the flame. This necessitates maintaining a large reservoir of air in the cheeks as the air is forced smoothly through the tube.

If the tip of the blowpipe is held about $\frac{1}{4}$ in. away from the flame, the air will divert the flame and cause it to assume a narrow conical shape, consisting of three parts, an inner, dark blue cone of unburnt gas, surrounded by a larger cone, violet blue in colour, formed by burning gas and carbon monoxide, and an outer cone, almost invisible and the hottest part of the flame. This type of flame is termed a reducing flame because it contains a surplus of carbon monoxide which takes away any oxygen from the mineral specimen being heated and will reduce a metallic oxide to the constituent metal.

If the tip of the blowpipe is inserted into the flame as shown, an excess of oxygen is given to the flame which is called an oxidising flame and will add oxygen to mineral specimens heated by it.

Tests for minerals can easily be carried out by heating small pieces on a charcoal block, and the reducing flame will burn out any oxygen and other combustibles, leaving a globule of say, tin, lead, zinc, copper or any other mineral which may be present in the specimen under test. This, however, is not always the case as some specimens may vaporise and settle as a fine deposit on the surface of the charcoal. Colour and chemical tests will complete the identification.

The colour of the flame itself gives some indication of minerals present. Petalite, an attractive pink material, will turn the flame reddish purple because of the lithium it contains, whilst the strong yellow flames of sodium, the blue/greens of copper and the violet of potassium will greatly stimulate the children's interest in this type of test.

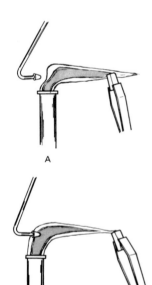

A

B

*Fig. 8
Identification of
specimens by means of
A reducing and B
oxidising flames*

Plate 1
(On previous page)
A collection of tumbled stones.

Key to cabochons in Plate 2 (opposite)

1 Unakite
2 Multicoloured Jasper
3 Vaquilla Agate
4 Sodalite
5 Snowflake Obsidian
6 Tigereye
7 Aventurine
8 Rutilated Quartz
9 Bloodstone
10 Tourmalinated Quartz
11 Blue Lace Agate
12 Crazy Lace Agate
13 Mahogany Obsidian
14 Amethyst Quartz
15 Brazilian Agate
16 Moss Opal
17 Sheen Obsidian
18 Malachite
19 Moss Agate
20 Multicoloured Jasper
21 Vaquilla Agate
22 Tigereye

23 Mahogany Obsidian
24 Tourmalinated Quartz
25 Turritella Agate
26 Amazonite
27 Mahogany Obsidian
28 Vaquilla Agate
29 Crazy Lace Agate
30 Snowflake Obsidian
31 Vaquilla Agate
32 Rose Quartz
33 Tigereye
34 Tigereye
35 Mahogany Obsidian
36 Blue Moss Opal
37 Australian Agate
38 Crazy Lace Agate
39 Moss Agate
40 Moss Opal
41 Sodalite
42 Mahogany Obsidian
43 Malachite
44 Blue Lace Agate

45 Mahogany Obsidian
46 Tigereye
47 Whitby Jet
48 Blue Lace Agate
49 Bloodstone
50 Rutilated Quartz
51 Rutilated Quartz
52 Bloodstone
53 Amethyst
54 Aventurine
55 Brazilian Agate
56 Banded Agate
57 Crazy Lace Agate
58 Brazilian Agate
59 Moss Agate (unusual specimen)
60 Crazy Lace Agate
61 Vaquilla Agate
62 Jasper
63 Turritella Agate
64 Amazonite

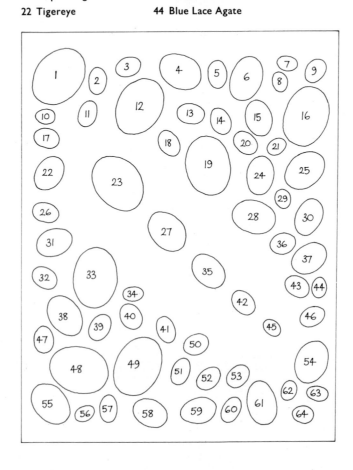

Plate 3
The Parkland Collection
Top left: amethyst crystal bed.
Top right: tabular barite crystal bed.
All the remaining stones are
slices of Queensland agate.

BEAD TESTS

These are carried out by melting a high melting point flux such as
borax, and picking up a bead of it on the end of a fine platinum or
nichrome wire. Whilst the bead is still hot, it is touched into the
powdered mineral specimen and reheated in both an oxidising and a
reducing flame, noting any colour change which takes place when hot
in the two flames and also when cold. Copper, for example, becomes
green when hot in an oxidising flame, turning blue on cooling,
although colourless in a reducing flame, cooling to brown.

Fig. 9
Bead testing

Children taking part in field studies, orienteering, adventure training
and similar activities frequently bring specimens back with them in
the hope that they may prove suitable for inclusion in jewelry making,
whilst others become keen on amassing a collection of rock specimens
which they like to polish.

In a school where lapidary work is carried out, the beginning of each
term brings to the craft room enthusiastic youngsters, eager to
ascertain the identity of their holiday collections, which are many and
varied. It is at this time that the teacher will appreciate the value of
having taught them some of the tests mentioned, as considerable time
can be wasted in attempting to polish unsuitable specimens, in
addition to unnecessary use of the machines.

Saw blades and coolants

Lapidary work, as a school subject, is still in its infancy in this country. It is safe to say that the majority of stone cutting and polishing is carried out by enthusiastic amateurs, whose numbers are growing so rapidly that suppliers are finding that demands for machines and materials have increased beyond their expectations.

The American lapidarists have a wide choice of machine. Many well-known firms produce a range of saws, sanding, polishing and lapping machines in addition to a variety of combination units. In this country we are not so fortunate and our choice of machine is fairly limited, unless an imported machine can be afforded. There is, however, one manufacturer in Scotland who, during the past few years, has produced a range of machines of excellent quality and sufficiently robust to stand up to the strains imposed upon them by beginners, both children and adult. One of these machines has been in almost continuous use in our school workshop for more than two years, and since its purchase, the only item of expenditure incurred has been the cost of cutting oil, replacement of grinding wheels and sanding discs. The total cost has been well under £5 and many beautifully cut gemstones have been produced for a very low cost.

*Plate I
Original PMR2
Combination
Lapidary Unit*

With the growing interest in the craft, other British manufacturers
are now producing lapidary equipment, but most commercial machines,
whilst excellent for individual or very small group work, have
disadvantages when a class of around twenty small boys are all eagerly
awaiting their turn to have a go. Whilst it is agreed that organisation
will prevent chaos, it is equally obvious that if the processes necessary
to produce a finished gem can be streamlined, the happier both
children and teacher will be.

The basic processes in gem cutting are sawing, grinding, sanding and
polishing, in addition to lapping, where a flat surface is required. All
the combination machines necessitate these operations being carried
out on vertically rotating grinding wheels, sanding and polishing discs,
but it is my experience that children seem to find it easier to sand and
polish horizontally.

Prior to the acquisition of a commercial unit, a considerable amount
of highly successful work was carried out on the simply constructed
machine described in Chapter 6.

THE DIAMOND SAW

When purchased, most rough gem material is in fairly large pieces and
the first process in producing a finished gem is to cut off a slice of
suitable thickness. For this purpose, the diamond saw is used.
Basically, this is similar to the woodworker's circular saw, with the
addition of a tank to contain the coolant fluid which is essential for the
saw's operation. The rim of the blade passes through the coolant and
carries it to the material being cut, washing out the tiny particles
removed by the cutting action, in addition to lubricating and cooling
the blade. It is essential that a diamond saw must never be used
without coolant as otherwise the blade would be badly damaged and
possibly ruined. THIS CANNOT BE TOO STRONGLY EMPHASISED
as the blade is the most expensive part of the combination lapidary
unit. With care, it will have a surprisingly long life, but if misused, it
can be rendered useless on the first cut.

Before embarking upon a description of the uses of the saw, it would
be advantageous to look at the types of blade available. These vary in
thickness and diameter from 0·010 x 4 in. to 0·105 x 36 in. and even
larger. The small diameter, thin blades are used on the more precious
materials, sometimes being termed "slitting saws", whilst blades up to
10-in. diameter are given the name "trim saws". In schools and by
many amateurs, they will be used to usurp the functions of the larger
diameter "slabbing saws", i.e. the cutting of rough material into slices
or slabs, prior to trimming to approximate shape.

The blades themselves are usually made of mild steel, although some
of the smaller blades are phosphor bronze. The rims are either
notched or sintered. In the case of the former, notches are cut into the

*Plate 2
Three types of
diamond saw blade*

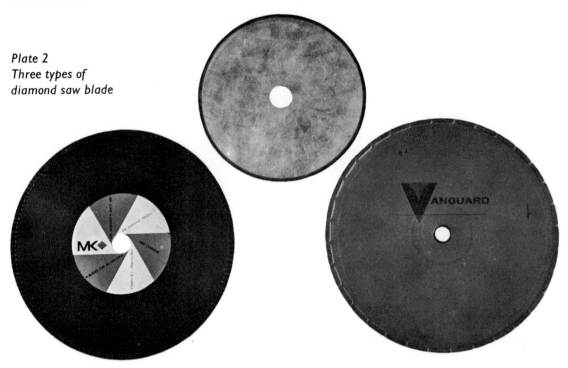

periphery of the blade and these are loaded with a mixture of powdered metals and diamond, after which the blade is subjected to intense heat and pressure in a process known as sintering which fuses the particles into position.

With this type of blade, care must be taken to observe the manufacturer's operating instructions, as some specify that the blade be run in one direction only, whilst with other makes it is stated that it is beneficial to reverse the direction of rotation periodically. The reason for this is probably due to the design of the blade, as some have small notches cut at right angles to the edge whilst others have large inserted segments. It is usually the latter type of blade which has a specific direction of rotation, usually denoted by an arrow marked on the blade.

The sintered rim blade is usually more expensive, but smoother in operation, lasts longer and may be run in either direction. The rim is made by mixing diamond powder with powdered metal which is then compressed into a thin hoop. This is heated until the metal and diamond particles fuse, and the hoop is then soldered onto a mild steel disc.

The saw which cannot injure

Cutting with the diamond saw is by far the safest machining operation carried out in any workshop. From the instructor's point of view, the high spot of a demonstration of gem cutting to beginners is to observe the looks on the faces of the class, especially if the class is composed of students who have used a circular saw for cutting wood. Amazement at the demonstrator's temerity in allowing his fingers to be in such close proximity to the fast spinning blade is clearly expressed by some, whilst others are obviously convinced that the operator is either very conceited or just plain careless. Their amazement is even greater if the demonstrator, having sliced through a piece of rock, allows his fingers to rest on the blade before switching off and then shows that he still retains them!

Beginners find it extremely difficult to appreciate that the rim is quite smooth to the touch and that the "teeth", which they can neither see nor feel, can cut through rock as easily, if not as quickly, as a circular saw cuts through wood. I have found that it is a good thing to allow children to touch the blade, as this gives them immediate confidence to tackle what is, to the unitiated, a rather frightening job, because prior to embarking upon lapidary work, they will always have been instructed never to touch any moving parts of a machine. The reason for this familiarity with the blade will become apparent when use of the saw is discussed.

Blade speeds

This is a highly controversial subject, different authorities having differing opinions, and whilst some will recommend 1000 r.p.m. for an 8-in. blade, others may suggest as high a speed as 3000 r.p.m. However, most blade manufacturers give a recommended speed for the operation of their products, usually expressed as surface feet per minute, i.e. the circumference of the blade in feet, multiplied by the number of revolutions per minute. Surely it is common sense to accept the maker's advice.

To obtain the necessary blade speed in revolutions per minute, the following formula is used, as blade diameters are always expressed in inches.

$$\text{r.p.m.} = \frac{\text{Surface feet per minute}}{\text{Blade diameter} \times 3 \cdot 1416 \div 12}$$

The table in the appendix should be sufficient to cover most requirements. One cannot be dogmatic about this subject as some materials cut easier than others. The thickness of the specimen must also be taken into consideration in addition to the rate of feed.

Rate of feed

This is governed by the pressure of the stone against the blade, and varies with the thickness and density of the stone which is being cut. Many commercial machines are fitted with mechanical feeds which operate automatically or gravity feeds which can be incorporated in the machine described in Chapter 6.

COOLANTS

A diamond saw must never, under any circumstances, be run dry, and the general practice is to incorporate a tank below the saw table so that the base of the blade picks up the coolant as it rotates. The main reason is to disperse the considerable amount of heat generated by the cutting action, as this, in addition to being detrimental to the saw, could cause the stone to fracture. The coolant also helps to overcome the friction between stone and blade. It acts as a lubricant, in addition to washing away the stone dust and keeping the blade at work.

Wherever lapidary workers congregate, the subject of suitable coolants will arise, each enthusiast being prepared to give the strongest reasons for his choice. Diesel oil, motor oil mixed with paraffin, flushing oil, transformer oil, cutting oil and anti-freeze, to name but a few, have all been recommended to me at various times. Most of the oils have disadvantages and as many blade manufacturers deprecate the use of water-soluble cutting oil, I used neat anti-freeze for some considerable time despite the obvious comments from my colleagues.

The properties required of a coolant   A good coolant must fulfil the following requirements.

(a) It must have a very high flash point, obviously the most important feature if used in schools.

(b) Must not give off mist or vapour.

(c) Should possess good lubricating qualities.

(d) Should have a low viscosity at all temperatures.

(e) Should be odourless and finally, but not the least important, it should be cheap.

Information received from the U.S.A. showed that Corvus oil, a Texaco product, was the favourite coolant used by American workers, but as this was before the re-introduction of the Texaco Service Stations in this country, plus the fact that it is only sold in the U.S.A. in five-gallon drums, the use of this coolant seemed to be impractical.

However, enquiries revealed that this particular oil is marketed in this country as Regent 519 Oil (now Texaco 519) at a cost of approximately £1·50 for a five-gallon drum. The Company's representative assured me that, as this is a processing oil used in the rubber industry, supplies are readily available at their depots, and this has proved to be the case.

In addition to fulfilling all the requirements previously mentioned, it possesses a further desirable quality. Some of the coolants mentioned soon become fouled by particles of rock dust, but it has been found that when using Corvus oil, the dust rapidly settles to the bottom of the tank where it forms a layer, almost of the consistency of Plasticine, with clean oil on the surface. When it becomes necessary to renew the oil, the old oil can be poured into a container and the base of the tank cleaned. By the following day, a layer of clean oil will appear on the surface of the container and this can be re-used.

One disadvantage in using an oil of this nature is a tendency for it to penetrate into some of the slightly porous stones. In any case, before any shaping can be carried out, it is essential that the stone be washed in methylated spirits or a strong detergent.

Research into the problems of lubricating and cooling diamond impregnated tools for use in various industries is a continuous process, and the Burmah Castrol Industrial Limited company kindly supplied much valuable information on the subject. After studying the results of tests carried out by several experts in tribotechnology, it became obvious that Burmah Castrol had succeeded in producing a water soluble coolant which is ideal for lapidary work, marketed under the name of Castrol Syntilo 303. This soluble oil is diluted with water in the ratio of 70:1 when it forms a pink transparent solution with a greater wetting power than water with a controlled "non-fatty" lubricity. Its cooling power is as good as other cutting fluids and the settling of the grit particles retains the stability of the emulsion, the residue settling at the bottom of the tank as in the case of Corvus oil.

In addition, it is stated that Castrol Syntilo 303 is a good rust inhibitor and as the water evaporates, a protective layer is formed on ferrous alloy machine parts. It also contains inhibitors against chemical attack on most non-ferrous alloys. It can be obtained by writing to Burmah Castrol Industrial Ltd, Burmah Castrol House, Marylebone Road, London, N.W.1. The present price is £1·50 per gallon tin which is extremely economical when one considers the dilution rate.

When a new diamond saw blade is purchased, a comprehensive list of instructions regarding fitting and operating the blade is always enclosed and these should be carefully studied and rigidly adhered to. Before attempting any work with the diamond saw, the following points must be stressed and in schools it is desirable that they are continually brought to the pupils' attention.
1   Make sure that the speed is correct.
2   Never cut dry, ensure a copious supply of coolant.
3   Keep the saw table clean, free from chips, grit and sludge.
4   Never allow small pieces of stone to fall between the blade and the slot in the table; this will buckle the blade.
5   Always make sure that the stone being cut is firmly held.
6   Make sure that the cut remains straight.
7   Never force the stone against the blade, feed it gently.
8   Keep the blade sharp.

BEFORE USE

AFTER USE

AFTER SHARPENING

*Fig. 10
Sharpening techniques
for the diamond saw*

Regarding this latter instruction, it may be found that after cutting some materials, the blade appears to "lack life". This is because the diamond saw cuts by scratching the work, almost in the same way as glasspaper does wood, and to do this, the diamond must project above the surface of the metal matrix. On some types of notched blade this tends to build up in front of the "teeth" and must be removed by cutting through about 20 square inches of any soft brick which approximates the character of ordinary mortar which has set for a few days. Common red brick is usually too hard fired to provide sand particles which will roll and cut away the matrix, but if a screwdriver, pressed fairly easily and rotated against a brick, grinds its way in, the brick should be suitable. The stubs of lapidary grinding wheels are ideal for sharpening blades and a few cuts across a 100-grit wheel stub makes the blade cut like new.

The reason is that due to the hardness of the diamond, a "wake" of metal will be developed behind the "teeth" when viewed in the direction of sharpening, backing up each "tooth" like a buttress. The faces of the "teeth" are essentially free of metal but with this type of blade, it will be apparent that using the blade in a reverse direction will do two things:

1 Because the buttress will be presented to the material being cut, the cutting action will be far less efficient and
2 The buttress will quickly be worn away, leaving the diamond standing unsupported and easily stripped out of the matrix.

As previously stated, however, some makers of notched blades specify that the blade rotation should be periodically reversed, hence the need for studying the maker's directions must again be emphasised.

USING THE DIAMOND SAW

Very few schools or amateurs will, in the early stages, be able to afford a slabbing saw, which is a luxury which can be dispensed with. Much of the material will be of such a size that it can be sliced with the 8-in. trim saw. There are also dealers in this country who will sell ready-cut slices of material or will slice your own rough for a modest fee but this should not be necessary as, with care, comparatively thick slices can be cut on the trim saw.

Unless for a specific purpose, the purchasing of ready-cut slices is not recommended for school work as most of the fun and excitement is missed. Until one has taken a piece of dull-looking rock and cut it into beautiful slices, the lapidary bug will not bite, but after that first slice, the beginner will be committed to exploring a new and wonderful world.

CUTTING A SLICE—THE FIRST STAGE IN MAKING A GEM

The use of vices and clamps will subsequently be discussed, but let us first cut a slice by hand. To some experts, this is regarded as a most heinous offence, but not all workers will possess a machine equipped with a vice, and if the rock is under 2 in. thick, excellent slices can be produced from an 8-in. blade.

The first essential is to study the material in order to ascertain that it is free from flaws which could cause it to break during cutting. This could damage the blade. The aim is to produce a slice approximately $\frac{3}{16}$ in. to $\frac{1}{4}$ in. thick for normal cabochon cutting. Special properties which the material may possess, for example the chatoyance of tiger eye, sunstone, labradorite, etc., must be taken into consideration.

PROTECTING THE SAW BLADE

It is vital for the well-being of the blade that it must not be deflected in the slightest degree from a straight cut, and this necessitates the largest possible area of the rock being in contact with the saw table and offered up to the blade at right angles. Never attempt to start against a sloping surface directly, but if this is necessary, a slight nick must be made at 90° before the rock is turned onto the mark as shown. This *must* be carried out with the utmost care to prevent blade damage. If the saw shows any tendency to wander from a straight cut it is better to start a fresh cut from another position rather than continue, as the blade would jam and may be buckled beyond repair.

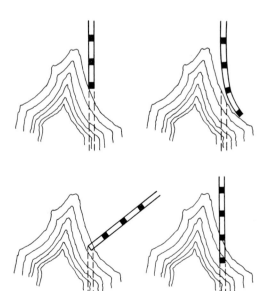

Fig. 11
Methods of cutting into sloping side of rock

Bearing all these considerations in mind and having ensured that the blade speed is correct, the tank contains an adequate supply of coolant and the splash guard is in position, switch on. Hold the rock firmly in both hands, fingers in front, thumbs behind, little more than the thickness of the blade between the forefingers to ensure that the rock is not deflected. With a firm pressure downwards onto the table start feeding the rock to the saw at a gentle pace, very slowly until you get the feel of the operation. Never force any material, and if sparks appear, the saw slows or the blade runs hot, slow down the rate of feed at once: these are signs of attempting to cut too fast.

*Fig. 12
Correct position of
hands when cutting a
rock*

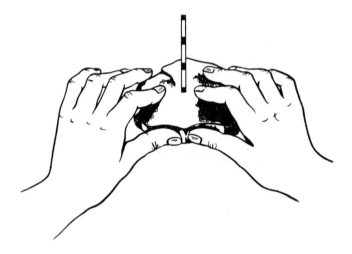

Only experience will show how fast one can feed. Gemstones differ in hardness and cutting qualities and it is always a good thing to remember that slow feeding saves saw blades. Once the cut has started, it is best if it can be continued straight through without pausing, maintaining the same steady pressure. On approaching the finish of the cut, keep the thumbs close together to prevent small "nibs" breaking off and becoming jammed between the saw and the table with possible disastrous results.

This first cut having been accomplished, all that remains is to repeat the procedure, cutting off a slice to the requisite thickness, either by eye or with the assistance of a fence (a piece of wood or metal clamped onto the table the appropriate distance from the blade).

*Plate 3 (above, opposite)
Position of fingers
when sawing*

*Plate 4 (below, opposite)
Angle aluminium used
as fence*

The slice should then be washed in water, detergent or methylated spirits, depending upon which coolant has been used, and dried for further inspection which may decide the ultimate size and shape of the finished stone. Ensure that both sides of the stone are examined for cracks or flaws. At this stage a good tip with many materials is to hold it against a strong light, especially in the case of transparent and semi-opaque materials. Choose the portion of the slice which is most appealing to you from the point of view of colour, pattern, size or shape of finished gem desired.

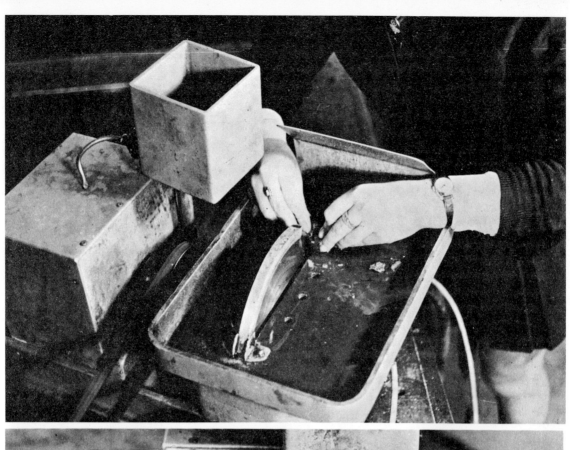

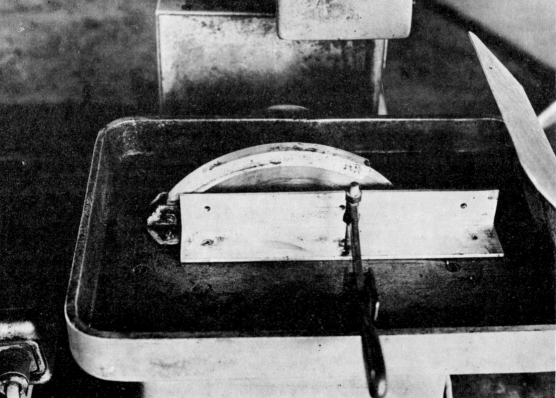

*Fig. 13
Selecting correct
template shape*

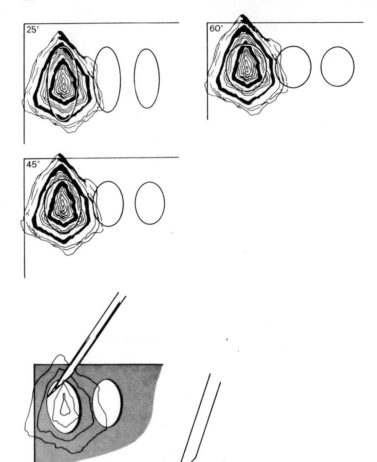

*Fig. 14
Marking out cabochon
blank from Bittner
Template*

If a formal shape, for example square, circular or oval, is desired, it is wise to use a template. Bittner's templates are plastic sheets with a variety of shapes and sizes punched into them, corresponding to the dimensions of commercial mounts. Having decided on the shape you wish to produce, move the template over the slab until you select the position which is most pleasing. Having decided on the position, mark round the template onto the stone, using a bronze or aluminium pencil. A piece of $\frac{1}{8}$-in. brazing spelter or aluminium, sharpened to a point, makes an ideal marker. The marks will not rub off and as they are quite clearly visible you are now ready to trim the stone to approximate shape.

TRIMMING WITH THE SAW

This is necessary to avoid a considerable amount of grinding, with a consequent saving of time and unnecessary wear of grindstones. The saw table should be quite free from chips of former sawing operations, as even small pieces of rock below the flat base of the slab may cause it to tip during the cutting and this could break the slab. Never attempt to economise on grinding by cutting too close to the mark, despite the advice given by some authors. This is a good teaching point to emphasise to beginners, because unless the utmost care is taken by feeding very gently, many gem materials will chip slightly during the cutting and these chips may encroach beyond the mark.

Circles and ovals are the most popular shapes for finished cabochons, and when producing blanks for these shapes, after preliminary cutting, the mark will be encompassed by straight cuts with consequent triangular projections. Most authorities advise that these should be "nibbled" off with pliers in the same manner as does a glazier when his glass has failed to break at the cut. This is beyond the capabilities of most beginners and a far more satisfactory method is to surround the mark with a series of notches. These are made by sawing cuts at 90° to the mark, as close as possible to each other, stopping about $\frac{1}{16}$ in. from the mark itself. The projecting "teeth" are then sawn off, again at 90°, and it will later be found that the angle of the saw cut effects a further saving of grinding time.

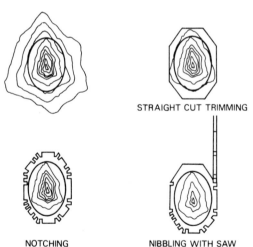

STRAIGHT CUT TRIMMING

NOTCHING

NIBBLING WITH SAW

Fig. 15
Methods of trimming

Grinding, sanding and polishing

GRINDING – OBTAINING THE ROUGH SHAPE

The second stage in the creation of a gemstone is usually carried out on grinding wheels, the basic shape being fashioned on a coarse wheel, slight inaccuracies and marks being subsequently removed on a finer grade wheel. The grinding wheels used in lapidary work are mainly vitreous bonded silicon carbide wheels, some being similar in appearance to the "green grit" wheels used for sharpening tungsten carbide tipped tools. It is strongly recommended that wheels be purchased from a reputable lapidary supply house to ensure the correct bonding is obtained.

Without delving too deeply into the method of manufacture, this must be considered in order to appreciate the techniques of grinding gemstones. Briefly, the wheels are classified as being of a specific grit and hardness, or bond. Many manufacturers use letters such as V. J., etc. to signify the degree or grade of hardness and this can be confusing until one become familiar with them. The most popular grit sizes are 60, 80, 100, 120 and 220, and as these figures represent the approximate number of particles of grit which, when laid side by side, will measure one inch, it will be appreciated that the smaller the number, the coarser will be the wheel.

During the process of manufacture, the grits are bonded with a glass-like substance at very high temperatures. Certain additives ensure that comparatively large air spaces are left between the grit particles. This is to ensure that water can penetrate into the surface of the wheel, an essential feature, as gemstones must always be ground wet. In addition to preventing the stone being damaged by heat, the water flushes the particles of abraded stone from between the air spaces on the wheel, thus retarding the "glazing" effect.

The proportion of the additives mentioned decide the grade of the finished wheel. A "hard" wheel lasts longer, but it tends to glaze, or become clogged with particles, necessitating frequent dressing. The softer grades wear away quicker, and it is this very fact which makes them cut faster, because new and sharp grits are constantly presented to the gem being ground.

Only two wheels are really necessary and it has been my experience that a 100-grit and a 220-grit wheel are entirely adequate. The finer wheel lasts about three times as long as the coarse wheel as this latter wheel bears the brunt of the grinding operations.

Wheels are made in a wide range of diameters and thicknesses but the most popular size is the 6 in. diameter, 1 in. thick wheel. When ordering, it must be remembered to specify diameter, thickness, grit size, hardness and size of the arbor hole.

Although lapidary wheels, "running wet", as they must do, are not so dangerous as the normal workshop grinders, there are certain dangers which must be emphasised.

Speed

Some authorities state, and probably quite correctly, that silicon carbide wheels operate best at a speed of 6000 surface feet per minute. In the case of a 6-in. diameter wheel, this would mean a speed of 3820 r.p.m., and if this is in excess of the maker's recommendations, the speed must be reduced. Many makers insist that a speed of 3000 r.p.m. must not be exceeded, giving a cutting speed of 4714 s.f.p.m. with a 6-in. wheel. This will be found to be quite adequate. Too low speeds tend to make the wheel wear quicker, and with a speed of less than 4700 it is preferable to use a harder wheel.

Fitting and checking the wheel

Flanges are used to spread the pressure of the nuts holding the wheel to the arbor. When fitting a new wheel, first ensure that it is free from cracks. Make sure that both wheel and flanges are clean before fitting onto the arbor, and if both flanges are quite flat against the sides of the wheel, screw on and tighten the locking nut.

Having made certain that the wheel is running true by giving it a spin by hand, fit the guard, switch on and allow it to run for a few minutes, *having taken the precaution of standing to one side.* The chances of a wheel bursting are extremely remote, but in schools, children should always be instructed to take this elementary precaution each time the machine is switched on. The importance of the correct operation of water supply to the wheel, usually by drip feed, cannot be over-emphasised because, as has been stated, the wheels are porous and consequently absorb a certain amount of water. If this is absorbed on one portion of the rim, the wheel will be out of balance and in consequence, extremely dangerous. *A wheel should never on any account rest in water*, and a good drill, which must be observed by both experts and novices alike is:

*Stand out of line
switch on
allow to run
water on
grind
water off
allow to run
switch off*

Allowing the wheel to run on for a few moments after grinding has finished will throw out any water which has been absorbed into the rim during grinding.

Grinding should always be carried out on the face of the wheel, the stone being continually moved from side to side. If this procedure is strictly adhered to, the wheel will wear fairly evenly. However, beginners frequently fail to observe this precaution and because of the hardness of the materials ground, lapidary wheels may quickly develop pits, bumps and grooves, when the wheel is said to "run bumpy". This bumpiness will be made apparent by vibrations being discerned on presenting the stone to the wheel, and although this may be tolerated to a slight degree, the wheel should be dressed before it becomes too noticeable.

Dressing the wheel

Dressing the wheel is best achieved by using a standard grinding wheel trimmer of either the diamond or star-wheel pattern. It will be necessary to clamp a rest horizontally across the face of the wheel, at centre height and as close to the face as possible, then switch on the motor, turn on the water and pass the trimmer, which must be supported by the rest, lightly across the face of the wheel, allowing it to hit the high spots. These will quickly be removed and the trimmer can then be brought a little closer to the wheel and moved to and fro until an even surface is obtained. Never exert too much pressure on the trimmer in the first instance as it will merely follow the undulations which will be accentuated, thus making the wheel worse instead of improving its efficiency.

If a commercial stone trimmer cannot be obtained, wheels can be trued by passing a piece of agate, preferably with a flat edge, across the face of the wheel in similar fashion. Although this is a much slower process, good results can be obtained. It has been previously stated that all grinding should be carried out on the face of the wheel and this should be strictly adhered to, especially in schools. Beginners often find it difficult to grind a flat surface on the periphery and will undoubtedly prefer to adopt the easier method of side grinding. This must not be tolerated in schools as grooves on the sides of wheels are obvious sources of danger.

SANDING – REMOVING THE GRINDING MARKS

When the stone has been given its finished shape by means of the coarse and fine grit wheels, the beginner could form the impression that it is ready for polishing. To the naked eye, it will possibly have a superficial polish but examination under a magnifying glass will prove that this is not the case. The surface will be covered with a series of fine scratches which must be removed before polishing is attempted because the more the stone is polished, the more apparent the scratches will become. As one author states, "You *may* live long

enough to polish out a scratch" and another, "When you think you
have sanded enough, carry on for another five minutes."

The American lapidarist has a choice of three methods of sanding,
namely belt, drum or disc, but as machines incorporating the belt and
drum methods are beyond the financial resources of most amateurs in
this country, we will only concern ourselves with the last mentioned
method.

The discs are usually aluminium alloy castings, 8 in. in diameter, onto
which an 8-in. disc of foam rubber (carpet underlay is ideal) is fixed
with an adhesive such as Evostik, applied to the hessian base. The
rubber surface is then spread with adhesive and covered with a thin
cloth such as sized tracing cloth or, alternatively, broad strips of the
2-in. wide cloth adhesive tape as used for holding strips of fitted
carpet together, trimmed to shape. Sanding cloth or paper discs are
then attached onto the cloth surface with a non-hardening adhesive.
One brand is known as Tacky Adhesive. This holds the cloth on firmly,
even when revolving at high speed, but permits the disc to be peeled
off when a change is necessary. The rubber base is advantageous to the
novice as it allows the disc to conform to the curvature of stones being
sanded, and the covering of tracing cloth prevents the surface of the
rubber being damaged when removing the discs.

The sanding operation may be carried out either wet or dry, but dry
sanding has very little to recommend it, as the cloths or papers,
although cheaper than the "wet or dry" type, wear out much quicker
and have the great disadvantage that it is impossible to keep the stone
cool whilst being sanded. The frictional heat is fatal to many heat-
sensitive stones and also it may cause the dopping wax to melt and the
stone to be pulled off the dop stick.

Wet sanding prevents the dust off the gemstone being inhaled by the
operator. The constant supply of water washes the dust off the disc
which cannot become clogged with gem dust. In addition, it has been
found that wet sanding gives a far superior finish to the stone, as the
degree of cutting can be varied by increasing or reducing the water
supply. The less water used, the more severe the abrasion, whilst a
copious supply of water reduces the cutting action.

The sanding discs may be obtained in two forms, either as "wet or
dry" silicon carbide coated paper, as used for rubbing down cars after
spraying, or waterproof silicon carbide coated cloth. Although these
are naturally more expensive, they have a very much longer life. In the
same manner as the grinding wheels, they are classified according to
grit size and range from the very coarse 60-grit to 600 and even finer,
but the most suitable grades for general use are 220, 320, 400 and 500.

Most types of sanding cloths naturally receive more wear towards the rim than at the centre, and a new lease of life can be given to apparently worn-out discs by laying them flat, brushing with a wet brush from the centre outwards and leaving to dry. In addition to removing particles of gem dust which may have lodged between the grits, fresh grits from the centre are brought towards the edge.

Worn-out discs should be carefully stored as some gem materials respond to sanding on a worn disc. A further reason is that it is possible to re-coat cloths by coating them with a very thin coat of waterglass or waterproof adhesive and evenly sprinkling the appropriate silicon carbide grit over the surface, inverting it to shake off the surplus and leaving to dry. Experience alone will show the requisite consistency of the adhesive and the amount of grit to apply, but the experiment is worth while in view of the financial saving involved.

The latest type, only recently brought on to the American market and not yet available in this country, consists of plastic discs, impregnated with grits and polishes in varying grades and materials. They have been well received by American workers but it is highly probable that they will be more expensive than the cloth type.

Perspex, thick leather and wooden discs, charged with a slurry of loose silicon carbide grit and water, can be used instead of cloths or papers, but leather and thin Perspex should be cemented onto a metal, preferably $\frac{3}{16}$ in. or thicker aluminium backing disc, and many workers prefer this type of sanding. When making wooden discs, choose a timber which will absorb the slurry evenly over the surface; mahogany, sycamore, lime, agba, gaboon, obeche and similar hardwoods are all suitable as they are termed "diffuse porous". This term is applied to hardwoods in which the vessels form ducts or tubes, evenly disposed across the cross section of the tree, because the growth of this type of tree shows very little change between spring and summer. In view of the fact that the discs will be subjected to a constant water drip, it is a good idea to soak them in hot paraffin wax to impregnate them partially and thus prevent the absorption of water and consequent warping.

It can safely be assumed that the use of wood laps was general among early lapidarists as this material would be universally obtainable, and like many other ancient practices, it has much to commend it. The discs are easily produced in any school workshop for a moderate cost. They are long lasting and have the added advantage that grooves may be cut into either the rim or face to accommodate different sizes of cabochons.

The range of loose silicon carbide grits available to the lapidarist is similar to that of the sanding discs previously mentioned, i.e. 60 to 600 and finer, and at this juncture it is perhaps desirable to emphasise what will be repeated later. *The greatest care must be taken to ensure that all grits are kept separate* as one grain of a coarser grit mixed in with a finer grade could result in a gemstone being badly scratched.

When working with children, a system which has been found to be quite satisfactory is to store the grits in different coloured tins and kept away from the machines. Grits for immediate use are available, ready mixed with water in soft plastic bottles of the "Squeezy" type, those with the spray included being ideal. These bottles are painted in similar colours to the storage containers so that the possibility of contamination is reduced to a minimum.

To return to the sanding operation, it will be apparent that as the process is identical with grinding, the peripheral speeds should be approximately the same, and it is here that the cloth discs have the advantage over the wooden discs. They can be run faster, being more stable in balance, and the grit tends to be thrown off wooden discs, especially if they are run vertically. If used horizontally, it is obviously desirable to work as far away from the centre of the disc as possible, as some gemstones "undercut" if sanded at too slow a speed.

A gemstone is said to be undercut when the surface resembles orange peel, i.e. is covered with tiny pits due to minute portions of the surface being pulled out, chiefly during the sanding operation. This is due to the structure of the stone, jade and some of the quartz varieties being noticeably troublesome in this respect. In most cases, a faster speed, a copious supply of water and careful sanding will overcome it.

If any one stage in the production of a gem can be said to be the most important, it is surely that of sanding. One of the most frequently used phrases, is "Back to the sander" because it is at this stage that the foundation for a perfect polish is laid.

The process may be regarded as being parallel with planishing a piece of silver. Poor planishing, bad finish and poor sanding, inferior polish.

POLISHING – THE FINAL STAGE

It is difficult to imagine a more perfect polish than that of a well finished gem, and if the foundations have been well and truly laid by correct sanding, this final process presents few problems, these being chiefly the selection of the appropriate polishing medium for a particular stone.

The theory of polishing is another section of the craft which is a basis for argument between lapidarists, some of whom adhere to the generally accepted belief that polishing is simply a matter of using finer and finer abrasives until the scratches produced are invisible. This theory is, of course, correctly applicable to the polishing of metals, but some authorities, after many experiments, have evolved a more complex theory. Briefly, they suggest that due to the frictional heat at the point of contact, ultra minute particles which project above the surface of the gem, fuse together and flow over the surface, forming what is termed the "Beilby layer". This, again, is a basis for discussion and experiment in the laboratory and to those who think the theory untenable, it must be pointed out that many gemstones receive their final polish by contact with much softer materials.

Polishing materials

These are usually in the form of powders which are mixed with water.

Cerium Oxide is the most popular, a pinkish coloured powder, comparatively cheap and excellent for polishing most of the gem materials other than those which undercut or the extremely hard stones. It can be regarded as the general purpose polish, as more of this will be used than any of the following.

Tin Oxide Before the introduction of cerium oxide, this was the standard polishing agent for most cabochon materials, but although it is cheaper, weight for weight, than cerium, it is heavier so that there is very little financial difference. It polishes more slowly than cerium and in addition it is more messy in use. It is, however, an excellent polish to use when tumbling, a process to be discussed in later pages.

Chrome Oxide Although a good material for polishing jade and stones which undercut, it has very little else to recommend it as it is dirty to use, staining hands and clothing green, these stains being difficult to remove.

Linde A Undoubtedly the best all-round polish, its only disadvantage being its cost, approximately ten times the price of cerium oxide. However, only a small amount is usually necessary to produce a superb polish on most stones, and a few ounces should be stocked for the difficult stone or the "special occasion" when an extra high polish is desirable.

All these polishes are supplied in powder form and are mainly used in conjunction with the hard white felt buff, usually 6 in. diameter by 1 in. wide, which is to be found in most school workshops. The buff is first well wetted and a slurry of polish and water then applied with a soft paintbrush. Alternatively, the slurry can be sprayed or squirted on from a Squeezy bottle, these being ideal as they prevent the powders from being contaminated. It is, of course, most essential that a separate container or brush is used for each polish and for no other purpose. If there is any suspicion that a polishing agent has been contaminated, it is better to cut one's losses and throw it away. They should be stored in a similar manner to the grits, but preferably in a different cupboard.

It may seem strange to the beginner, but not all gem materials will take a polish from the felt buff, these being chiefly those which have a tendency to undercut, lapis lazuli being most noticeable in this respect. In such cases, it is usual to resort to the use of a thin, soft, flexible leather buff, mounted on a disc of sponge rubber on an aluminium backing plate, in the same manner as described for sanding discs.

Diamond powder   As would be expected, this is extremely expensive, but here again only minute quantities are required and usually only when faceting or lapping. It is produced by crushing diamonds, which could not be used as gems, into fine powder, termed bort, which is sieved and graded into sizes. These sizes are measured in microns, one micron being 0·001 millimetre. Bort is marketed as fine as $\frac{1}{4}$ micron, and it is fascinating to realise that more than 100,000 of these grains would be required, side by side, to cover 1 lineal inch.

The most suitable grade for polishing gemstones is 2 micron and this can be obtained either as powder or in a ready mixed compound. These compounds are usually sold in different concentrations, that is the amount of diamond powder in 1 gramme of the carrying agent, one manufacturer listing no fewer than 8 concentrations and 12 mean micron sizes. The price increases with the concentration and the micron size. To give some idea of the price range per 5 grammes, this manufacturer's range varies from $\frac{1}{4}$ micron Super Fine, £2·95, to 90 micron in their heavier concentration, £16·65. Fortunately for the lapidarist micron compound is supplied in Super Fine, Fine and Light concentrations at £2·95, £4·05 and £5·65 respectively per 5 gramme transparent disposable syringe.

The cost of diamond powder also varies according to micron size; a current price list quotes 0–1 micron at 75p per carat, 0–2 at 84p and up to 60 microns £1·20.

If powder is preferred, it is necessary to mix it with a suitable carrier to spread it over the lap, and the constituents of commercial pastes are trade secrets. Oil bases were formerly used, but these proved wasteful as the mixture was thrown off the lap and it is obvious that a more tenacious base is needed. One of the most interesting suggestions is that ends of good quality lipstick be used, a piece about pea size being blended with one carat of powder. The lipstick should be spread over the base of a tiny screw top jar by means of a spatula made from a broken watch spring and the powder gradually blended in. The ideal container is a $\frac{1}{2}$-oz. face cream jar, made of opalized glass with a rounded inside base which facilitates blending and ensures that there is no waste.

Diamond can be used on discs of leather, cast iron, copper or wood, but in the latter case, close grained hard woods are essential, the ideal being lignum vitae. Cherry, apple, pear, beech, maple, laburnum, hawthorn, holly, yew and the like are all suitable.

With diamond polishes, a high peripheral speed is not necessary, about 700 feet per minute being adequate as this will prevent excessive heating. Consequently, the discs can be as small as 3 or 4 inches in diameter and may be grooved in the same manner as suggested for sanding discs, not only to make the polishing of cabochons easier but also to retain the polish where it is required.

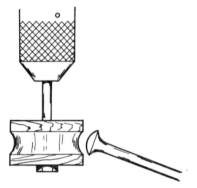

*Fig. 16
Polishing a cabochon
with diamond
compound. Wood disc
in drilling machine*

No water is used with diamond compound; instead the stone is occasionally dipped in olive oil to help the lubrication of the disc and to spread the compound evenly, and in view of this, wood discs mounted in a suitable arbor can be used in the drilling machine. Only the smallest amount is used, and as diamond does not wear away, once the disc is charged, it should polish a considerable number of gems. A conservative estimate is that 5 grammes will polish between 400 and 500.

Here again, it must be emphasised that the greatest care be taken to avoid contamination of either powder, compound or discs by any grit and the latter should be stored in suitable containers when not in use.

Pre-polishing
Many workers recommend that after sanding has been completed, the gem should be pre-polished with Tripoli powder or powdered pumice, but if the sanding has been well done and finished with a nice well-worn cloth, this should not be necessary.

LAPPING

Some beginners are confused regarding the difference between sanding and lapping. Whilst in lapidary work, sanding mainly refers to the pre-polishing stage of cabochon or facet cutting, lapping is the process which results in the production of a flat surace on a gemstone.

In our school workshop, many children are attracted by the beautiful patterns and colours revealed when many of the varieties of small agates are sliced. They frequently create pendants and other articles of jewelry from these slices which are polished on both sides, the surrounding edge often being left in its natural rough state.

The laps are simply flat discs, sometimes of cast iron machined flat in the lathe, or any of the materials previously mentioned as being suitable for sanding discs. In use they are rotated horizontally at comparatively slow speeds, between 400 and 600 r.p.m. Commercial lapping machines have laps varying in size from 12 in. to 18 in. and even larger, but of necessity, we are limited to 9 in. laps which prove to be quite satisfactory for the work which the children undertake.

Loose silicon carbide grits are used to grind the stones flat and are applied mixed with water to a fairly thick slurry, working through the grades of grit from coarse to fine, following the same procedure as when grinding and sanding a cabochon.

If the slice has been cut cleanly and no saw marks are visible, the coarser grits will not be necessary and a start could possibly be made with 220 grit. If the slice has been badly sawn or a large amount of material has to be removed, 80 or 100 grit must be brought into play. A range of grits from 80 to 600 should prove to be quite adequate for most school workshops and these are used in sequence as is found necessary until a flat smooth surface is obtained.

The grits are best applied from Squeezy type bottles. Brushes can be used, but if they are, a separate brush *must* be used for each grade of grit. We actually reserve a separate lap for each grade of grit but this is not necessary if metal laps are thoroughly washed before proceeding to the succeeding grit and obviously it is essential that the stone and hands be thoroughly washed after each grinding, otherwise scratches will certainly result.

Fig. 17
Applying grit and water to lapping machine

Fig. 18
Lapping – moving slice across rotating lap

The final polish is generally obtained from cerium oxide on a 6 by 1 in. hard felt polishing disc, as we find this suitable for the majority of the gemstones we use, although leather discs cemented onto a backing plate are sometimes used if the stone being worked fails to respond to normal treatment.

Points to note when lapping are:
1 Remove any nibs left on the edges of the slice after sawing by grinding on the coarse wheel.
2 Work the slice across the lap, from centre to periphery and back, keeping it moving as this helps to keep the surface of the lap true.
3 Remember that the lap cuts more at the outside than it does at the centre because of the increase in peripheral speed. To avoid the slice being unevenly ground, it is necessary to turn it frequently.
4 Wash the stone if it falls off the lap into the bowl.
5 Never let the lap run dry, but at the same time bear in mind that too much water results in the grit being thrown off the lap and wasted.

Many other materials are used as laps: copper, bronze, tin, lead, Perspex, wood and even chaser's pitch as used in repoussé work, all being appropriate for some specific purpose. Most of these are beyond the scope of school workshops, but information on them can be obtained by reference to several of the books listed in the bibliography.

Cutting a cabochon

The uninitiated will immediately ask "What is a cabochon?" The Oxford Dictionary states "Gem polished but not shaped or faceted, from the French caboche" but to the lapidarist, this is not strictly correct. According to Larousse, the word is derived from caboche, the head or pate, and a cabochon is a smooth round-headed nail. This is exactly what is implied when a gem is said to be cut "en cabochon", a smooth, rounded shape.

The cutting of stones "en cabochon" is by far the most popular activity carried out by amateur gem cutters and this is the best shape for a beginner's first attempt. In addition to being the easiest gem cut to accomplish, it is also the most suitable cut for many materials, in fact, very few of our native gemstones are cut in any other way. Cabochons are also extremely suitable for inclusion in most of the items of jewelry attempted in schools, as the mounting of them presents very few problems, even to the beginner.

In addition to the outline shapes, cabochons must also be considered for their cross sections. These may be termed either high, medium, low or hollow, the degree of curvature being dictated by personal choice, or of necessity by virtue of certain characteristics of the stone being cut. From the artist craftsman's point of view, the cabochon is the most satisfactory shape because it frequently allows him to express his own ideas of shape, colour, pattern or line in his finished gem.

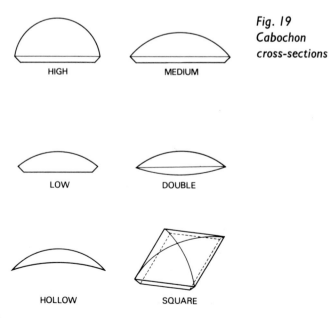

HIGH   MEDIUM

LOW   DOUBLE

HOLLOW   SQUARE

Fig. 19
Cabochon
cross-sections

Many gem materials, when cut, reveal the most amazing patterns and many of the same rules which govern the composition of good landscape photography or painting can be applied, as for example, the creation of dominating areas, to catch the eye and create a centre of interest. The creation of balance, either of colour or pattern, is an important point to be considered, in addition to the shape or size of the finished gem. In schools, the decision on how to mark out a slice could be made during art lessons.

Although it is admitted that circles and ovals are the most popular shapes, cabochons may also be square, cushion, pear drop, baroque, in fact any conceivable shape which can be domed.

To the lapidarist, there is no gem quite like the first one, as it will be remembered when many superior gems which one has produced have long been forgotten. This makes it essential that a suitable material is chosen for the first attempt, in order to ensure a successful beginning, especially when youngsters are being taught the craft.

CHOOSING THE MATERIAL

Choose a material which is of uniform structure, fairly hard, say around $7\frac{1}{2}$ Mohs, sufficiently tough to withstand a few hard knocks, for reasons which will later become apparent, and of attractive pattern or colour. Stones which are too soft will grind down far too quickly and should be avoided, as also should any material bearing flaws or soft inclusions which may pull out during the finishing stages.

Excellent beginnings have been accomplished by using Brazilian, Bechuanaland and Mexican agates, but as these have to be bought, the author usually guides his young pupils to some of our native rocks, offering a choice from the many varieties of barite, granite, quartz and feldspar, even though some of them may be slightly lower than the requisite degree of hardness.

CUTTING AND GRINDING

It is strongly recommended that the first stone is not too large, $\frac{3}{4}$ in. by 45° on a Bittner template is about right. Mark out and cut to approximate shape as outlined in the previous chapter, making sure that the outline is at least $\frac{1}{16}$ in. inside the base of the notches. With beginners and young children, the stone should now be "dopped" (the term used to indicate the fixing of the stone to a temporary handle), but as experience is gained, time can be saved by regarding the stone as now ready for the first grinding operation or profiling, as it is termed. Follow the correct procedure, check the speed of the wheel, switch on, water on and then, holding the stone firmly between the thumb and forefinger, sweep it lightly across the face of the coarse (100 grit) wheel, virtually "stroking it" with a wrist action, ensuring smooth curves. The pencil mark must be facing up, and if the

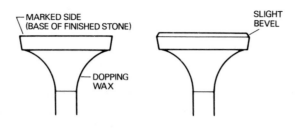

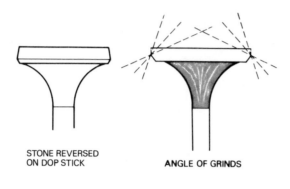

Fig. 20
Grinding a cabochon

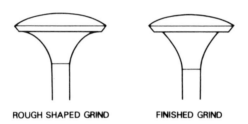

stone is held slightly above the wheel centre, the curvature of the
wheel will cause the edge to assume a slight bevel, following the line
of the notches. Projecting points will soon be removed and grinding
should continue until an even shape is obtained, with a border of
approximately $\frac{1}{16}$ in. remaining outside the mark. If grinding is
continued below the mark, it is advisable to re-mark the stone a size
smaller as it is extremely difficult to restore the balance of symmetry
freehand.

Assuming that all has gone according to plan, an oval stone will have
been produced, with the sides tapering very slightly away from the
pencil mark. Turn off the water supply and allow the stone to run dry
for a few seconds to throw off any surplus water which may have been
absorbed.

DOPPING THE STONE

The stone is now ready for dopping on to a handle or "dop stick". These can be short lengths of wooden dowel or metal rod, about 5 in. long and of a suitable diameter to accommodate the stone being shaped, usually about $\frac{1}{3}$ the width of the stone. Several wooden dop sticks from $\frac{1}{4}$ in. to $\frac{1}{2}$ in. diameter and metal from $\frac{1}{8}$ in. to $\frac{5}{16}$ in. diameter should always be to hand. Aluminium alloy rod is ideal for dop sticks, being light, non-corrosive and non-absorbent, an important factor because, being subjected to constant wetting, wooden dops frequently swell and cause the wax to crack.

Fig. 21
Wood, metal and
faceting dops

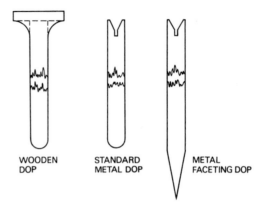

WOODEN
DOP

STANDARD
METAL DOP

METAL
FACETING DOP

With both wood and metal dops, it is desirable to round off one end to ensure that it does not dig into the palm of the hand, whilst the other end is cut square or slightly hollowed. On the metal dops, a "centre" made with a Slocombe drill has a beneficial effect on the bond between the stone and the dop.

The stone is fixed to the dop stick by a commercial dopping wax, sealing wax, or flake shellac, although some workers prefer to make their own by melting together equal parts by weight of shellac and sealing wax. This is comparatively cheap, does not shrink away from the stone, is strong and of a fairly low melting point and with care, can be used many times.

A small container (water pipe stop end caps are ideal) is partly filled with broken wax and placed on a stand with a spirit lamp below. Only a small flame is necessary and care should be taken to prevent the wax from becoming overheated and bubbling up, as this weakens it. As soon as the wax is fluid, warm the end of the dop stick in the flame and then insert it about $\frac{1}{2}$ in. into the wax. Rotate the stick between finger and thumb for a moment, withdraw the stick and place it onto a bench block or a flat piece of sheet metal when the wax will form a bed for the stone. Several of these prepared dops can be stored ready for use.

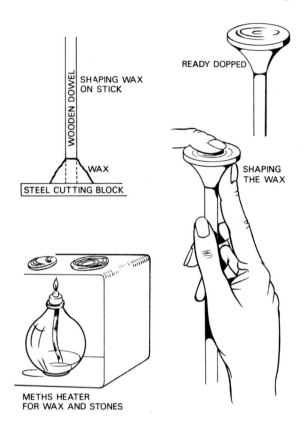

SHAPING WAX
ON STICK

WOODEN DOWEL

READY DOPPED

WAX

STEEL CUTTING BLOCK

SHAPING
THE WAX

Fig. 22
Dopping

METHS HEATER
FOR WAX AND STONES

Warm the stone by setting it on a stand alongside the wax container with the marked side down, i.e. with the slight taper uppermost. Care must be taken, especially with heat sensitive gems, not to allow the stone to become too hot, and a good guide is to place a few flakes of shellac on the uppermost surface of the stone. When this melts, the stone is ready for dopping, the shellac, in addition to acting as a guide, gives additional strength to the joint.

Take a prepared dop stick, rotate the waxed end in the flame until it softens, press it onto the stone and with a rapid inversion of the hand, swing the stick vertically and with a moistened forefinger, or flexible spatula, centre the stone and mould the wax into a conical support.

The dop stick is now placed vertically in a vice, tin of sand or other suitable support and left to set hard. It must be emphasised that the wax should never be suddenly chilled, as this causes the wax to contract away from the stone with a consequent loss of adhesion. If the stone becomes detached from the dop stick during subsequent operations, it is due to one of the following mistakes:

(a) Stone too cold.
(b) Stone not being clean and free from oil or grease.
(c) Wax too cold or too weak because of excessive heat or age.
(d) Insufficient wax to form adequate support.

Inspection of the stone will show the reason for failure and the necessary correction made when the stone is re-dopped.

Assuming that the stone is securely fixed, if necessary, the profiling can be carried out as previously described, after which, a slight bevel is made from the side of the stone to the pencil mark, at an angle of about 45°. This is preferably carried out on the smooth (220 grit) wheel, by holding the dop stick at the requisite angle to the wheel, supporting the stone with the forefinger and thumb of the left hand and rotating the dop stick with the right hand whilst lightly pressing the stone against the wheel.

PERSPEX GUARD

*Fig. 23
Angle of grind should
be approximately 45°*

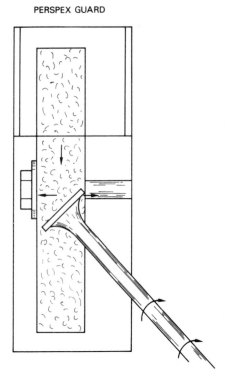

This bevel has a dual function, the primary one being that it prevents the edge of the cabochon chipping. The other reason is that as cabochons are usually mounted in a box setting, the bevel gives clearance in the corner between the wall and the base of the setting. This allows the cabochon to sit flat on the base, even though tiny particles of silver solder may not have been completely removed, and these could cause the cabochon to crack when the wall of the setting is being burnished over.

The stone is now removed from the dop, either by slightly warming the wax, which will allow the stone to slide off the dop, or alternatively by chilling the stone. Usually, holding the stone under a cold water tap for a few seconds is sufficient to allow the stone to be forced off by slight pressure from beneath with the thumb nail. If the tap water is not cold enough, a few minutes in the freezing compartment of a refrigerator or immersion in water containing ice cubes will cause the stone to fall off the dop. Any surplus wax may be scraped off with a penknife blade or washed off in methylated spirits, after which the stone is re-dopped with the bevel side down.

Following the regular procedure regarding speed and coolant, make the first cut by holding the dop stick at an angle of about 25° to the 100 grit wheel and, holding the dop stick in the same manner as described when grinding the bevel, sweep the stone across the face of the wheel, at the same time rotating the dop stick between the finger and thumb of the right hand.

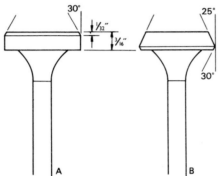

Fig. 24
Cabochon cutting
A *Base chamfer*
B *First grinding angle*

Pausing frequently to inspect and ensure that an even degree of grinding is maintained, continue the operation until the edge of the base bevel is reached, when the stone should appear as shown. The angle is increased and a second cut is made in similar fashion, subsequent cuts being made until the centre is reached.

By rotating and sweeping the entire surface of the stone across the wheel, the edges are removed, care being taken to avoid the most commonly made mistake made by beginners, namely a flat-topped dome. In profile, the cabochon should at this stage describe a perfect curve without any flats, but should these or any other faults such as lack of symmetry or humps be apparent when examined, by first drying the stone and holding it at eye level, the necessary correction must be made by further careful grinding.

Remember that the final shape of the stone depends solely on the care taken at this stage, and it is as well not to rush the operation. When satisfied that the shape is all that can be desired, pass on to the 220 grit wheel. Again observing the usual precautions, use the same light, rotating, sweeping movements across the face of the wheel until all the marks made by the coarse wheel are removed and when this has been achieved, the stone is ready for sanding.

Some workers recommend that preliminary grinding on the coarse wheel is carried out by rotating the stone in the same plane as the rotation of the wheel, at the same time moving it to and fro across the

Plate 5 (opposite)
a *Grinding a cabochon
– coarse wheel*
b *Grinding a cabochon
– fine wheel*
*Note position of fingers
supporting the
cabochon*

face of the wheel. In this case, the dop stick must be twisted clockwise, allowing the wheel to pull the stone, and this method has much to commend it, but if children are taught this method, they tend to allow the stone to remain in the same position on the wheel and this can soon cause grooves which means the wheel needs constant dressing.

SANDING THE CABOCHON

Irrespective of whether commercial discs, or wood or leather with grits are used, the process is identical. Adjust the speed of the machine to give the requisite speed, as outlined in the chapter on sanding, and commence with a 320 disc or grit. Turn on the water supply and with the finger and thumb supporting the stone as in previous operations, lightly rotate the stone against the disc, working from the edge towards the centre of the stone by moving the hands through an arc. Raising and lowering the hands whilst moving them in sweeping arcs at the same time as rotating the dop stick sounds extremely complicated, but it is quite a natural movement and once it has been demonstrated to beginners, the knack is soon acquired. Care must be taken to ensure that the edge of the stone is always prevented from digging into the disc by presenting the centre of the stone towards the direction of rotation. It has been previously stated that sanding is the most important operation in producing a high finish on a gemstone, and the main points cannot be over-emphasised. Keep the stone wet, moving and rotating until every mark left by the 220 grit wheel has been removed. Take care not to burn the stone by too much pressure, especially with new discs running wet. Although the water helps keep the stone cool, considerable frictional heat is created at the point of contact.

Remember that certain gems need different speeds of sanding and these are easily obtained with the discs, the speed of cut increasing from the centre to the rim. With a material which undercuts, always work at the extreme edge of the disc, with a copious supply of water direct onto the stone.

Before proceeding to the next stage, the stone, dop stick and hands should be washed to ensure that there is no "carry over" of 320 grit to the next disc. This is a "must" if grit slurrys are being used, as one particle can ruin the surface of the gem. The stone is now worked on a finer grade sanding disc, 400 grit or finer, and using exactly the same technique, remove the marks left by the 320 grit disc. Again, continuous inspection is necessary and it is at this stage that any previous errors will stand out most noticeably. The surface of the stone should have an even polished appearance, although inspection under a magnifying glass will show that the surface is covered with minute scratches of the same depth. If any deeper scratches are apparent and do not disappear after a few extra sweeps, revert to the 320 disc, which necessitates repeating the 400 grit operation. When

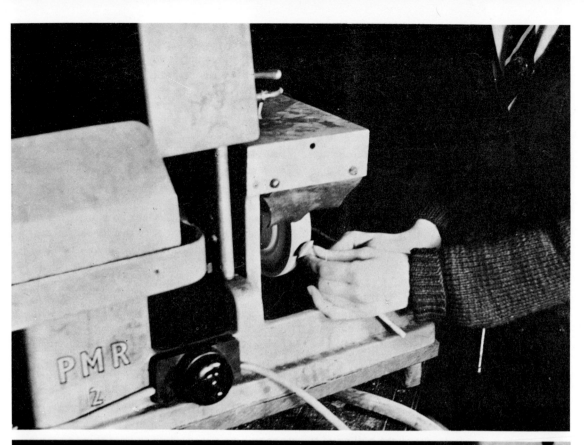

satisfied with the appearance of the stone, it should be placed on a
clean cloth or paper tissue whilst preparation is made for the final
operation.

POLISHING

Before attempting to polish, thoroughly wash the stone and dop
stick – and it is a good thing to use a nail brush on the hands as fine
grit particles can lodge under fingernails before being released onto
the polishing disc, with disastrous results. If this precaution is not
strictly observed, sooner or later, marks as noticeable as furrows on a
newly ploughed field will appear on the surface of the almost finished
gem and most likely, it will be the "important one, urgently needed"
so beginners, please be warned.

Adjust the speed of the machine to give a speed of around 1150
surface feet per minute, approximately 750 r.p.m. in the case of a
6-in. disc. This should be dressed with the appropriate polish.
Supporting the stone as in previous operations, use firm but gentle
strokes, moving and rotating the stone against the buff, still supporting
the stone and ensuring that it is always tilted away from the run of the
buff. If this is not done, the stone could be pulled off the dop stick and
possibly chipped, a disastrous occurrence at this stage. Only experience
will enable the worker to decide the amount of pressure to exert, but
a slight pulling of the stone will be noted when the polishing agent is
doing its work; extra pressure is not necessary and can be harmful, as
the stone may be overheated and the wax softened.

If the sanding has been correctly carried out, a high polish will be
obtained with surprising speed. After the stone has been removed
from the dop, carefully washed in methylated spirits and dried, it
should be examined in a good light with a magnifying glass to ensure
that it is up to standard before being wrapped in tissue or cotton wool
to prevent accidental damage. This latter procedure should be insisted
upon from the outset with children because as they progress and
produce gems from the rough, some soon become blasé and fail to
appreciate the value of the results of their efforts.

Facet-cutting—a more advanced technique

Facet cutting is the most complicated and skilful operation carried out
by the lapidary worker. It involves the creation of a number of highly
polished plane surfaces, or facets, on a gemstone, from which rays of
light are reflected and refracted, giving fire and brilliance to stones
which, in their natural state, may be devoid of colour or interest.
These facets are cut symmetrically around the surface of the gem at
specific angles, which vary according to the refractive index of the
stone being worked, and it is obvious that a knowledge of mathematics and physics is advantageous to the would-be facet cutter.

This branch of the craft has been practised for many centuries in India
and the East, although most authorities believe that the natural
crystalline shapes of many gems were merely accentuated, frequently
to remove obvious flaws.

Jean Baptiste Tavernier, a Frenchman who lived in the seventeenth
century, was the greatest trader in gemstones of the era in which he
lived, and travelled extensively in India. He was highly thought of by
the rulers of many states, from whom he purchased many famous
gems, notably the Tavernier Blue Diamond, which weighed 112 carats
and from which the Hope Diamond was subsequently cut. His diaries,
published in London in 1678, show drawings of gems which have been
crudely faceted.

The founder of the art of true faceting is regarded by most authorities
as Louis de Berghen, a Belgian who lived in the fifteenth century and
cut diamonds to precise geometrical designs. Other experts attribute
the first brilliant cut diamond of 58 facets to Vincenzo Petruzzi who
lived in Venice in the sixteenth century, and this cut is the basis for
dozens of variations.

FACET NOMENCLATURE

The layman is frequently confused by the names given to various cuts,
and this is not surprising, as differing names are sometimes applied to
the same cut. For example, emerald cut or step cut, French cut or
calibre cut, Double French or Cardinal cut and many more. But
basically, all cuts are variations of the two earliest forms, the table cut
and the brilliant.

Before going further, let us look at a faceted stone and name its parts.
Starting from the top, the flat portion is termed the table, usually the
largest facet on the stone, from which it tapers outwards, usually for

*Fig. 25
Possible evolution of
faceting. Natural
crystal form with base
and apex removed*

*Fig. 26
Progression to more
usually accepted table
cut*

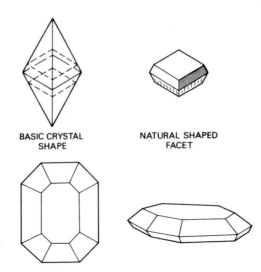

BASIC CRYSTAL
SHAPE

NATURAL SHAPED
FACET

$\frac{1}{3}$ its thickness, to the widest part, the girdle, the space between being referred to as the crown. From the girdle downwards is known as the pavilion and if a small facet is made on the base, this is the culet facet. Hence the terms "crown main facets", "pavilion mains", etc. In a brilliant cut stone there are 32 crown facets above the girdle and 24 below, plus the table and the culet, making the 58 facets first cut by Petruzzi. Many books, however, state that the standard brilliant cut has 57 facets and this is because the modern tendency is to grind the pavilion facets to a point, omitting the culet, as this increases the brilliance and fire.

The table cut (was this name derived from Tavernier's "Great Table", a huge diamond weighing more than 240 carats?) is by some experts regarded as the basic form, as it can easily be carried out by simply grinding off the points at the base and apex of a natural crystal.

This cut is used extensively on opaque stones such as sard, bloodstone, onyx, hematite and lapis lazuli for mounting in rings, cuff links and seals, as the flat table is usually sufficiently large to permit engraving for this latter purpose.

Stones cut in this fashion may be single or double bevel, flat topped or slightly domed (buff top) or combinations of these shapes. By increasing the number of facets above and below the girdle, the stone is said to be step cut or emerald cut, as emeralds are frequently cut in this manner.

The vast majority of step cut stones are square or rectangular, some-times with the corners removed to form an elongated octagon, but as all the facets are parallel to the girdle, it is obviously a more simple cut than the brilliant. The cutting of a faceted gem in this style is often successfully attempted in school by children who have previously only cut one cabochon.

Rock crystal, amethyst, smoky quartz, rutilated quartz and rose quartz are all popular with children for their first attempts.

GIM-PEG METHOD

Early gem cutters used a simple piece of apparatus when faceting, and indeed, many professional cutters use the same method today, the process being termed the gim (jam, jamb, gem) peg method. Children can be taught to produce reasonably faceted stones with the aid of the peg which we fixed to our combination unit. Mounted on the machine, adjacent to the lap, is a vertical shaft which carries a pear-shaped piece of hardwood, adjustable for height and having a series of holes drilled spirally around the major portion of its surface.

To create a faceted gem, the stone is first sawn and ground to shape and overall size (when it is termed a preform), after which all the succeeding operations are carried out on the lap. Ideally, the laps should vary in hardness according to the stone being worked, increasing in hardness with the hardness of the stone. They are used as described in the section on lapping, although the speed is reduced to between 200 and 300 r.p.m.

Specially made dop sticks are used for faceting and these should be of less diameter than the preform so that the girdle projects slightly and is clearly visible, otherwise there is the strong possibility that some facets will be cut beyond the girdle. These dop sticks are made from Duralumin rod, about 6 in. long in a range of diameters from $\frac{1}{8}$ in. to $\frac{5}{16}$ in., one end being turned to a point in the lathe. The other end is drilled with a Slocombe drill until it almost reaches the diameter of the rod. This greatly facilitates the dopping of the preform and ensures a good degree of adhesion, which is an important consideration, especially if accurate and correctly faceted gems are attempted by using a mechanical aid known as a faceting head.

This particular piece of apparatus will be discussed later in the chapter, but meanwhile, let us continue with our method of producing a stone, using our primitive gim peg.

Having dopped the stone as squarely as possible, it is usual to polish the table first, and this the children do by holding the dopped stone face down on the lap, which is charged with a slurry of 220 silicon carbide grit and water, moving it across the face of the revolving lap and at the same time slowly twisting the dop stick to and fro between the finger and thumb.

Only gentle pressure needs to be exerted because of the comparatively small area being treated, constant examination of the stone being made to ensure that a flat face is obtained. The process is repeated, using 400 and 500 grits in succession, finishing off with cerium oxide on hard leather.

The coarse grit lap is then replaced on the machine and the peg
adjusted for height so that the point of the dop stick, when jammed
into a suitable hole, will give the requisite inclination to the stick
which will result in the gem resting on the lap at the desired angle,
usually about 45° in our case, as we mostly use varieties of quartz. It
must be emphasised that the stone points in the direction of the
rotation of the lap as this minimises the possibility of the stone being
chipped at the edges, lessens the strain on the dopping wax and
prevents the stone "digging in" the surface of the lap.

*Plate 6
Facet cutting using
gem peg – cutting
main crown facets*

Having lifted the stone off the lap, an important point, the machine is
switched on, the stone lowered onto the lap and the stick rotated
between finger and thumb. Again, only very gentle pressure is needed.
After a few seconds, the gritty sound of grinding will fade, a signal that
the stone has been rounded off at the crown angle, ready to receive
the crown main facets.

Using the same hole on the peg, the stone is again lowered gently onto
the revolving lap and a small flat is ground on the crown. The stone is
raised from the lap, rotated through 180° and a flat of similar size
ground, after which the stone is rotated through 90° for the 3rd facet
and 180° for the 4th.

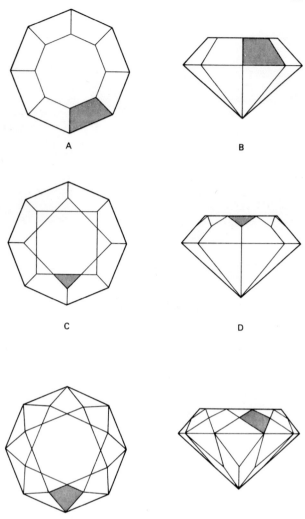

Fig. 27
Facet stages
A is plan view of B
C is plan view of D
E is plan view of F

Facets numbered 5, 6, 7 and 8 are obtained by repeating the procedure as in obtaining 1 and 2 and with care and a good eye, the table will have been reduced to a reasonably shaped octagon.

The coarse lap can now be removed and the 400 or 500 lap substituted, the stone, dop stick and hands thoroughly washed and the facets again worked in the same sequence. In the case of a standard brilliant cut, the 8 table facets (sometimes termed skill facets or star facets) are the next to be cut, and as these are very small, the fine grade grit will prove adequate. The table facets break the joining edges of the main facets and should extend for a distance of $\frac{1}{3}$ the distance between the table and the girdle, the angle of cut being 30°. The peg is rotated or lifted, as necessary, to obtain this angle, and only the lightest of pressure and constant examination is needed to produce these tiny facets. When they are created on a gem of perhaps less than $\frac{1}{8}$ in. diameter, the reason for the term "skill" facets becomes quite obvious.

Plate 7
Facet cutting using
gem peg – cutting
table facets

The girdle facets, 16 in number, cut at an angle of 50°, are the next to be cut, one each side of the divisions between the crown main facets, the dividing line forming a common side for each of the adjacent triangles. The apex of the triangles forming each pair of girdle facets should just touch the apex of the table facet above them, whilst the base, which must not quite touch the girdle, should meet its neighbouring facet half-way along the crown facet. The reason for stopping short of the girdle is to prevent making a thin edge which would possibly chip when being set in a piece of jewelry.

After completing the girdle facets, the crown is ready for polishing. Before the polishing lap is handled, the usual precautions regarding cleanliness must be observed, as a scratch on the stone at this stage must be avoided at all costs. Having fitted the polishing lap, each facet is polished in turn, beginning with the girdle facets, as the peg will be correctly adjusted for this operation. Only a few seconds are needed to polish each facet and care must be taken not to exert too heavy a pressure, as this could generate sufficient heat to either burn or crack the stone. The peg is then adjusted to give the angle for the table facets, and subsequently the main facets, which are in turn polished and the crown completed.

The stone is then removed from the dop stick, the best method being to heat the stick until the wax softens. The stone can then be eased off the stick and as much of the wax as possible removed before it sets hard, the remaining wax being dissolved by wiping with or immersion in methylated spirit.

To complete the stone, the pavilion must next be cut and polished, so the next stage is to re-dop the stone squarely, a comparatively simple matter with Dural sticks, as they can be held upright in a vice and gently heated by a blowpipe flame. When the wax melts, the stone can be pressed down firmly, the reservoir of heat retained in the stick helping to overcome the chilling of the wax by the stone.

The coarse lap is restored to position once again and the peg adjusted to enable the pavilion main facets to be cut at an angle of 41°. These, 8 in number, are cut in the same way as were the crown facets. Care must be taken when grinding the first pavilion facet to ensure that the girdle width is not reduced and thus the facet must be stopped when the desired thickness of girdle has been reached. This thickness naturally varies according to the stone being worked and the setting in which it will eventually be mounted, although some authorities insist that it should be proportionate to the diameter of the stone, usually about 2 per cent.

The placing of the pavilion main facets is also very important as these should line up with the crown main facets in a correctly cut brilliant, and this calls for careful judgement at all stages. Once these have been cut almost to size on the coarse lap, the finer lap is substituted to cut the facets to finished size and remove the marks left by the coarse grit.

This lap will be quite adequate for the cutting of the pavilion girdle facets which are cut in pairs, one each side of each main, in the same manner as the crown girdle facets, forming tiny inverted and adjacent right-angled triangles with a common height, bases extending half-way along the girdle and their hypotenuse meeting half-way down the line of each main facet.

Only a slight change of angle, usually about 3 or 4 degrees is required for cutting these facets and this being accomplished, the pavilion is ready for its final polish. To really complete the stone all that remains is to give the girdle a trim by lightly twisting the dop stick round, on and parallel to the lap to smooth off the edge before fitting the polishing lap. Bear in mind that a considerable amount of time and effort has been used, which can be nullified if care is not observed at this final stage. Having washed hands, stone and dop stick, the polishing can be carried out as on the crown and the stone removed, cleaned free of wax ready to mount.

It will be obvious that this is a highly skilled process, dependent solely on the operator's hand and eye, many years of experience being necessary to acquire the technique. It will be equally obvious that the cutting of a perfect brilliant will be beyond the capabilities of youngsters. However, this does not mean that they should not be encouraged to try, and as a beginning, they will get a tremendous thrill from making a simple faceted stone, perhaps with just the table, crown and pavilion mains cut and polished.

Whilst this may be a complete anathema to the serious worker, it will be a great source of pride to the child who has created it from the rough and who may be stimulated to further efforts.

This is another instance in which lapidary work can be correlated with yet another allied craft subject, Technical Drawing. Facet cuts could be designed and orthagonal projections carried out, in addition to Isometric sketches, and whilst some of the proposed cuts may not be either suitable or practical, the children would undoubtedly benefit from such exercises.

FACETING HEADS

Plate 8
Milling exercise piece
used as faceting guide

Mechanical aids have been designed to ensure absolute accuracy in faceting. These are termed faceting heads, and many are advertised in

lapidary publications, but the cost is, in most cases, equal to the cost of a combination machine and consequently beyond the reach of the average school.

However, a standard milling exercise, carried out in many engineering apprentice's schools, can be adapted to help children create flats on their stones. As will be seen from the accompanying photograph, the exercise consists of milling a series of flats on a 2 in. diameter piece of steel, beginning with a decagon and working down to a triangle.

This is purely an exercise for the apprentices and the apprentice supervisors in our local factories can always be relied on to produce one on request. In any case, this would be a simple pattern to make and cast in aluminium alloy.

A $\frac{1}{4}$-in. hole is drilled through the centre through which an aluminium dop stick is retained in the required position by means of a grub screw and the faces of the template are supported by a horizontal bar mounted on the vertical shaft. Subsequent procedure is as when using the gim peg method and simple step cuts can easily be made.

Plate 9
Making a table cut
gem using milling
exercise piece

The commercial faceting head is a precision instrument, but the making of one is not beyond the capabilities of any metal-work master and although we have not yet made one in our school, it is a worthwhile project which we hope to undertake when time permits.

Members of the Kingston Lapidary Society have made them, virtually from odds and ends of scrap. The faceted gems produced would do credit to a professional cutter, working with expensive equipment, although some degree of care and skill is needed to compensate for the lack of the more sophisticated refinements possessed by the commercial unit.

The faceting heads made by my fellow club members consist of a rigid shaft, either attached to the machine as for the gim peg or mounted on a heavy base. Mounted on the shaft is a sliding collar, which can be supported at any height on the shaft, at the same time being free to swing, and extending from this collar is a quadrant arm, marked off in degrees from 0° (parallel to the lap plate) to 90°.

*Fig. 28
Artist's impression of
amateur made
faceting head*

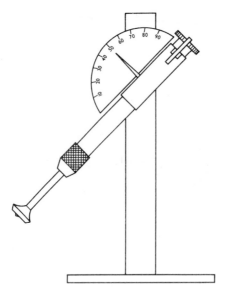

Fixed to the central point of the quadrant, the dop arm can be rotated to any angle on the quadrant and locked in position, a pointer reading off the angle of elevation, this being equal to the angle between the girdle and the facet being ground.

The dop arm is bored throughout its length, and the dop stick holder passes through this bore with a push fit. On the upper end of the dop holder is a fixed disc of metal, approximately $\frac{1}{4}$ in. thick and $2\frac{3}{4}$ in. in diameter, which has 96 $\frac{1}{16}$ in. holes equally spaced on a $1\frac{1}{4}$ P.C.D.

A spring-loaded plunger fixed to the dop arm indents into these holes, thus enabling the dop stick holder to be held in any of 96 rotary positions, and as 96 is divisible by multiples of 2 and 3, this enables a great variety of facet cuts to be made. (The number of facets must divide into the number of holes in order for them to be equal in size.)

An improvement would be to have an additional circle of 80 holes, equally spaced, and a moveable or a second plunger, as this would permit the cutting of pentagons and facet cuts with multiples of 5 facets.

The dop sticks are retained in a collar or chuck fitted at the lower end of the holder, and this portion, in view of the fact that it will be constantly in contact with water, is best made from stainless steel or a non-ferrous metal.

Readers who decide to include faceting in their lapidary work will appreciate that having finished the crown of a faceted stone by use of a faceting head, it is essential that the stone must be transferred to another dop stick to work on the pavilion, and that it is very important that the stone be fixed "square" on this second dop stick. This transfer can be easily accomplished by means of the small jig illustrated.

Plate 10
Dop transfer jig

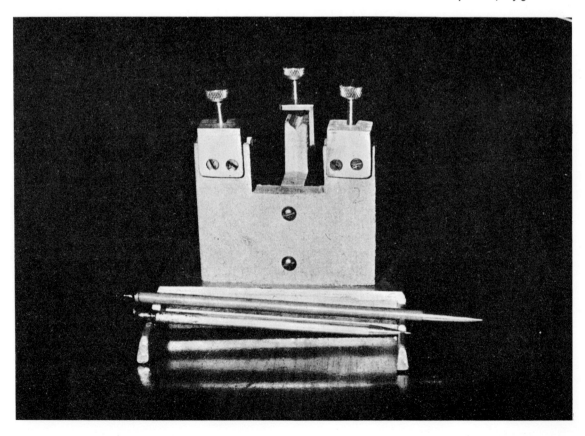

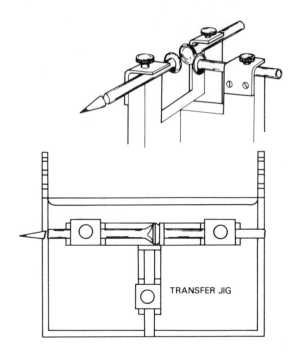

*Fig. 29
Dop transfer jig*

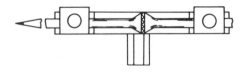

Ours was made from two small pieces of Sindanyo, a form of asbestos sufficiently hard to withstand machining, the vee grooves being cut with a 90° countersink, gripped in the lathe chuck, both pieces being clamped onto the milling attachment, thus ensuring that the vees were at the same height.

For both convenience and appearance the blocks, having been fixed together, were mounted on a cast base which also holds face plates, which are turned from aluminium rod, and metal dop sticks ready for use.

To mount a gem for faceting, a face plate is securely held in one of the vees by the appropriate clamping screw, a prepared dop stick is held in the opposite vee and the ready-warmed stone placed between them. A face plate mounted in the vee at right angles to the dop stick enables the stone to be correctly centred, whereon the dop stick can be heated by any suitable flame, until the wax becomes sufficiently soft to allow the dop stick to be pressed against the stone.

*Plate 11 (above, opposite)
Milling vee grooves in
Sindanyo for dop
transfer jig*

*Plate 12 (below, opposite
Centring gem against
face plate*

To transfer the stone to another dop stick merely involves the substitution of a second dop stick for the face plate opposite, heating it to fix the stone, afterwards heating the first dop stick to release it.

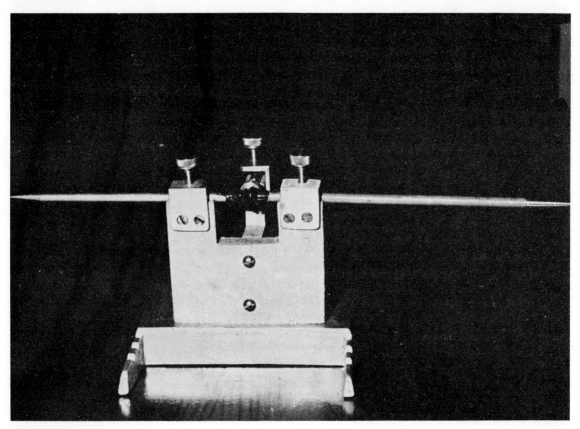

*Plate 13
Transferring gem for
cutting the pavilion*

Lapidary machines A combination unit for the Do-It-Yourself enthusiast

In the few short months which have elapsed since the first words of this book were written, there has been a great increase in lapidary work in this country; newspapers and magazines have printed articles and a British magazine, devoted solely to the craft, has appeared on the bookstalls.

Craft teachers now have a fairly wide range of machines from which to choose if finances permit, but I am aware of the fact that many schools and amateur craftsmen cannot afford the initial outlay to purchase a commercial unit if they wish to begin lapidary work. This should not prevent them from having a go, because the unit which is described in the following pages can be produced for a very moderate cost.

When first introducing lapidary work into my school, I had no alternative other than to construct a machine, and at that time, ploughing what was virtually a lone furrow, produced a simple but effective unit which has been in use for several years and still functions efficiently.

The basic requirements of a lapidary unit are shafts to carry the saw, grinding wheels, discs and pulleys, the shafts being driven by an electric motor and suitable belts. Obviously, the shafts need to be housed in bearings which in turn must be supported. In the first instance, the problems of a suitable design were discussed with two interested Fifth Form boys, one of whom pointed out that there were several short lengths of $1\frac{1}{2}$-in. Dexion which had been left over from a project in the Science department.

These were soon acquired and governed the finished size of the unit, as, not being sure of the ultimate successful functioning of the unit, or the interest it would arouse in the rest of the children, it was essential that the cost be kept to an absolute minimum.

Four 1 ft. 6 in. and four 1 ft. 3 in. lengths of the Dexion were bolted together to form two 1 ft. 6 in. by 1 ft. 3 in. rectangles, which were then bolted to four vertical pieces, each 1 ft. 9 in. long to form a "box" 1 ft. 6 in. by 1 ft. 3 in., with a height of 1 ft. 9 in.

*Plate 14
Frame assembly of
combination unit*

Several ideas were then considered and rough sketches made, to decide how the saw and two grinding wheels were to be mounted, but every solution posed further problems. It was eventually decided that as only one shaft could conveniently be accommodated on what was to be the table, or top of the box, one end must serve two operations and that the saw and coarse grinding wheel could alternately be mounted on one end of the shaft as and when required.

A $\frac{5}{8}$-in. diameter by 15-in. long Picador shaft was purchased, together with a pair of self-aligning "sealed for life" pillow block bearings. This is the best type of bearing for this machine, because it excludes grit-laden moisture from the ball races, and, in addition, the cheaper type of plummer block can be extremely difficult to line up; as little as $\frac{1}{1000}$ in. out of line will cause stiffness and consequent excessive wear.

Plate 15
Assembly turned to
show main shaft
bearing supports

The shafts are supplied with the ends turned down to $\frac{1}{2}$-in. diameter for a distance of 2 in. at one end and $2\frac{1}{2}$ in. at the other, being threaded with fine left- and right-hand threads alternately, complete with a nut and two flange washers for each end.

Facing the direction of rotation, another 1 ft. 3 in. length of Dexion was bolted across the top, $6\frac{1}{2}$ in. from the left, and a second similar piece bolted across the top $3\frac{1}{2}$ in. from the right, the pillow blocks being mounted on top of these two bearers at 8-in. centres.

Two $1\frac{3}{4}$-in. "A" section vee pulleys were fitted to the shaft between the bearing, care being taken to ensure that the short threaded end, which is threaded left-hand, was at the left-hand side. This end takes either the saw or the coarse wheel, the smooth wheel being mounted permanently at the right-hand side. This arrangement is purely arbitrary but it seemed more natural to follow the sequence of operations from left to right.

The bearings were bolted down securely, the wheels fitted and spun by hand to ensure that they revolved truly, after which they were removed and the top covered with a sheet of $\frac{1}{8}$-in. thick aluminium. Aluminium seemed the obvious choice in view of the amount of water which is splashed around. Some constructors may prefer to use galvanised sheet steel, marine ply, blockboard faced with a plastic laminate, or any similar material; the choice is left to the individual.

Two slots, 6 in. by 2 in., were cut into the sheet to accommodate the wheels, the necessary holes drilled and the table fixed to the top of the box frame, the grinding assembly fitted into position, enabling us to visualise the position of the motor.

*Plate 16
Bearers for Picador
polishing head and
motor*

Sawing and grinding having been catered for, all that remained was to arrange for sanding and polishing before adding the "refinements". A search through catalogues revealed that Picador make a $4\frac{3}{4}$-in. centre height polishing head with a right- and left-hand threaded shaft and this gave the solution to our final serious problem.

Two further 1 ft. 6 in. lengths of Dexion were bolted across the front and back of the box, 8 in. from the base and two 1 ft. 3 in. lengths bolted across them at $4\frac{1}{2}$-in. centres 4 in. in from the right-hand side, forming the bearers for the polishing head which was thus mounted parallel with and below the main shaft.

We were fortunate in obtaining an old flameproof type $\frac{1}{4}$ h.p. electric motor, which saved us the trouble of arranging shields to prevent the entry of water into the motor, and this was mounted on two 8-in. pieces of $1\frac{1}{4} \times \frac{1}{4}$ mild steel, bolted from the base to the front polishing

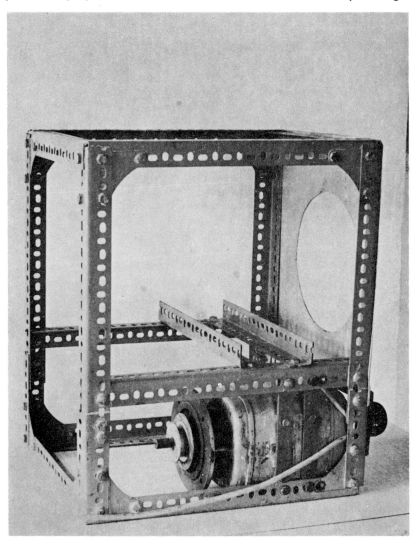

Plate 17
Motor mounted and
bowl support fitted

head bearer. Slots were then cut into the top plate to permit the fitting of the driving belts. A 3-in. pulley on the motor, driving the $1\frac{3}{4}$ pulley on the main shaft through a vee-belt gave us a speed of approximately 2500 r.p.m. and an A29 vee-belt from the second pulley on the main shaft driving a $4\frac{1}{2}$-in. pulley on the polishing head produced a spindle speed of approximately 970 r.p.m.

By turning the whole frame on to its end, the polishing head spindle assumed a vertical position, enabling the discs to run horizontally.

A piece of aluminium sheet was then cut to the size of the end and a hole large enough to take a plastic washing-up bowl (10 in. diameter in our case), cut out, the centre of the hole coinciding with the centre of the spindle.

Plate 18
Polishing head and
grinding splash fitted

Plate 19
Assembly with diamond saw and fine wheel

After a 1¼-in. hole had been cut in the centre of the base of the bowl, a 1-in. length of plastic tube was cemented in, and the bowl, having been pressed into the hole in the aluminium plate, was placed over the spindle which projected about an inch over the top of the plastic tube.

A suitable length of ½-in. bore aluminium tube was slid over the spindle, the end of this tube just projecting over the top of the plastic tube and forming a bearer for a flange washer which supported our discs. These were 6-in. diameter ⅛ aluminium sheet onto which were cemented similar sized discs of leather, held down by a further flange washer and nut.

The aluminium plate was then drilled and bolted into position and the sanding and polishing end being ready for action, we turned our attention back to the grinding head.

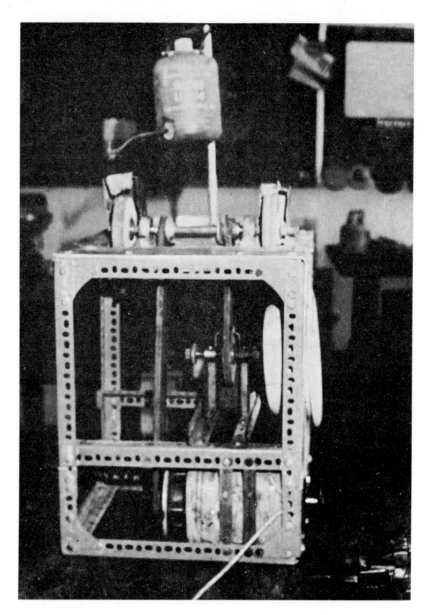

Plate 20
Ready for use. Fine
and coarse wheels
fitted

In our ignorance, we assumed that troughs mounted below the wheels could be filled with water to enable them to run wet, and two were made of sheet brass with hinged covers. This, of course, was before we appreciated the danger of allowing wheels to rest in water or the necessity of observing precaution No. I, *stand out of line*, but fortunately, all we suffered when first switching on was a ducking, the contents of the trough being ejected with considerable force despite the hoods.

A simple bracket was fitted to the frame and a polythene container suspended from it, a piece of copper tube with a cylinder block drain tap soldered into the end, having first been fixed through a hole at the

Plate 21
Assembly turned onto
side for sanding and
polishing

lower end of the container. This was achieved by threading the end of the copper tube and pushing it into the hole in the container with a nut at each side of the container wall.

We now had a drip feed which could be swung from one wheel to the other and capable of being controlled to produce a minimum of splashing, which was further prevented by fastening pieces of soft leather on the hoods and allowing them to just touch the wheels. To prevent water remaining in the troughs, a hole was drilled and tapped in each of their bases to accommodate a screw plug to enable them to be drained before turning the unit over after grinding had been finished.

We were now in business. A 6-in. sintered rim saw, essential for this type of machine with children because the direction of rotation is immaterial, enabled us to cut small slices of suitable materials which were soon ground and polished into cabochons.

Our machine has been described as Heath Robinson, but it soon attracted the attentions of "the powers that be", who appreciated the possibilities of the craft as a school subject, and enabled us to purchase a P.M.R.2 machine for the school.

F

The P.M.R. range of machines are now being used in many schools and are supplied complete with all accessories ready for immediate use.

One criticism which may be levelled against the P.M.R.2 machine is that it can only be used by one person at a time, but this is the case with all machine tools, most of which cost appreciably more, and are monopolised by one student for much longer periods.

The wheels, sanding and polishing discs are mounted in turn on an arbor, and in practice, with several children engaged in jewelry making, it is possible for some of them to cut their slices, mark out, trim saw and dop their stones, whilst one is using the coarse wheel. They then carry on with designing and making their mounts, ring shanks, etc., coarse grinding in turn as the wheel becomes vacant.

The remainder of the processes are then continued in the same manner and this helps a smooth, uninterrupted sequence of operations, right through to the silver soldering and finishing processes, each child in the group always being fully occupied.

The maker of the P.M.R. range of machines has obviously been aware of the need for improvement in this respect with the result that on the P.M.R.3 model, only the sanding and polishing discs need to be changed so that it is possible for four children to use the machine at any one time. The latest model, the P.M.R.4, is a much smaller and cheaper machine than the P.M.R.3; a 6-in. unit costing £32·50 against the £79·50 of the 8-in. P.M.R.3 unit.

The only disadvantage experienced with these machines is that silicon carbide sanding discs are mostly used as, running vertically, wet grits are soon thrown off wood or leather discs. Many of the younger children prefer to sand and polish on the "Heath Robinson" machine as they insist that they find it easier to work over the top of the disc rather than on the side.

This was one of the reasons why the two collaborators in the "Heath Robinson" design, by this time members of the Upper Sixth, were again pressed into service, this time to help design and make a much more sophisticated unit which would enable a gem to be cut from the rough, with the minimum amount of delay occasioned by changing wheels.

A PROJECT FOR THE METALWORK ROOM

From the outset, it was agreed that castings were essential, and as our furnace can only accommodate an A5 crucible, aluminium alloy casting of more than 3 lb. would involve more complications.

Not being equipped with either a milling or a shaping machine, all the machining operations would have to be carried out on our $4\frac{1}{2}$-in.

Harrison lathe, which fortunately is equipped with a boring table. With these considerations in mind, rough sketches were prepared.

Several amendments were made, bearing in mind that for various reasons, the machine must be portable and the overall length limited to 3 feet. Eventually, rough working drawings were produced and we were again under way.

It was obvious that a rigid base would be needed, and although the possibilities of bolting castings together were considered, we decided that this was unsatisfactory and the boys soon produced a suitable wood pattern for a solid base.

Plate 22
Saw tank castings and grinding wheel trough casting

This they took to a small local foundry which specialises in the production of aluminium alloy castings and, having explained their problems to the interested proprietor, spent an afternoon there, returning with the information that they had poured the casting and could collect it the next day after it had been fettled.

This visit proved extremely beneficial, because the boys, in addition to obtaining the casting at a very reasonable price, were given many useful hints on foundry practice.

THE SAW

Having obtained the base, which fortunately was extremely flat, it was scraped smooth and a start was made on the tank which was to support the saw and table.

We had decided that our unit should have an 8-in. saw, and this governed the size of the tank, which could not be fitted into our casting boxes, so this was cast in two parts from the same pattern. These were then mounted in turn on the lathe boring table, and the meeting faces machined true by means of a fly cutter, made especially for the job. This tool has been used for many of the machining operations involved in the construction of the unit, and the accompanying photograph should enable anyone who is interested to make one for themselves.

*Plate 23
Fly cutter assembled*

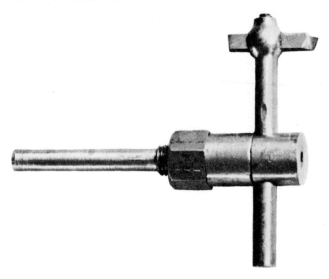

*Plate 24
Fly cutter dismantled*

Plate 25
Fly cutter in use.
Machining meeting
faces of tank

The two halves of the tank were then drilled and screwed together with 4 B.A. socket screws and again clamped onto the boring table. The top and bottom were then machined flat.

As the shaft which was to carry the saw blade would have to pass through the tank, a Pollard S F TAG, $\frac{5}{8}$-in. flange bearing could, with advantage, be mounted on the side to support the shaft. The centre height having been calculated, the holes for the bearing were then marked out on a surface plate. The sides of the tank were separated and one of them clamped to a milling attachment mounted on the lathe top slide and the centre of the bearing hole located by lining up with a Slocombe drill mounted in the lathe mandrel. The Slocombe drill was then removed and a $\frac{5}{8}$-in. end mill substituted in its place and the bearing hole drilled, after which the screw holes were drilled and tapped in the normal manner.

The holes to take the screws to fix the tank to the base and the saw table to the tank were drilled and tapped and the two sides re-assembled together, a smear of Osotite gasket cement having been previously applied to the mating surfaces to ensure that they would remain water tight.

Plate 26
Machining tank base

Plate 27
Positioning holes for
bearing bolts, using
Slocombe drill

Plate 28
Milling hole for saw
spindle

Whilst these machining operations were being carried out, the pattern for the saw table had been made and the table casting poured. In order to accomplish this, two crucibles of metal were needed, one being first melted, removed from the furnace and kept at heat in the forge until the second crucible charge was ready for pouring, when the two crucibles were poured into the casting flask together. Realising that this was not quite acceptable workshop practice, it was carried out by members of staff after the children had gone home and the casting was ready for them when they returned to school the next day.

No machining was necessary on the saw table, other than the marking out and drilling of the four clearance holes for the countersunk headed screws which hold the table to the tank. This was then smeared with Osotite and mounted on the base, four $\frac{3}{8}$-in. clearance holes, counter-bored to take $\frac{3}{8}$-in. socket screws, having been previously drilled in the base for this purpose.

Plate 29
*Saw spindle and tank
assembly*

About this time, we realised that it would be advantageous to include a vice on the table and although this was hastily designed, it is nevertheless quite efficient.

The slide bar was turned down to a shoulder, threaded and screwed into the two cast blocks which were then mounted onto the table after the sliding carrier had been fitted onto the slide bar, the actual vice being made at a later date.

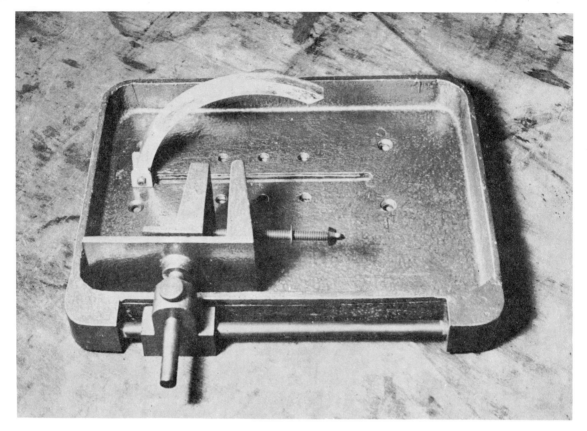

Plate 30
Sawing table with
vice assembled

THE GRINDING WHEELS

Having completed the sawing table, our attention was next focused on the grinding wheels, and as will be seen from the drawings, the design called for two shafts, one of which was to carry the saw and the coarse wheel.

The centre height of this shaft having already been decided, a simple calculation gave us the requisite height for the bearing pedestal and a pattern was made, allowing a $\frac{1}{4}$ in. more in height for machining. The two shafts were to be fixed at the same height, running in Pollard S L Pillow blocks, so three castings were taken from this pattern and again, the fly cutter was brought into operation, the three castings being clamped together on the boring table and machined as one. The holes to take the fixing screws and bearing retaining screws were drilled and tapped, clearance holes drilled in the base plate, which was counterbored underneath to accommodate $\frac{3}{8}$-in. socket head screws, and the three bearing pedestals mounted in their respective positions.

Plate 31
Machining bearing
pedestals

The shaft to take the saw and coarse wheel was made from $\frac{5}{8}$-in. diameter bright steel, mounted in the lathe between centres and $1\frac{3}{8}$ in. was turned down to $\frac{1}{2}$-in. diameter at one end, the other end turned down to $\frac{1}{2}$-in. diameter for a distance of $2\frac{1}{4}$ in.

A gear train to cut 16 threads per inch ($\frac{1}{2}$ in. B.S.F.) was arranged and $\frac{11}{16}$ in. of left-hand thread was cut on the shorter of the two ends, the other end being threaded for $\frac{5}{8}$ in., right-hand thread. The lengths of these threads are most important and will depend on the thickness of the flange washers, which are mounted on each side of the saw and the wheels. The thread should finish as close as possible to the outside face of the outer washer, as this prevents the washer from being forced out of line by the pressure of the locking nut. Failure to observe this precaution will result in a very wobbly saw, as we found on our first attempt.

A finer thread would, of course, be more suitable and would minimise this problem, but as we had no fine thread chasers, and we did have $\frac{1}{2}$-in. B.S.F. left- and right-hand taps and dies, we chose this size to facilitate the cleaning up of the threads which have proved to be quite satisfactory in operation.

Plate 32
Bowl support and lap
bearing spindle
support castings

The second shaft was made in similar fashion but only needed one end turning down to $\frac{1}{2}$ in. for $2\frac{1}{4}$ in. This was threaded with a left-hand thread for $\frac{3}{4}$ in., the other end being left plain.

On temporarily fitting the bearing pedestals, we realised that we had made a blunder in designing the base. No provision had been made to prevent water splashing from the wheels or to keep it from flooding the whole base of the machine. Not wishing future operators to have permanently wet knees, we cast an open-ended box which was screwed to the base from underneath, the seal in this case being made with Araldite in view of the fact that the walls of the box would only take 4 B.A. screws.

PROVIDING FOR SANDING, POLISHING AND LAPPING

The two supports for the bowl which would prevent splash from the sanding and polishing discs were the next items to be cast, and were machined as a pair, the ubiquitous fly cutter again being pressed into service.

It had already been decided that we should use a plastic bowl similar in size to the one on our original machine, and as the crucible furnace was always ready, a top plate was cast which would take the bowl. The supports had been mounted on the base, and after holes had been drilled and countersunk in the top plate, this was placed on the supports and the position of the holes marked off, using the top plate as a template.

The supports were then removed, drilled and tapped and the top plate fixed on to them, re-assembled as a whole on the base, and we now faced our final problem, obtaining a vertical from a horizontal drive.

Bevel gears seemed to be the obvious answer, but the cutting of these was beyond our capabilities, and although we could have had some made, by this time we were feeling independent and regarded the solution of this problem as a challenge to our ingenuity; lay shafts, toothed or twisted belts and jockey pulleys were all considered and eventually we thought of a friction drive.

Plate 33
Machining bowl
support bracket
castings

A suitable bracket was designed to fit a $\frac{5}{8}$-in. Plummer block which we had in stock, a pattern made and the subsequent casting machined to give a parallel base and top by the usual method. This was then

mounted on one of the bowl supports with the centre of the bearing central with the bowl and a piece of $\frac{5}{8}$-in. diameter bright mild steel, turned to a sharp point at one end, enabled us to locate the centre of a housing to take the vertical shaft.

A $\frac{1}{2}$-in. diameter hole was drilled through the base plate at this location point, and a spigot $\frac{1}{2}$-in. diameter and $\frac{1}{8}$ in. less in length than the thickness of the base plate, turned on a short length of $\frac{7}{8}$-in. diameter phosphor bronze. Whilst still in the lathe, a $\frac{1}{4}$-in. B.S.F. hole was drilled and tapped centrally into the spigot and the bar parted off $1\frac{1}{8}$ in. from the shoulder of the spigot. This piece, which would form the housing was then reversed in the lathe, faced off, centred, drilled and reamed $\frac{1}{2}$-in. diameter for a depth of $\frac{5}{8}$ in. and the spigot drawn into the base plate with a $\frac{1}{4}$-in. B.S.F. screw and washer.

A piece of $1\frac{1}{4}$-in. diameter phosphor bronze was then chucked in the lathe, faced off, centred and then turned down to $\frac{7}{8}$-in. diameter for $\frac{11}{16}$ in. along its length. It was then drilled to be subsequently reamed $\frac{5}{8}$-in. diameter and parted off 1 in. from the end, reversed in the chuck and $\frac{1}{8}$ in. turned down to $\frac{7}{8}$-in. diameter, thus forming a bush with a projecting collar which was coarse knurled.

Three 4 B.A. holes were drilled and tapped at equal distances in the $\frac{11}{16}$-in. length, countersunk to take 3 retaining screws and after reaming it was pushed onto the opposite end of the shaft which carries the fine grinding wheel to form a driving wheel. All that now remained for us to sort out, was a friction disc to rotate the shaft which would be supported by the housing in the base plate and the plummer block above it.

Another casting, this time a simple $4\frac{1}{4}$ by $\frac{1}{2}$-in. thick disc with a central boss $1\frac{1}{8}$ in. diameter, $1\frac{1}{4}$ in. long was quickly made, turned true in the lathe, the boss then held in the chuck and a recess $\frac{1}{4}$ in. deep turned into the face, leaving a wall approximately $\frac{1}{16}$ in. thick. The casting was then reversed and a $\frac{1}{2}$-in. diameter hole drilled through, counterbored to a full $\frac{25}{32}$-in. diameter for $1\frac{1}{4}$ in. and a $\frac{7}{32}$ in. slot cut across the end. A disc of $\frac{1}{4}$-in. thick tough rubber sheet was fixed into the recess with Evostik and a $\frac{1}{2}$-in. drill passed through.

The vertical shaft was made from $\frac{5}{8}$-in. diameter bright steel, turned down to $\frac{1}{2}$-in. diameter for $6\frac{7}{16}$ in. cut off to length, 11 in. A No. 3 hole was drilled through the $\frac{5}{8}$-in. diameter, 1 in. from the shoulder, through which a $\frac{7}{32}$ silver steel peg $1\frac{1}{4}$ in. long was later driven. The end was faced off and a $\frac{15}{32}$-in. diameter hole was deep drilled for $\frac{3}{4}$ in. into the end to accommodate the discs and laps, as will be seen later.

It was visualised that a strong compression spring would be placed on the $\frac{1}{2}$-in. portion of the shaft and sit in the counterbore of the driving disc, so that the silver steel peg, engaging with the slot on the boss, would take up the drive. This meant that a thrust collar be pinned

Plate 34
Cooker hot plate.
Centre boss machined
to take drive

onto the shaft above the pin, immediately below the plummer block, and having carried out this job, a phosphor bronze thrust washer was made to minimise wear on the plummer block face when the machine was in operation.

The amateur lapidary worker soon cultivates a very discerning eye regarding articles which may be of use to him in his hobby, and we are no exception as we had acquired some scrap electric cooker hot plates. These were the 6-in. and 9-in. in diameter, solid type with the elements encased in grooves underneath. After removing the element and insulation, the tops were skimmed flat in the lathe. The central bosses on the underside were then turned down to $\frac{15}{32}$-in. diameter, a nice push fit into the end of the shaft, and a $\frac{7}{32}$-in. slot cut across the diameter of each boss about $\frac{3}{8}$ in. deep. This slot engages with a $\frac{7}{32}$-in.

Plate 35 (above, opposite)
Horizontal to vertical
drive assembly

silver steel pin which was fitted across the end of the $\frac{15}{32}$-in. hole at the top of the shaft. These former hot plates were thus converted into ideal laps.

Plate 36 (below, opposite)
Saw, coarse and fine
wheels, splash guard
and drip feed

This decided how we were to make provision for sanding and, as we wished to be able to use either loose grits or discs, aluminium alloy discs of a similar pattern were cast and covered with foam rubber onto which we cemented either leather or cloth discs.

We were now ready to assemble our combined sanding, polishing, lapping head. A $\frac{1}{2}$-in. diameter ball bearing was inserted into the phosphor bronze housing which takes the spigot at the end of the shaft, the spring fitted and the whole assembly bolted up tight, with the rubber base of the driving disc now pressing down firmly onto the knurled driving collar.

On being pulled round by hand, it worked, but very heavy pressure on the cast iron disc revealed two snags, (a) a tendency for the drive to slip and (b) the disc canted sideways. These very minor problems were soon overcome by turning the driving collar into a "gear wheel" by making saw cuts at $\frac{1}{8}$-in. intervals around the periphery and casting a three-armed support which fitted over the shaft, immediately below the disc.

*Plate 37
Hot plate support*

MOUNTING THE MOTOR, DRIP FEED AND SPLASH GUARD

The final arrangements for driving the unit were made after we had decided on the motor to be used, and eventually this turned out to be a $\frac{1}{4}$ h.p. from a discarded washing machine. This motor had been side-mounted, and in order to keep the unit as compact as possible, we decided to make two rather peculiarly shaped castings which would lift the motor above the base plate.

These having been completed, the pattern used for the bearing pedestals was reduced in height and two castings were produced to carry a pair of $\frac{5}{8}$-in. plummer blocks and a lay shaft.

Pulleys and belts were all that remained to be fitted, no problems other than ensuring that the size of the vee-belts were accurately measured and the finishing touches were soon completed, these being concerned with the water supply to the wheels.

We could have constructed a water tank from sheet but thought it more appropriate to cast one, and after two "wasters" this was accomplished. The reason for our failures was, of course, the thin section of the walls and base of the box. Future patterns for this purpose will be made from expanded polystyrene when no difficulty is anticipated.

A hole was drilled and tapped in the front, just above the base, and a cylinder drain tap off an old car engine screwed in, the tank being mounted as shown in the drawings, by keyhole slots, onto two screws in the bowl supports.

The final item was the splash guard and this we decided should be made of Perspex. Here, a word of warning. Perspex does not bend easily if soaked in boiling water. Having broken one piece, we resorted to a local firm for information on how to do it and found that, on being heated to around 300° Fahrenheit in a domestic oven, Perspex becomes extremely pliable until it loses its heat.

A thin piece of sheet metal was curved into the required shape to fit over the two wheels and this was used as a former. The Perspex was heated, removed from the oven and smoothed over it, asbestos gloves being worn for this operation.

The Perspex quickly cools and the curved shape was used as a template to mark the curves on the sheet from which the sides were made, as it is easier to adopt this sequence rather than try to make the curve fit the pre-cut sides.

Slots were made to clear the shafts and the outside shape cut on the bandsaw, and the two sides cemented into the hood with Perspex cement.

To supply a drip feed to both wheels, a plastic Tee, as used in car windscreen washers, was fixed through a hole in the splash guard, short lengths of polythene tube being added to join the tee to the tank and cover the wheels. To complete the project, the machine was given a coat of primer and finished with Titanine Blue Hammer Finish paint, giving it quite a professional appearance.

*Plate 38
The completed
lapidary unit*

Improvements in the design and methods of construction could be suggested, but this is the story of our Mark I machine which it is hoped will provide a basis from which teachers can combine standard workshop techniques with the provision of a worthwhile project which, when completed, will prove to be of the utmost value in extending the curriculum.

On the following pages are working drawings for the making of the combination lapidary unit just described.

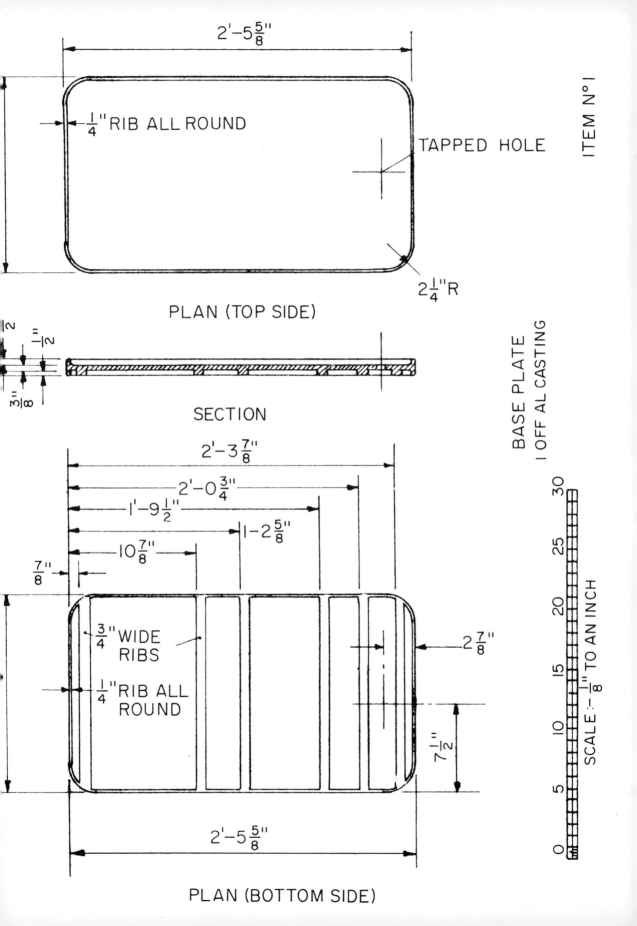

2'-5⅝"

¼"RIB ALL ROUND

TAPPED HOLE

2¼"R

PLAN (TOP SIDE)

ITEM N° I

BASE PLATE
I OFF AL CASTING

½

½"

⅜"

SECTION

2'-3⅞"

2'-0¾"

1'-9½"

1-2⅝"

10⅞"

⅞"

¾"WIDE
RIBS

¼"RIB ALL
ROUND

2⅞"

7½"

2'-5⅝"

PLAN (BOTTOM SIDE)

30

25

20

15

10

5

0

SCALE :- ⅛" TO AN INCH

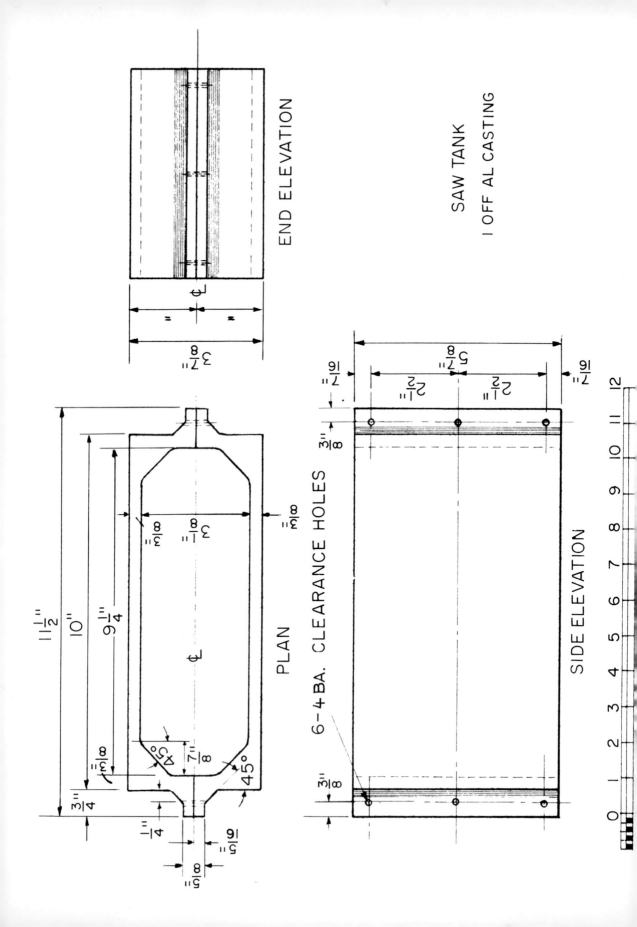

END ELEVATION

SAW TANK
1 OFF AL CASTING

PLAN

6 — 4 BA. CLEARANCE HOLES

SIDE ELEVATION

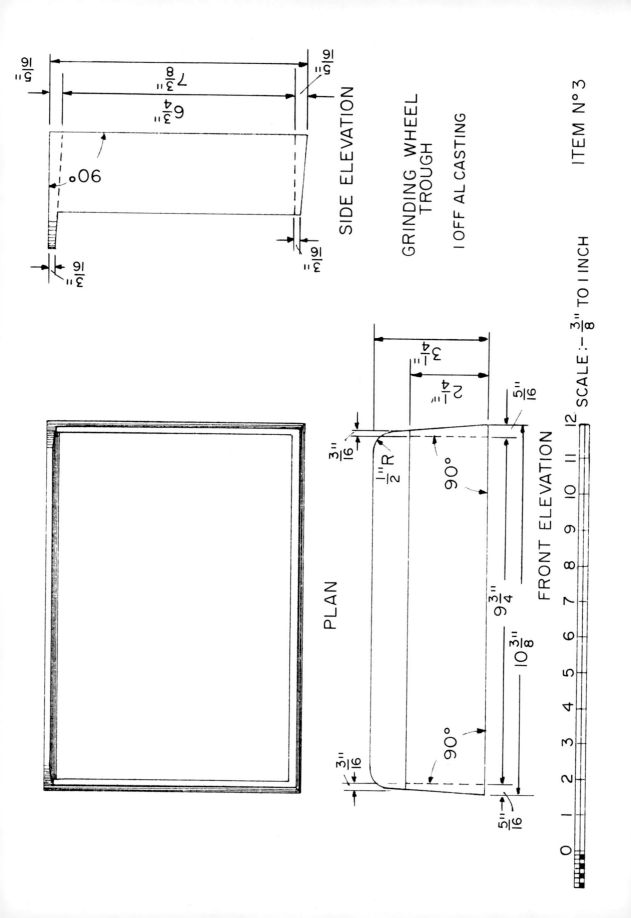

SIDE ELEVATION

GRINDING WHEEL
TROUGH

I OFF AL CASTING

ITEM N° 3

PLAN

FRONT ELEVATION

SCALE:- $\frac{3}{8}$" TO I INCH

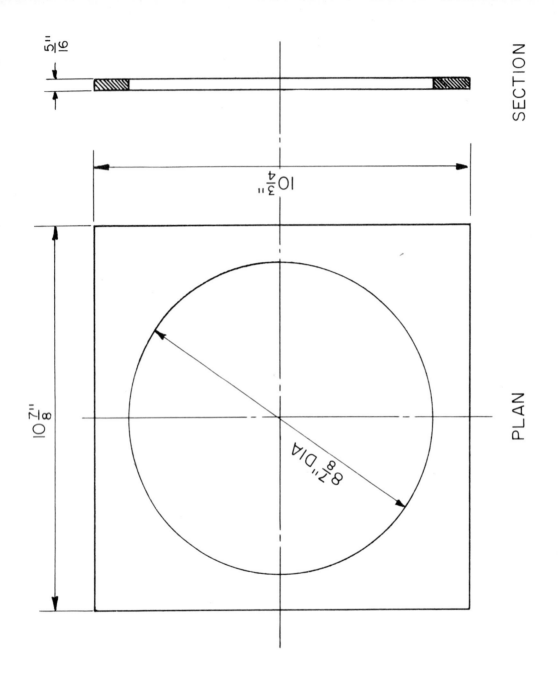

SECTION

$\frac{5''}{16}$

$10\frac{3}{4}''$

$10\frac{7}{8}''$

$8\frac{7}{8}''$ DIA

PLAN

BOWL SUPPORT PLATE

1 OFF AL CASTING

SCALE: $\frac{3}{8}''$ TO 1 INCH

0 1 2 3 4 5 6 7 8 9 10 11

ITEM N° 4

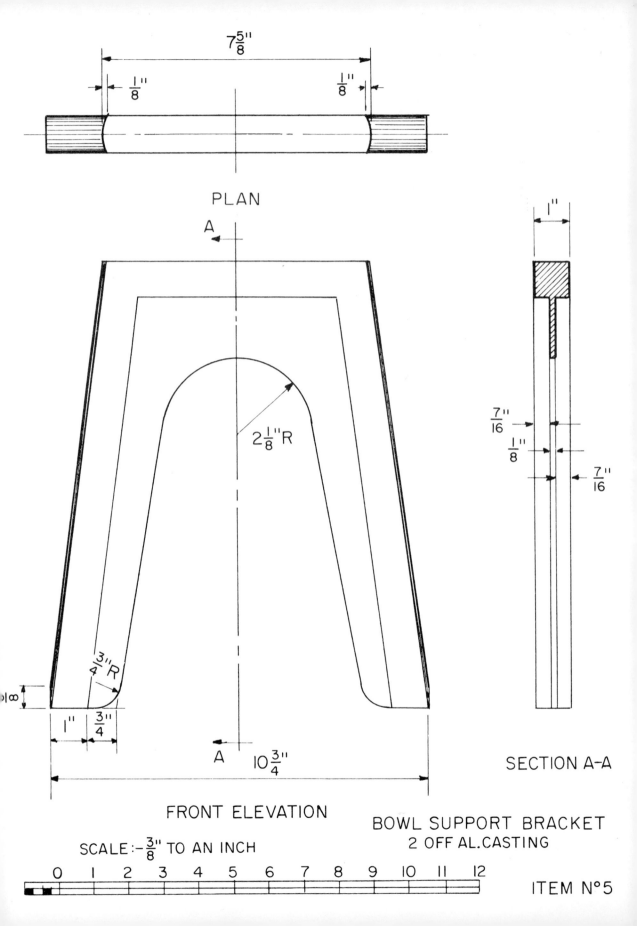

$7\frac{5}{8}$"

$\frac{1}{8}$"

$\frac{1}{8}$"

PLAN

A

$2\frac{1}{8}$"R

$\frac{3}{4}$"R

$\frac{9}{8}$

1"

$\frac{3}{4}$"

A

$10\frac{3}{4}$"

FRONT ELEVATION

SCALE:- $\frac{3}{8}$" TO AN INCH

1"

$\frac{7}{16}$"

$\frac{1}{8}$"

$\frac{7}{16}$"

SECTION A-A

BOWL SUPPORT BRACKET
2 OFF AL. CASTING

0 1 2 3 4 5 6 7 8 9 10 11 12

ITEM N° 5

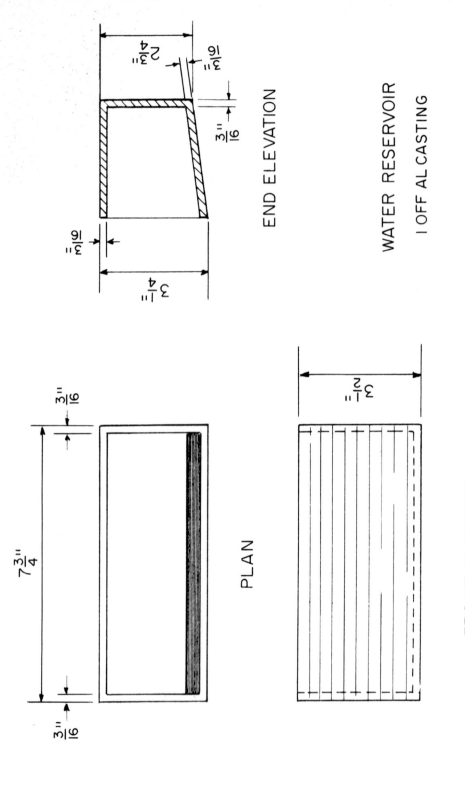

$2\frac{3}{4}''$

$\frac{3}{16}''$

$\frac{3}{16}''$

END ELEVATION

$\frac{3}{4}''$

$\frac{3}{16}''$

$\frac{3}{16}''$

$7\frac{3}{4}''$

$\frac{3}{16}''$

PLAN

$3\frac{1}{2}''$

FRONT ELEVATION

WATER RESERVOIR

I OFF AL CASTING

ITEM N°6

SCALE:- $\frac{3}{8}''$ TO AN INCH

0 I 2 3 4 5 6 7 8 9 IO

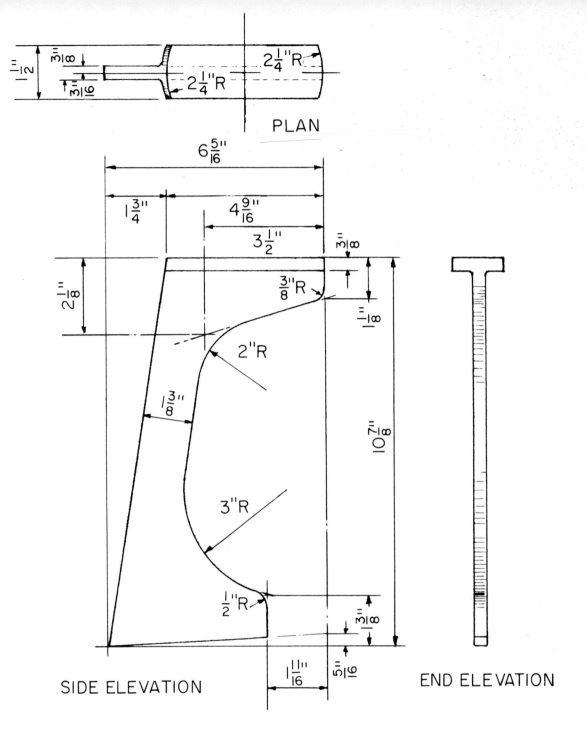

PLAN

$1\frac{1}{2}''$ $\frac{3}{8}''$ $\frac{3}{16}''$ $2\frac{1}{4}''R$ $2\frac{1}{4}''R$

$6\frac{5}{16}''$

$1\frac{3}{4}''$ $4\frac{9}{16}''$

$3\frac{1}{2}''$

$\frac{3}{8}''$

$\frac{3}{8}''R$

$2\frac{1}{8}''$

$\frac{1}{8}''$

$2''R$

$1\frac{3}{8}''$

$10\frac{7}{8}''$

$3''R$

$\frac{1}{2}''R$

$\frac{3}{8}''$

$1\frac{11}{16}''$ $\frac{5}{16}''$

SIDE ELEVATION

END ELEVATION

MOTOR SUPPORT BRACKET

1 OFF AL. CASTING

SCALE :— $\frac{3}{8}''$ TO 1 INCH

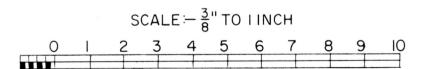

0   1   2   3   4   5   6   7   8   9   10

ITEM N° 7

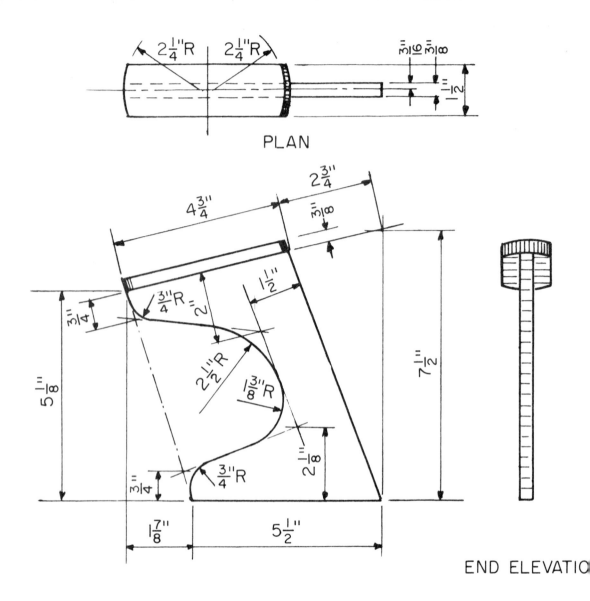

PLAN

SIDE ELEVATION

END ELEVATIO

MOTOR SUPPORT BRACKET

I OFF AL. CASTING

SCALE:— $\frac{3}{8}$" TO AN INCH

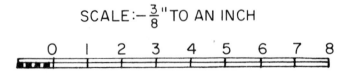

ITEM N° 7A

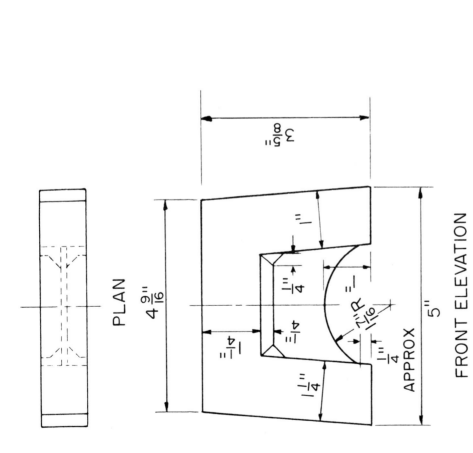

PLAN

$4\frac{9}{16}"$

$1\frac{1}{4}"$

$3\frac{5}{8}"$

$1"$

$\frac{1}{4}"$

$\frac{1}{4}"$

$\frac{1}{1}"$R $\frac{1}{16}"$

$\frac{1}{4}"$ APPROX

$1\frac{1}{4}"$

$5"$

FRONT ELEVATION

SCALE:- $\frac{1}{2}$ TO 1"

0   1   2   3   4   5   6

$\frac{1}{4}"$

$\frac{1}{8}"$ WEB

$1"$

SECTION

BEARING SUPPORT

(GRINDING WHEEL)

3 OFF AL CASTING

ITEM N°8

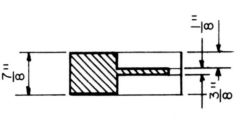

$\frac{7''}{8}$

$\frac{1''}{8}$

$\frac{3''}{8}$

SECTION

BEARING SUPPORT

(LAY SHAFT)

2 OFF AL CASTING

ITEM Nº9

$2\frac{3}{8}''$

$4''$

$4\frac{1}{8}''$

$1''$

$1''$

$1''$

₵.

PLAN

FRONT ELEVATION

SCALE:- $\frac{1''}{2}$ TO AN INCH

0   1   2   3   4   5   6

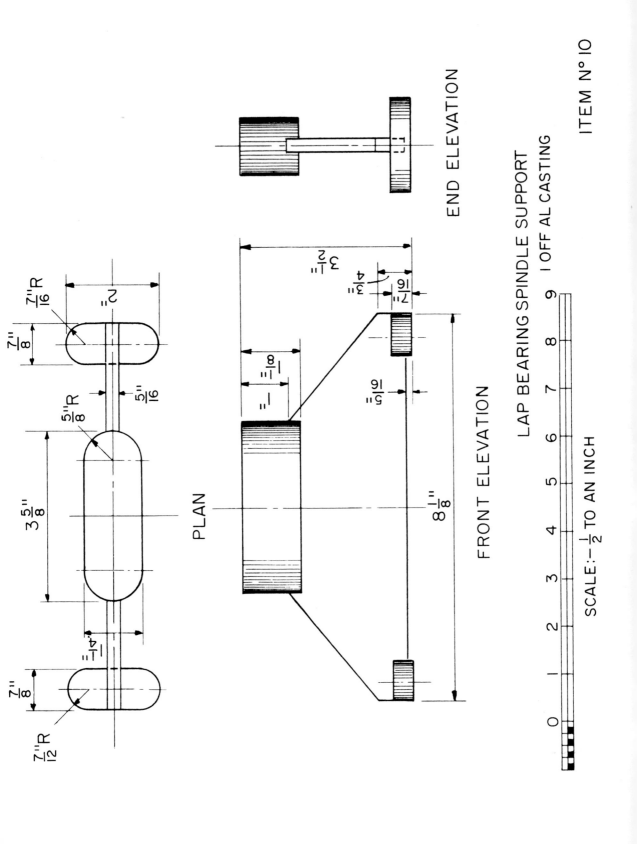

END ELEVATION

$\frac{7"}{16}$R

$\frac{7"}{8}$

2"

$\frac{5"}{8}$R

$\frac{5"}{16}$

$3\frac{5}{8}"$

$\frac{7"}{8}$

$1\frac{1}{4}"$

$\frac{7"}{8}$

$\frac{7"}{12}$R

PLAN

$3\frac{1}{2}"$

$\frac{7"}{16}$

$3\frac{3}{4}"$

$1\frac{1}{8}"$

1"

$\frac{5}{16}"$

$8\frac{1}{8}"$

FRONT ELEVATION

LAP BEARING SPINDLE SUPPORT

1 OFF AL CASTING

ITEM N° 10

SCALE:— $\frac{1}{2}$ TO AN INCH

0   1   2   3   4   5   6   7   8   9

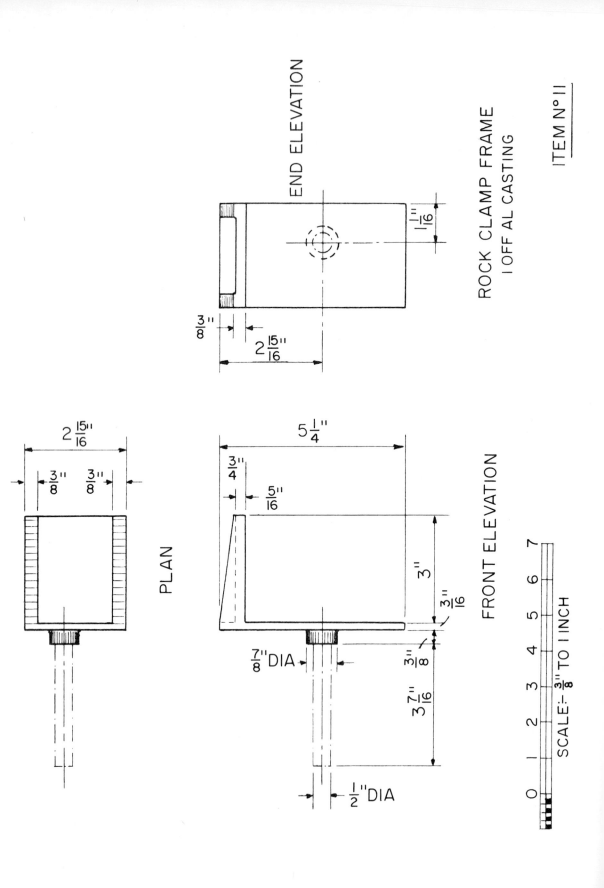

END ELEVATION

ROCK CLAMP FRAME
1 OFF AL CASTING

ITEM N° 11

$\frac{1}{16}$"

$\frac{3}{8}$"

$2\frac{15}{16}$"

$2\frac{15}{16}$"

$\frac{3}{8}$" $\frac{3}{8}$"

PLAN

$5\frac{1}{4}$"

$\frac{3}{4}$"

$\frac{5}{16}$"

3"

$\frac{3}{16}$"

$\frac{7}{8}$"DIA

$\frac{3}{8}$"

$3\frac{7}{16}$"

$\frac{1}{2}$"DIA

FRONT ELEVATION

0 1 2 3 4 5 6 7

SCALE:- $\frac{3}{8}$" TO 1 INCH

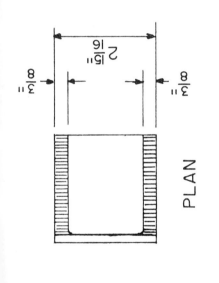

PLAN

$\frac{3}{8}"$

$2\frac{5}{16}"$

$\frac{3}{8}"$

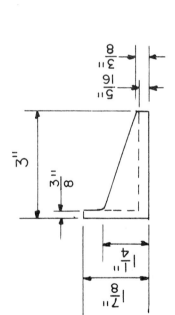

FRONT ELEVATION

$3"$

$\frac{3}{8}"$

$\frac{3}{8}"$

$\frac{5}{16}"$

$1\frac{1}{4}"$

$1\frac{7}{8}"$

END ELEVATION

ROCK CLAMP JAW

1 OFF AL. CASTING

ITEM Nº 12

SCALE:- $\frac{3}{8}"$ TO AN INCH

0   1   2   3   4   5   6

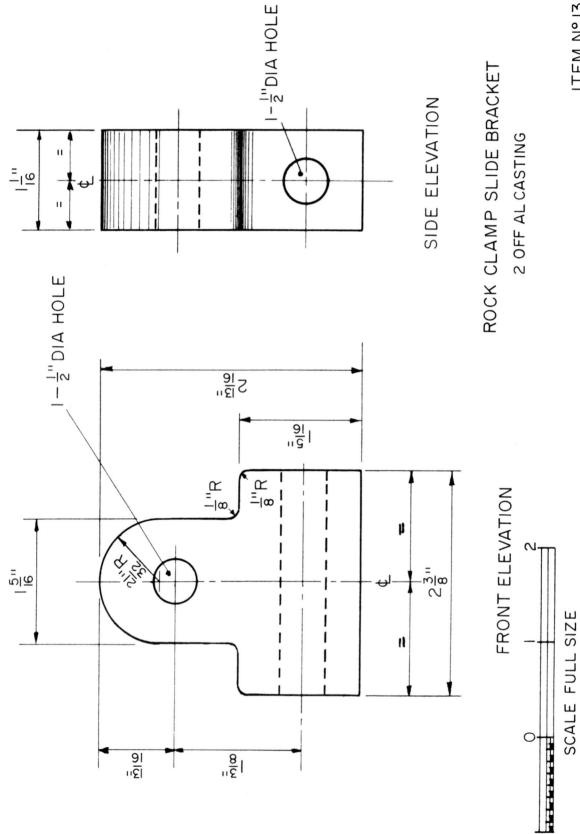

$1-\frac{1}{2}"$ DIA HOLE

$1\frac{1}{16}"$

$\mathbb{C}$

SIDE ELEVATION

$1-\frac{1}{2}"$ DIA HOLE

$1\frac{5}{16}"$

$2\frac{13}{16}"$

$1\frac{5}{16}"$

$\frac{1}{8}"$R

$\frac{1}{8}"$R

$\frac{21}{32}"$R

$\frac{13}{16}"$

$1\frac{3}{8}"$

$2\frac{3}{8}"$

$\mathbb{C}$

FRONT ELEVATION

ROCK CLAMP SLIDE BRACKET
2 OFF AL CASTING

ITEM N° 13

0   1   2

SCALE FULL SIZE

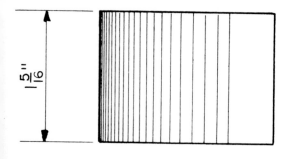

$1\frac{5}{16}"$

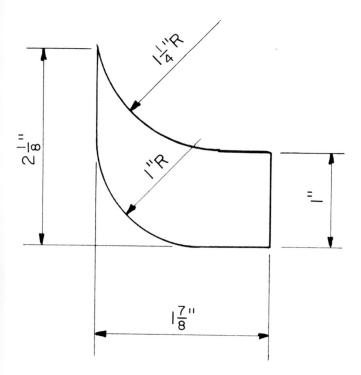

$1\frac{1}{4}"R$

$1"R$

$2\frac{1}{8}"$

$1"$

$1\frac{7}{8}"$

CLAMP SLIDE EXTENSION

2 OFF AL CASTING

ITEM N° 14

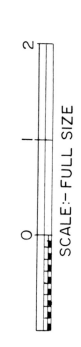

0   1   2

SCALE:- FULL SIZE

H

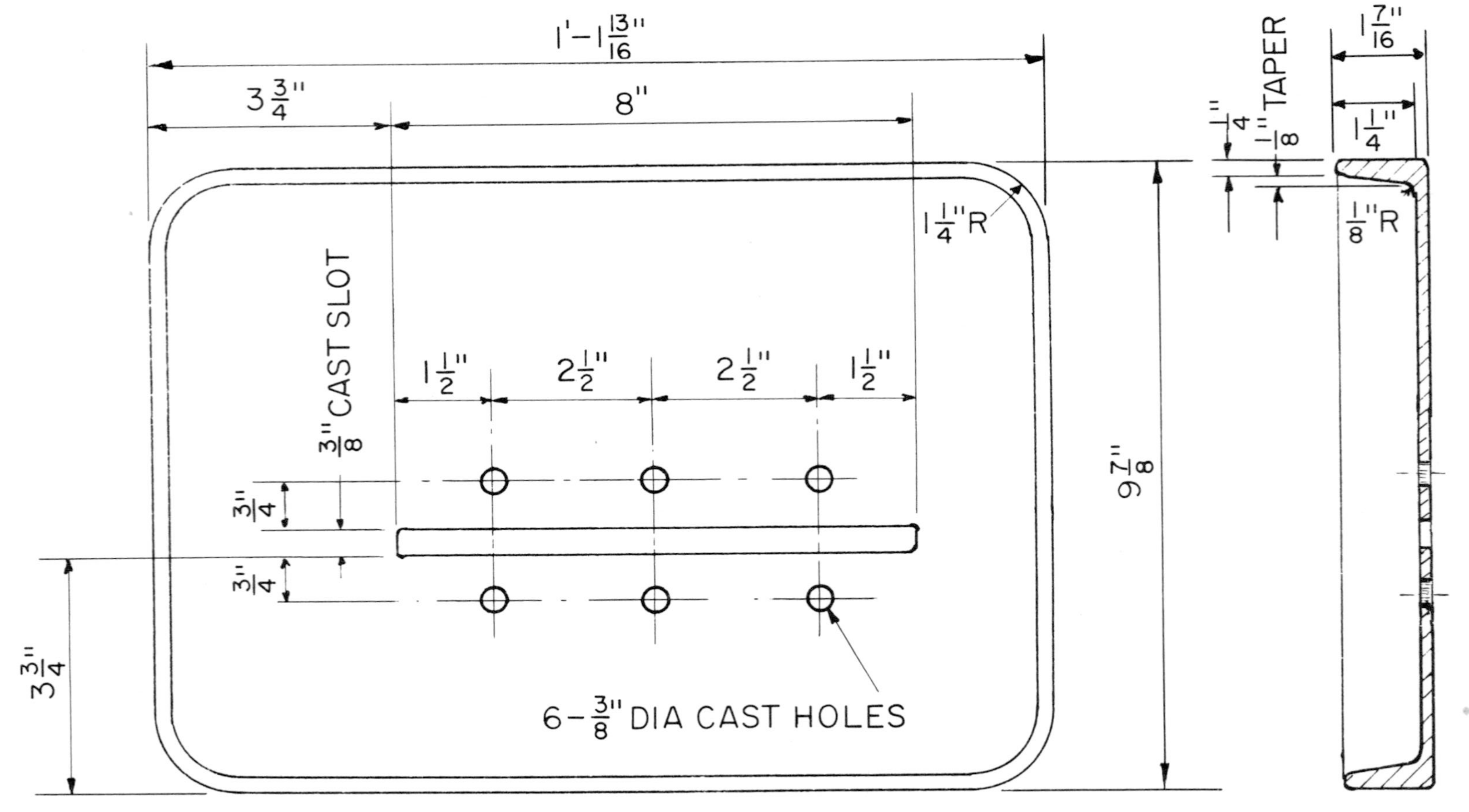

SAW TABLE SECTION

1 OFF AL. CASTING

ITEM Nº 15

$1\frac{7}{16}"$

$1\frac{1}{4}"$

$\frac{1}{8}"R$

$\frac{1}{8}"$ TAPER

$\frac{1}{4}"$

$9\frac{7}{8}"$

$1\frac{1}{4}"R$

$8"$

$1'-1\frac{13}{16}"$

$3\frac{3}{4}"$

$1\frac{1}{2}"$

$2\frac{1}{2}"$

$2\frac{1}{2}"$

$1\frac{1}{2}"$

$\frac{3}{8}"$ CAST SLOT

$\frac{3}{8}"$

$\frac{3}{8}"$

$6-\frac{3}{8}"$ DIA CAST HOLES

$3\frac{3}{4}"$

PLAN

SCALE:- $\frac{3}{8}"$ TO AN INCH

0 1 2 3 4 5 6 7 8 9 10 11 12 13 14

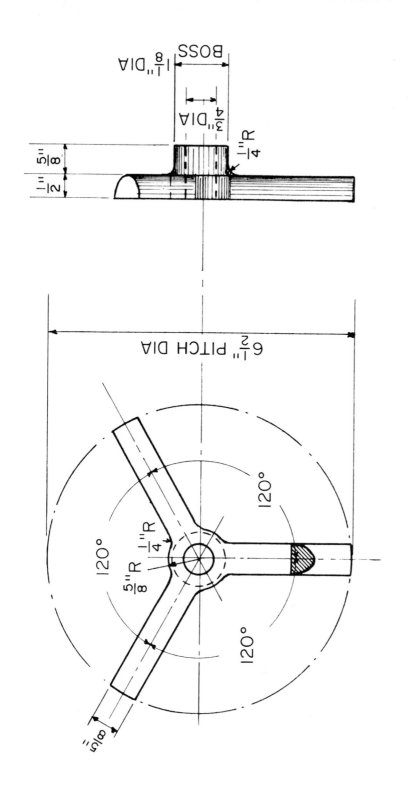

BOSS

$1\frac{1}{8}$" DIA

$\frac{4}{8}$" DIA

$\frac{1}{4}$" R

$\frac{5}{8}$"

$\frac{1}{2}$"

$6\frac{1}{2}$" PITCH DIA

120°

120°

120°

$\frac{1}{4}$" R

$\frac{5}{8}$" R

$\frac{5}{8}$"

HOTPLATE SUPPORTING SPIDER

I OFF AL CASTING

ITEM N° 16

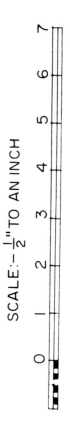

SCALE:- $\frac{1}{2}$" TO AN INCH

0   1   2   3   4   5   6   7

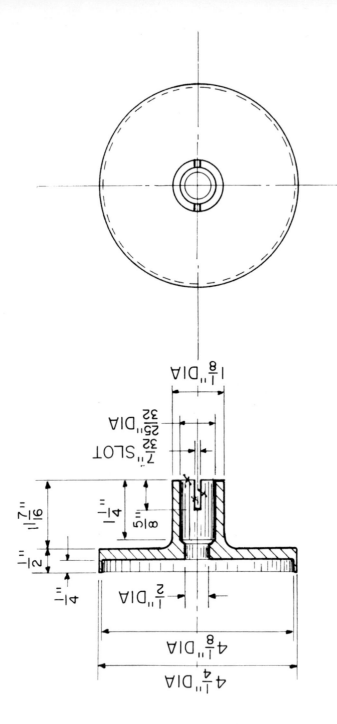

1⅛" DIA

25/32" DIA

7/32" SLOT

1⅛" DIA

1⁷⁄₁₆"

1¼"

5/8"

½"

¼"

1½" DIA

4⅛" DIA

4¼" DIA

LAPPING SPINDLE DRIVE PLATE

1 OFF AL. CASTING

ITEM N° 17

0   1   2   3   4   5

SCALE:- ½" TO 1 INCH

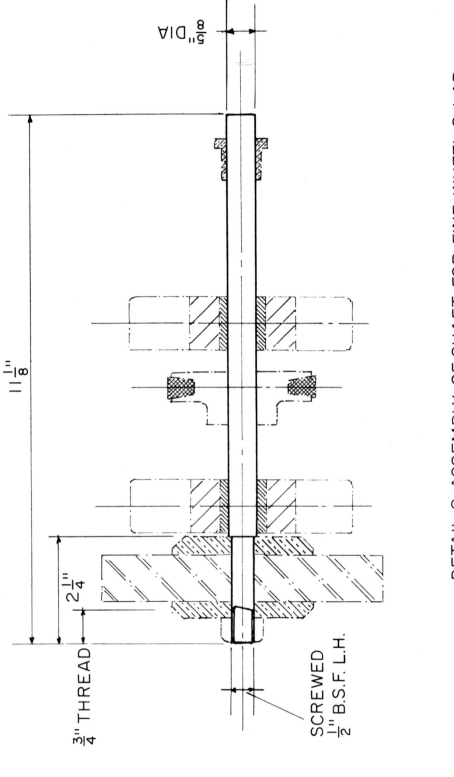

$5\frac{5}{8}''$ DIA

$11\frac{1}{8}''$

$2\frac{1}{4}''$

$\frac{3}{4}''$ THREAD

SCREWED
$\frac{1}{2}''$ B.S.F. L.H.

DETAIL & ASSEMBLY OF SHAFT FOR FINE WHEEL & LAP

1 OFF M.S.

SCALE:- $\frac{1}{2}''$ TO AN INCH

ITEM Nº 18

0   1   2   3   4   5   6   7   8   9   10   11   12

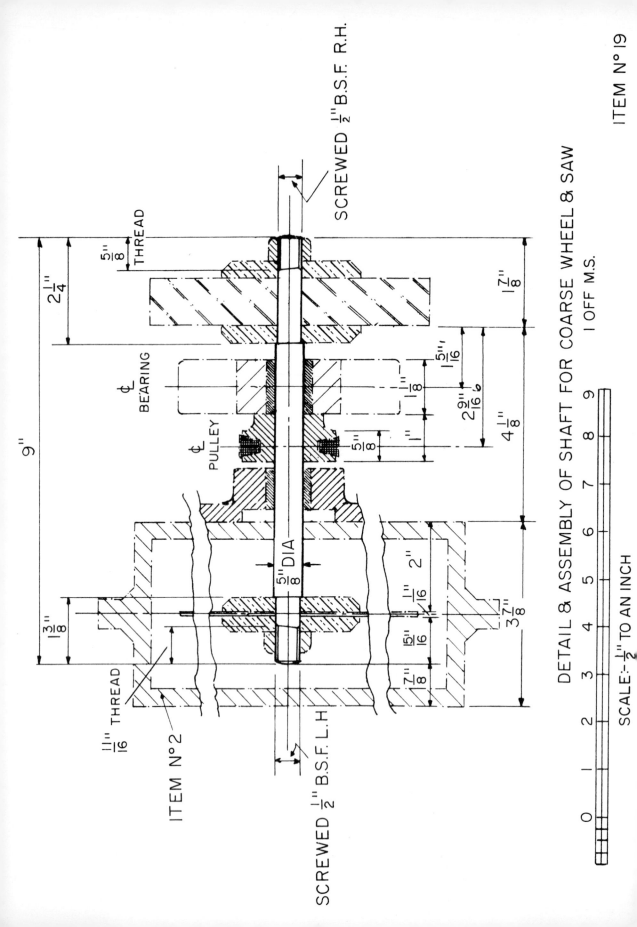

SCREWED $1\frac{1}{2}$" B.S.F. R.H.

THREAD

$\frac{5}{8}$"

$2\frac{1}{4}$"

9"

₵ BEARING

₵ PULLEY

$\frac{5}{8}$" DIA

$1\frac{3}{8}$"

$\frac{11}{16}$" THREAD

ITEM N° 2

SCREWED $1\frac{1}{2}$" B.S.F. L.H.

$1\frac{5}{16}$"

$1\frac{1}{8}$"

$2\frac{9}{16}$"

$\frac{5}{8}$"

1"

$4\frac{1}{8}$"

$1\frac{7}{8}$"

$\frac{5}{16}$"

2"

$\frac{5}{16}$"

$\frac{7}{8}$"

$3\frac{7}{8}$"

DETAIL & ASSEMBLY OF SHAFT FOR COARSE WHEEL & SAW

1 OFF M.S.

ITEM N° 19

0 1 2 3 4 5 6 7 8 9

SCALE:- $\frac{1}{2}$" TO AN INCH

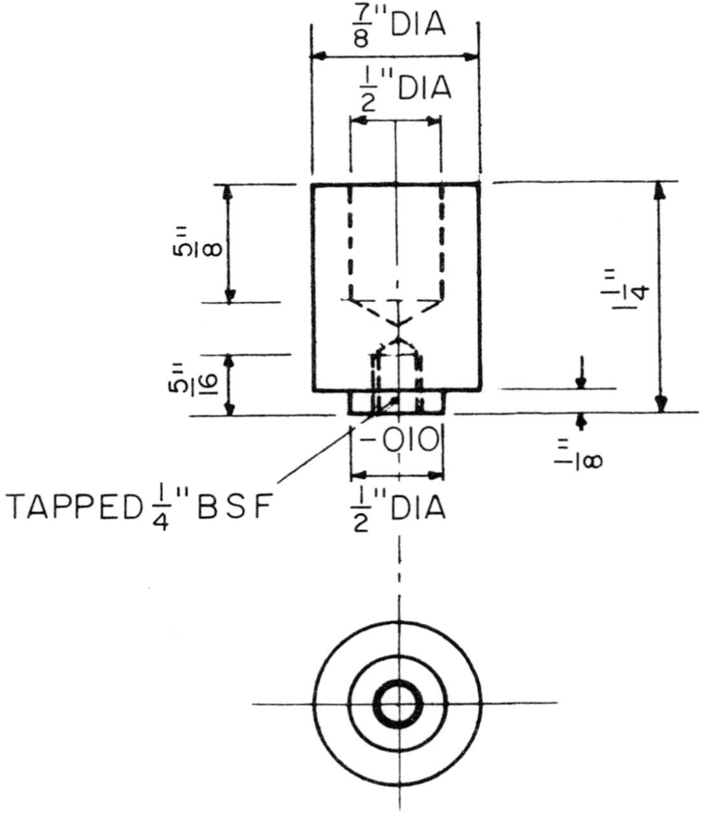

$\frac{1}{16}''$ DEEP SAW CUTS
AT APPROX $\frac{3}{32}''$ PITCH

$\frac{7}{8}''$DIA

$\frac{5}{8}''$DIA

$\frac{3}{8}''$

$\frac{3}{16}''$

$\frac{1}{16}''$

$\frac{1}{8}''$

$1''$

3–4 B.A.TAPPED
HOLES AT 120° APART

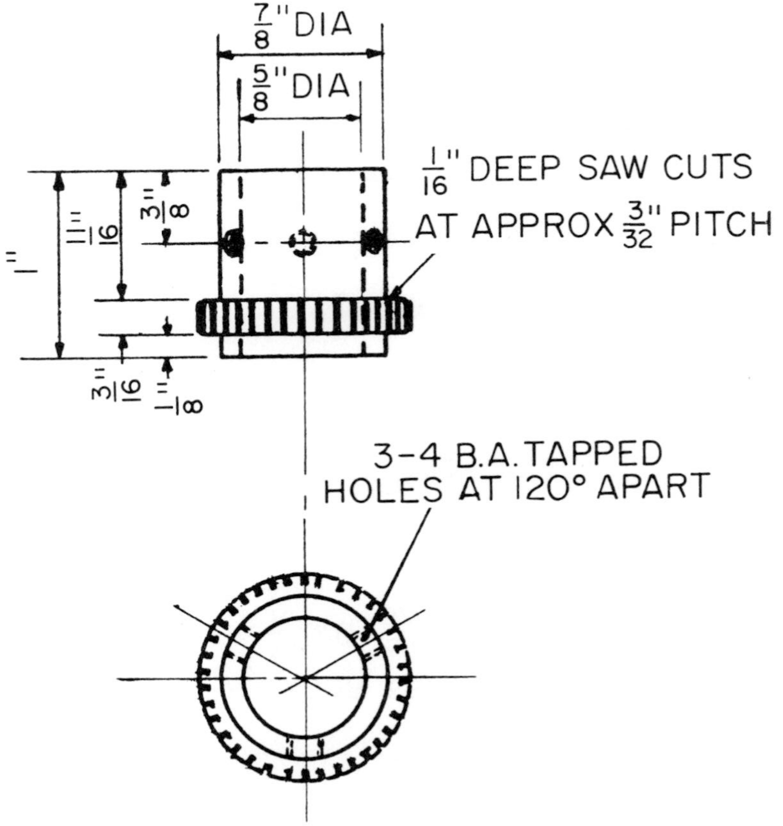

LAPPING SPINDLE DRIVING BUSH
I OFF PHOS BRZ

ITEM N° 22

SCALE:- FULL SIZE

$\frac{7}{8}''$DIA

$\frac{1}{2}''$DIA

$\frac{1}{2}''$DIA

$1\frac{1}{4}''$

$\frac{1}{8}''$

·010

$\frac{5}{8}''$

$\frac{5}{16}''$

TAPPED $\frac{1}{4}''$ BSF

LAP SPINDLE BOTTOM BEARING
I OFF PHOS BRZ

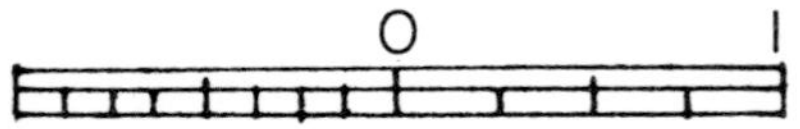

ITEM N° 21

SCALE:- FULL SIZE

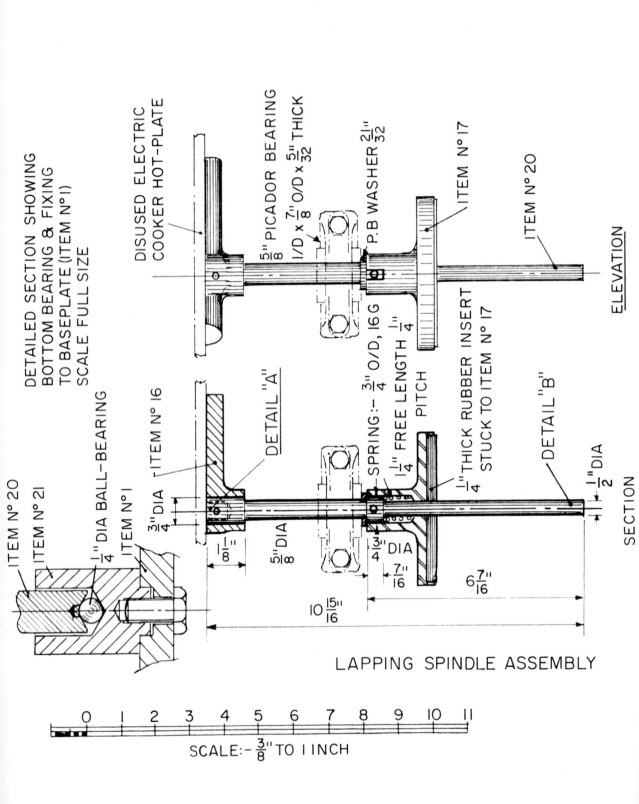

DETAILED SECTION SHOWING
BOTTOM BEARING & FIXING
TO BASEPLATE (ITEM Nº I)
SCALE FULL SIZE

ITEM Nº 20
ITEM Nº 21
$\frac{1}{4}$" DIA BALL–BEARING
ITEM Nº I

DISUSED ELECTRIC
COOKER HOT-PLATE

$\frac{5}{8}$" PICADOR BEARING
I/D x $\frac{7}{8}$" O/D x $\frac{5}{32}$" THICK

P.B WASHER $\frac{21}{32}$"

ITEM Nº 17

ITEM Nº 20

ELEVATION

ITEM Nº 16

DETAIL "A"

SPRING:- $\frac{3}{4}$" O/D, 16 G
$1\frac{1}{4}$" FREE LENGTH $\frac{1}{4}$"
PITCH

$\frac{1}{4}$" THICK RUBBER INSERT
STUCK TO ITEM Nº 17

DETAIL "B"

$\frac{1}{2}$" DIA

SECTION

$\frac{3}{4}$" DIA

$1\frac{1}{8}$"

$\frac{5}{8}$" DIA

$\frac{3}{4}$" DIA

$\frac{7}{16}$"

$6\frac{7}{16}$"

$10\frac{15}{16}$"

LAPPING SPINDLE ASSEMBLY

0 1 2 3 4 5 6 7 8 9 10 11

SCALE:- $\frac{3}{8}$" TO 1 INCH

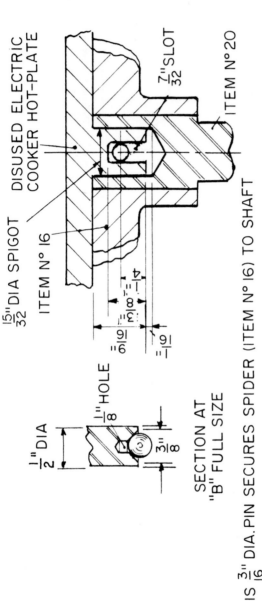

DISUSED ELECTRIC
COOKER HOT-PLATE

$\frac{15}{32}$" DIA SPIGOT

ITEM N° 16

$\frac{7}{32}$" SLOT

ITEM N° 20

$\frac{11}{4}$"

$\frac{3}{8}$"

$\frac{9}{16}$"

$\frac{1}{16}$"

$\frac{1}{2}$"DIA

$\frac{1}{8}$"HOLE

$\frac{3}{8}$"

SECTION AT
"B" FULL SIZE

THIS $\frac{3}{16}$" DIA. PIN SECURES SPIDER (ITEM N° 16) TO SHAFT
(ITEM N° 20) AND PROVIDES DRIVE TO HOT-PLATE. SECTION ON "A"
FULL SIZE

ITEM N° 20

This scale applies to all the plans and elevations which follow on the
next eight pages.

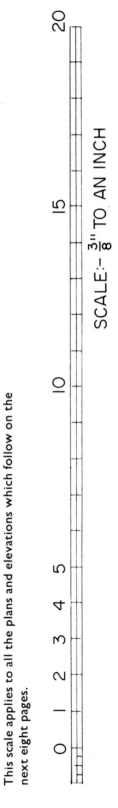

SCALE:- $\frac{3}{8}$" TO AN INCH

0 1 2 3 4 5   10   15   20

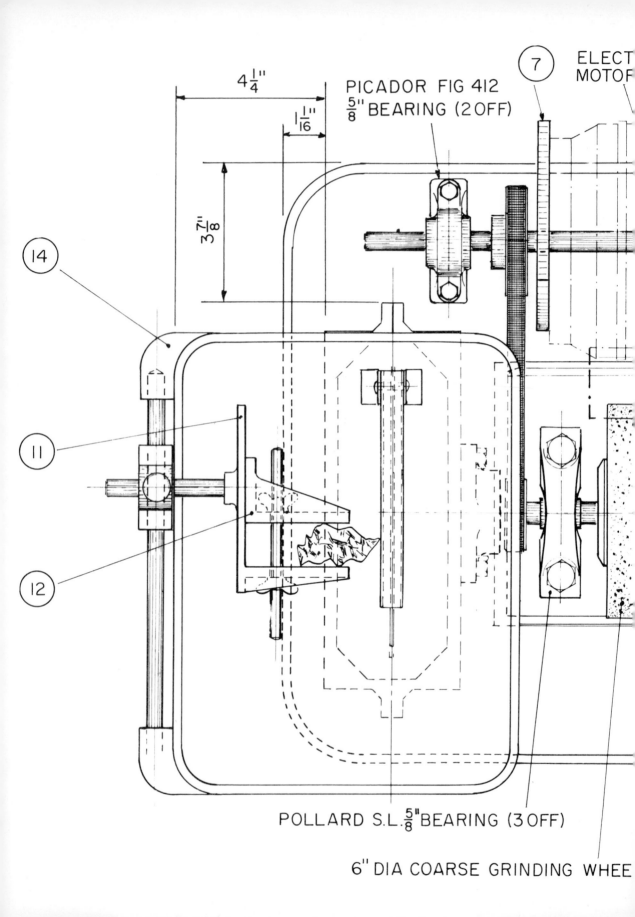

4 1/4"

1 1/16"

3 7/8"

PICADOR FIG 412
5/8" BEARING (2 OFF)

7

ELECT
MOTOR

14

11

12

POLLARD S.L. 5/8" BEARING (3 OFF)

6" DIA COARSE GRINDING WHEE

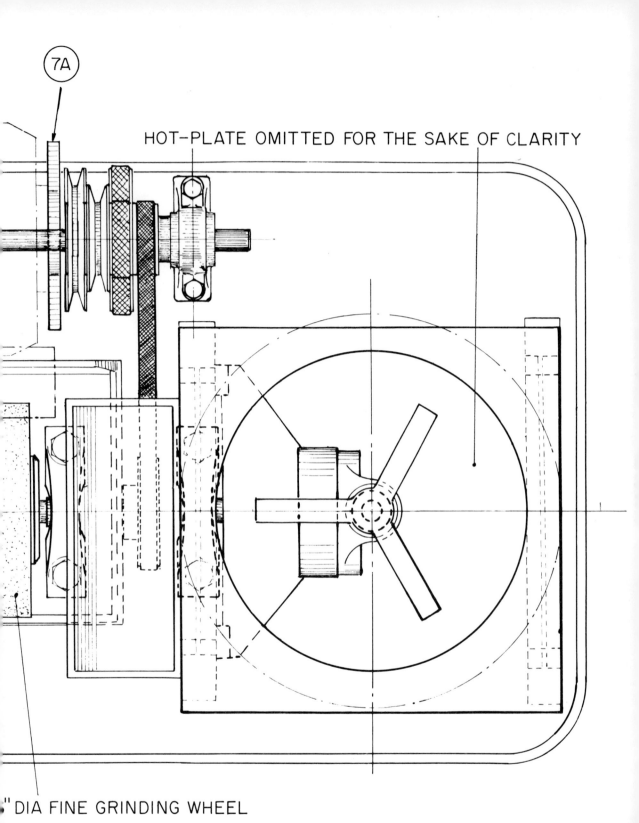

7A

HOT-PLATE OMITTED FOR THE SAKE OF CLARITY

"DIA FINE GRINDING WHEEL

GENERAL ASSEMBLY OF
COMBINATION LAPIDARY UNIT-PLAN

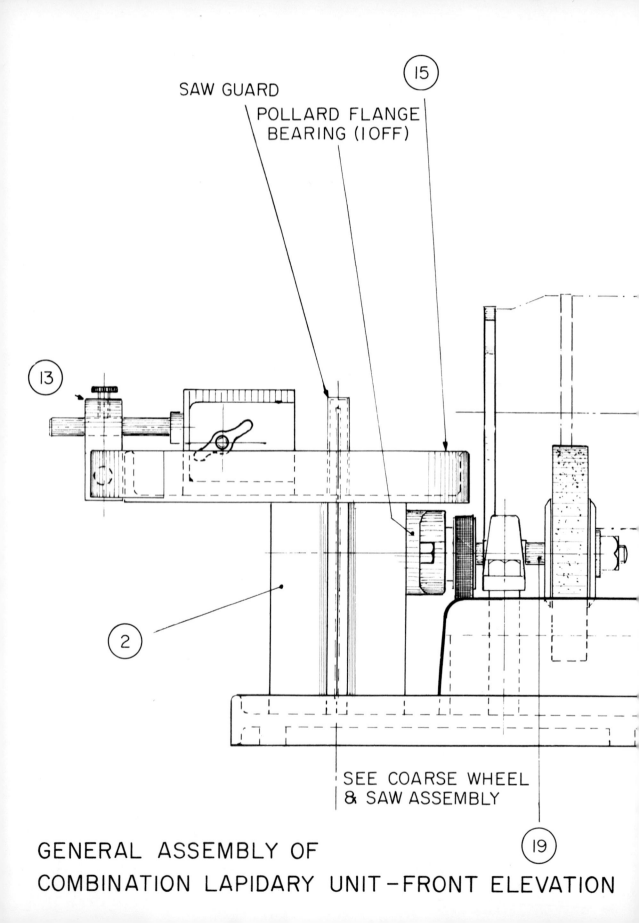

SAW GUARD

POLLARD FLANGE
BEARING (IOFF)

13

2

15

19

SEE COARSE WHEEL
& SAW ASSEMBLY

GENERAL ASSEMBLY OF
COMBINATION LAPIDARY UNIT—FRONT ELEVATION

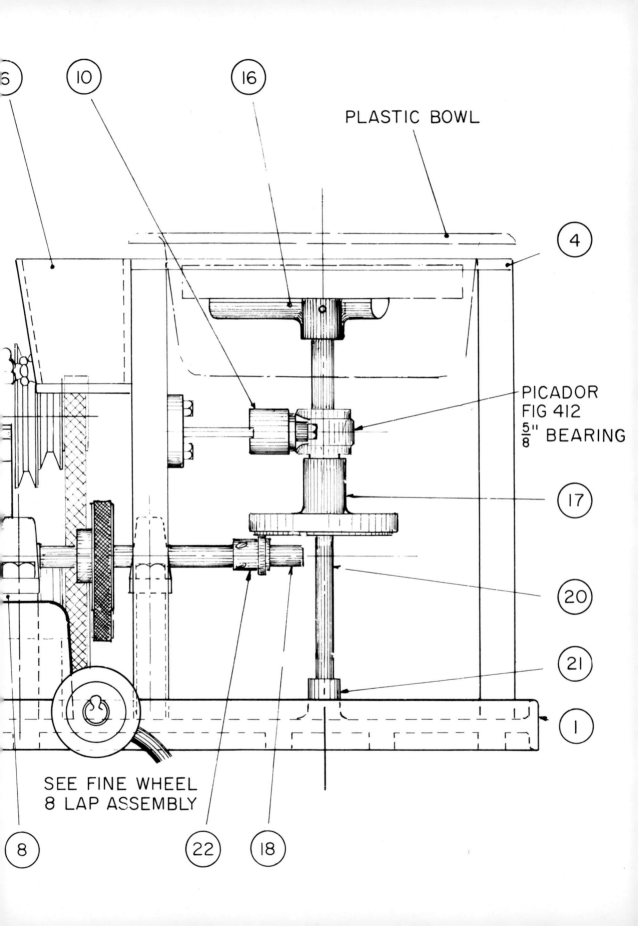

PLASTIC BOWL

PICADOR
FIG 412
$\frac{5}{8}$" BEARING

SEE FINE WHEEL
8 LAP ASSEMBLY

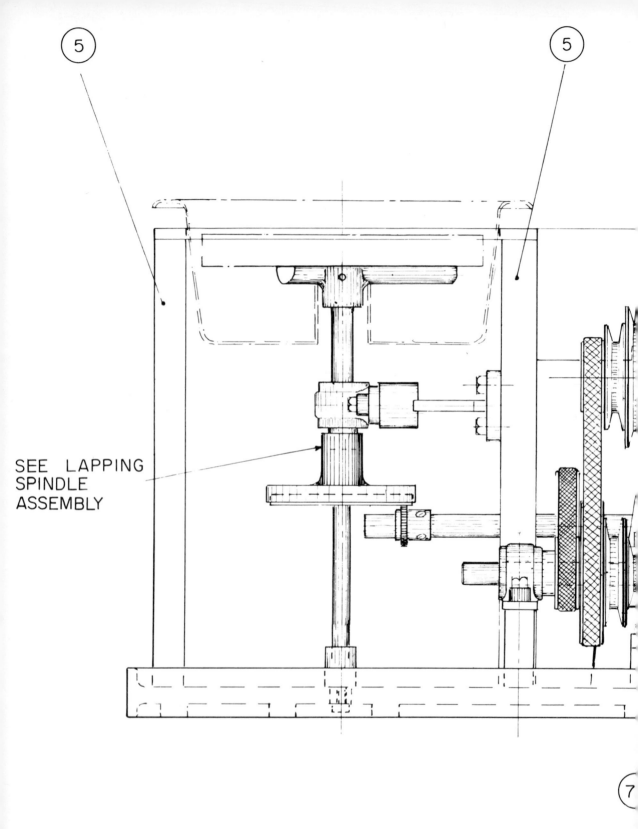

SEE LAPPING
SPINDLE
ASSEMBLY

GENERAL ASSEMBLY OF
COMBINATION LAPIDARY UNIT – BACK ELEVATION

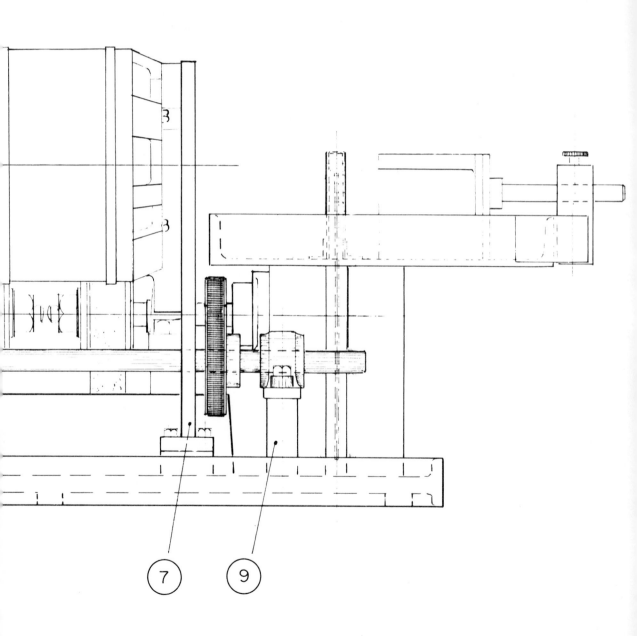

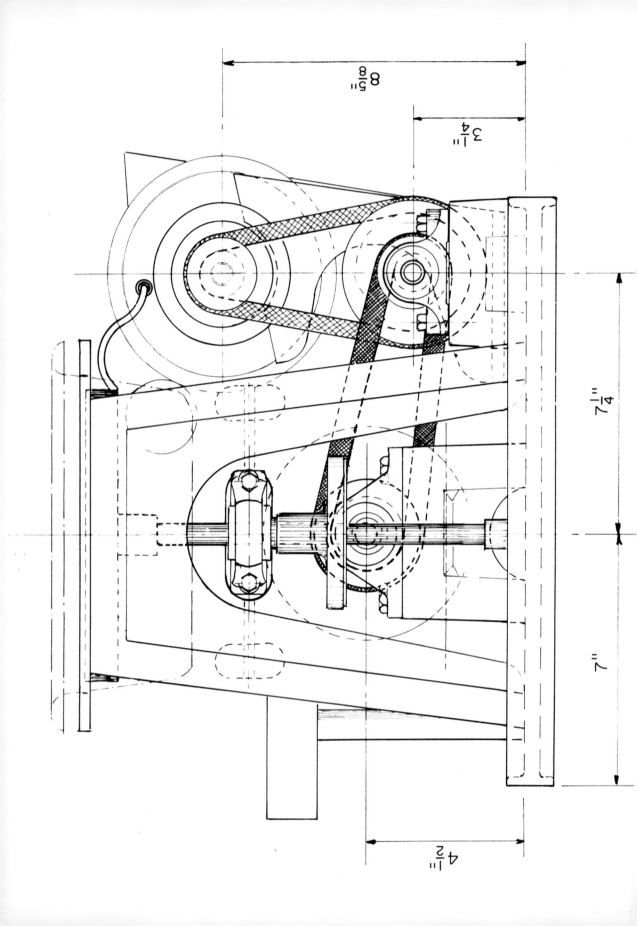

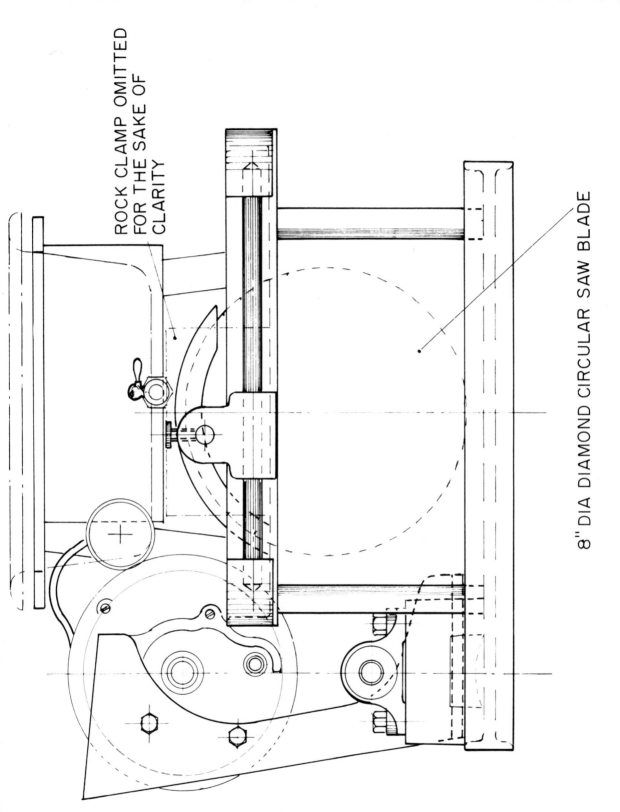

ROCK CLAMP OMITTED
FOR THE SAKE OF
CLARITY

8" DIA DIAMOND CIRCULAR SAW BLADE

GENERAL ASSEMBLY OF
COMBINATION LAPIDARY UNIT—END ELEVATIONS

Tumble polishing—
the simplest form of
lapidary work

Whilst it may seem illogical to finish a course of instruction in lapidary processes with the simplest method, I feel I am justified in so doing, for two reasons.

The first reason is that, as no manual skill or dexterity is required to produce tumbled stones, it can hardly be classed as a craft and the skilled operations should have pride of place. Secondly, tumble-polished stones cannot be produced individually and in fact must be dealt with in quantity, and there is no point in having a tumbling machine without an outlet for the end product.

Consequently, this branch of lapidary work is eminently suitable for younger children in addition to the amateur craftsman, as tumbled stones can be used to make a great variety of items of jewelry by very simple, or more advanced methods.

The pebbles which we find on the beach are naturally tumble-polished, having been rolled and abraded against each other by a countless succession of tides, until all the corners and rough edges are removed and they assume the smooth finish with which we are all so familiar.

In the tumble polisher, this process is simulated, and by the use of suitable abrasive grits and polishing powders, a degree of finish is obtained which is never reached in nature.

Although no degree of skill is needed during the tumbling operation, a certain amount of knowledge is necessary regarding the nature and hardness of the materials used and an appreciation of what actually takes place in the tumbling barrel. One cannot just place a load of mixed stones in the machine, switch on and hope for a batch of gems to be forthcoming.

TUMBLING MACHINES

A gem tumbling machine is the simplest and cheapest lapidary machine to construct, as basically all that is needed is a water-tight container, referred to as a tumbling barrel, made to revolve at a specific speed. The operations are similar to those required to produce a cabochon from a blank, namely, a coarse grind to remove all corners and rough projections, a second and third grinding with differing grades of grit, followed by a final polish and wash.

Plate 39
Commercial tumbling
machine

Coffee jars, screw-topped fruit bottling jars, paint tins and plastic containers are but a few of the many vessels used as tumbling barrels by amateurs, each having advantages, disadvantages, even possible dangers. If they can be afforded, however, the commercial rubber barrels are best in the long run. Aluminium containers should never be used as aluminium causes marks on many varieties of stone which can only be removed by re-polishing.

In constructing a tumbling machine, it must be remembered that what is required is to simulate the natural process which produces the pebbles on the beach. There can be very few of us who have not stood on a pebble-strewn shore and watched them, carried along by the incoming tide, rolling against each other until they are forced into a heap, only for some of them to roll back, pulled by the force of gravity, assisted by the drag of the receding water.

THE SPEED OF ROTATION

To create this rolling action within the barrel, it is desirable that a certain speed of rotation is maintained and this can be obtained from the formula $\frac{1}{2}(54 \div \sqrt{R})$ where R is the radius of the barrel in feet. This is, of course, an ideal which it may not be possible to obtain but the formula is given as a guide to would-be tumbler constructors.

Example: With a 6-in. barrel, speed equals

$$\frac{1}{2}\left(\frac{54}{\sqrt{\frac{3}{12}}}\right) = \tfrac{1}{2}(54 \div \sqrt{\tfrac{1}{4}}) \div \tfrac{1}{2}(54 \div \tfrac{1}{2})$$
$$= \tfrac{1}{2} \times 54 \times \tfrac{2}{1} = 54.$$

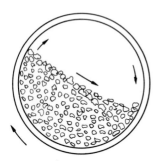

*Fig. 30
Grinding action in
tumbling barrel*

At the correct speed for the size of barrel, the stones will continually
be moved, those which are against the wall being carried up to a point
where they will roll down the layer nearest the centre, in a continuous
stream.

If the speed is too fast, the stones will be carried beyond the point at
which they should roll over and drop to the bottom of the barrel.
This lessens the tumbling action and causes the stones to be chipped.
If the speed is too slow, the mass of stones will approach a point below
the "roll over" position and will then slide, in a mass, to the base,
resulting in flat-sided stones.

Much can be learned from listening to the tumbler in operation; a
"swish-swish" denotes too slow a speed and the clicking of falling
stones means that the speed is too high. What is required is a steady
rumbling noise which tells that the stones are, in fact, rolling over
and over.

The slow speed at which tumblers rotate means that normal electric
motors, which usually rotate at speeds of around 1480 r.p.m., must be
appreciably geared down. To avoid the use of excessively large pulleys,
the usual procedure is to produce a reduction by designing the
machine so that the barrels rest on rollers or spindles.

For example, if a 6-in. barrel is rotated on $\frac{1}{2}$-in. diameter steel rollers,
covered with garden hose to provide grip, the diameter will be
approximately $\frac{3}{4}$ in., thus effecting an 8 to 1 reduction or 185 r.p.m.
A further $3\frac{1}{2}$ to 1 reduction must be obtained by the use of suitable
pulleys.

In view of the gearing down, it will be apparent that the torque is
fairly low, and quite small motors can be used to drive tumblers, but
as these machines must operate for long periods without stopping,
motors must be continuous rated and preferably fan-cooled.

TO PREVENT "GASSING"

One feature of the tumble polishing process which will not be
apparent to beginners is "gassing" – not the verbal outpourings of
enthusiasts – but actually the formation of gas within the barrel.

There are many theories regarding the factors which create this gas –
chemical reaction, fermentation, excessive heat and the breaking down

of the silicon carbide into its constituents, have all been formulated as reasons, but one fact is constant. Gas forms much more quickly in steel barrels, and paint cans or the like should be rubber-lined.

Many workers claim that they can prevent the formation of gas by suitable additives, but these claims are very debatable. By far the safest procedure is to release the gas pressure every twenty-four hours, and as some experts state that the gas formed is hydrogen, ensure that no naked lights (including cigarettes) are in the vicinity when the tumbler is opened.

General rules to minimise gas pressure can be summarised as follows:

1 Open the barrel at regular intervals.
2 Remove all loose particles from materials by washing them thoroughly before placing them in the barrel.
3 Prevent the material from tumbling in contact with metal.
4 Fix the machine well away from any external source of heat.

THE FIRST GRIND

The correct load for a tumbler is that which fills the barrel to between $\frac{1}{2}$ and $\frac{5}{8}$ of its capacity, and for the best results, the pieces of stone should not vary too greatly in size.

Care must be taken to ensure that, if different types of stone are to be tumbled together, they should be of approximately the same degrees of hardness, otherwise the softer stones will finish as minute particles. The process can be "speeded up" by first grinding off projections and sharp edges on the rough grinding wheel or even pre-forming the stones by sawing and grinding to approximate shapes.

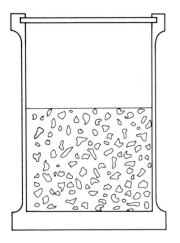

Fig. 31
Tumbler barrel load

Ken Parkinson, whose tumbled stones are always a joy to behold, includes pieces of broken grinding wheels, stone dust and chippings, together with a small amount of 80 grit silicon carbide in his first grind. He states that contrary to general belief, too much grit actually retards the grinding action and that 3 ounces of grit to 3 pounds of stone is more than ample. The barrel should then be filled with water just up to the level of the stones and a teaspoonful of soda added to make the subsequent cleaning of the barrel easier.

About 4 to 5 days of continuous running may be necessary to coarse grind a load of stones, but this will be dependent on size, hardness, etc. From time to time, it will be necessary to add a few more stones to retain the correct level, as this will naturally fall as the rough surfaces are turned into dust. The water in the barrel will possibly be so contaminated that it is too thick to do its job and extra water may be necessary.

Periodic inspection will show when the stones have had all their rough edges removed, and some stones may possibly be fit for the second grind before others in the same barrel. These could be removed and fresh stones added until a sufficient quantity is available to make a load for the second grind.

STAGE TWO

Before proceeding to this stage, the stones should be examined and any which are unsuitable because of breakages, flaws, cracks, bad shape or colour should be discarded. There is, at first, a tendency to carry on with the whole batch, but this is a waste of time as the tumbler opens up, for good or ill, the latent possibilities within the stone.

Having selected the second load, the stones must be carefully washed and the barrel thoroughly cleansed of every particle of grit but *never in a sink*. The residue from the tumbler will set solid in the U-bend and its disposal presents a problem which the reader will have to resolve. So again, *never* down sinks or drains; and it is not particularly beneficial to the garden either.

For the second grind, place the stones in the barrel with 1 oz. of 220 grit to each pound of stones, a teaspoonful of soda and plenty of carrier. Carrier is the term applied to a great variety of materials which literally carry the grit and keep it in close contact with the stones. Ken uses walnut shells or polythene slugs in the proportion of half the bulk of carrier as stone, but the variety of materials used as carrier is legion. Wood shavings, sawdust, felt and leather chippings, cornflour, sugar syrup and even instant mashed potato, to mention but a few.

The regular 24-hourly inspections will show when all the marks left by the first grind have been removed, and when the stones have a smooth, even, semi-matt surface, they will be ready for the final grinding. During the 4 or 5 days in which the second grind is in progress, it may be necessary to add a little water if the mixture seems too thick, but do not be tempted to add fresh grit, because as the grit breaks down it naturally grinds smoother.

THE FINAL GRIND

When satisfied that the 220 grit has done its work, again thoroughly wash the stones and the barrel, which should then be refilled to the appropriate level with stones, carrier, the usual teaspoonful of soda and 1 oz. of 500 grit to the pound of stones.

Run the tumbler for about 3 days, not forgetting the 24-hour de-gassing and checking. During these checks, a few of the stones can be tested by washing and drying them, followed by a quick test polish on the polishing buff if one is available. It may be that a longer period is necessary and if they do not polish without any scratches being visible under a magnifying glass, run the tumbler for further 24-hour periods. Remember that this is the most important stage and that stones removed too soon from the final grind will never polish satisfactorily.

THE FINAL POLISHING AND WASHING

A careful inspection should precede the polishing run, and after the stones have been again thoroughly washed and dried, any which are chipped, broken or sharp-edged must be placed on one side for re-tumbling. A sharp-edged stone at this stage can ruin the whole batch, so it pays to be extra careful. A few grains of grit left in the barrel at this stage will also leave their marks, so once more, absolute cleanliness.

Place the stones in the barrel, never drop or shovel them in, and add $\frac{1}{2}$ oz. of tin oxide for each pound of stones. This is another hint for which I am indebted to Mr Parkinson, as he has found that, although cerium oxide is almost a universal polishing agent on buffing wheels, it does not polish so effectively as tin oxide in the tumbler.

Top up with water to just above the level of the stones and start the final run, the length of which may vary from 3 to 5 or more days. Every 24 hours, remove a few of the stones, wash them under a running tap and allow to dry, and if they still appear wet and shiny they are almost ready for mounting into jewelry.

A final run of 6 to 8 hours in a thick goo of washing powder and water is extremely beneficial, as this will remove any traces of polish, and after a final wash in warm running water the stones will be ready for mounting into jewelry.

The need for care in the disposal of tumbling barrel waste has already been emphasised and one further word of warning is necessary before leaving this process.

If the machine is stopped for more than a few hours residue will set in the barrel in the same way as it will in the U-bend of the sink. Like concrete. Consequently, if the machine has to be stopped for any length of time, the only thing to do is to remove the stones from the barrel, wash them thoroughly as well as the barrel and leave everything clean in order that the process can be continued when convenient. Of course it is not necessary to use just the one barrel for all the tumbling stages. A good idea is to have 4 barrels using each in turn for coarse, medium, fine and polishing work. There is sometimes a chance of an odd piece of grit damaging your stones in the final stages no matter how carefully the barrel may have been cleaned out. In the long run, no extra expense is involved because the barrels will have a correspondingly longer life.

It will be apparent to many teachers that a tumbling machine will be an asset to Junior as well as Secondary Schools because, as will be seen in the next chapter, there are many items of baroque jewelry which can be made even by quite young children.

There is scope for a considerable amount of experiment in the tumbling process. Speeds could be varied, different carriers used and careful records should be made and retained. Charts could be produced showing, for example:

1 Weight of stone at commencement.
2 Weight of grit or polish added.
3 Ratio of grit to load.
4 Speed of barrel.
5 Length of run.
6 Weight of stone at end of run.
7 Type and weight of carrier (if any).
8 Type of stone, hardness, etc.

Separate charts could be made for each run of a batch of stones and the results utilised as the basis for many lessons. Percentages, graphs, ratio and proportion costing, electric current consumed, etc., all spring to mind as a means to adding realism to maths lessons.

Jewelry from tumbled stones and cabochons

Having tumbled a supply of what we can now refer to as baroque gemstones, let us see how we can use them to produce articles of jewelry, beginning with the simplest method.

Until the introduction of the epoxy resin adhesives, the mounting of baroques called for a considerable amount of skill and ingenuity, but now they can be securely fixed onto findings by quite young children if the few simple instructions concerning the use of these adhesives are fully observed. When correctly applied, the adhesive will prove to be stronger than the findings themselves.

Beginners may not be conversant with the term "findings", which refers to mass produced articles which the silversmith formerly had to make for himself, but which can now be bought in bulk, ready for use. Bolt rings, jump rings, fasteners, ear clips and wires, tie tacks, brooch backs, cuff link fittings, ring shanks and sets, bails, bell caps, hinges, joints and chain in lengths: these are but a few of the many findings available in either precious or base metals, the latter being either plated or anodised.

All the suppliers whose names are listed at the end of this book will provide catalogues on request and it is advisable to become familiar with what is available, especially if working with young children who may have neither the skill nor the facilities for making their own.

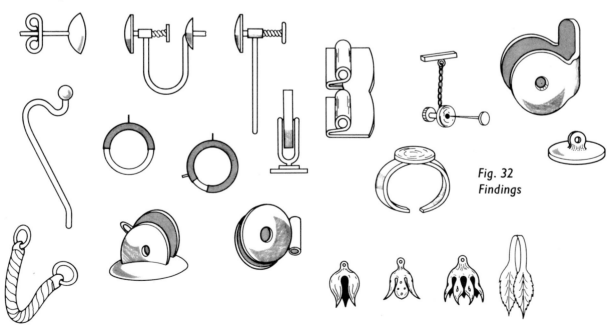

Fig. 32
Findings

A PENDANT

The simplest article to begin with is a pendant consisting of a large (1 to 1¼ in.) tumbled stone surmounted by a bell cap and hung on a chain of suitable length.

Having selected a bell cap of suitable size, the prongs are first opened slightly and manoeuvred around the top of the stone until the most appropriate position is found. A small steel burnisher should then be used to mould the bell cap into close contact with the stone and the small area of contact on the stone abraded lightly with either a silicon carbide abrasive stick or a piece of a sanding disc. Both stone and bell cap should then be cleaned.

*Fig. 33
Mounting bell cap onto
baroque stone using
the burnisher*

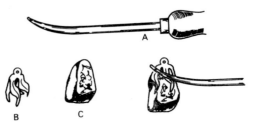

Although the tiniest spot of epoxy resin adhesive will hold several pounds weight if correctly mixed and applied, findings will not adhere to highly polished stones if any trace of grease, even the natural oil of the skin, is present. A wipe of methylated spirits on both stone and bell cap will ensure successful adhesion.

Mix only the smallest possible amount of epoxy, following the instructions carefully; these usually suggest mixing equal parts from each tube thoroughly on a piece of clean glass or tin lid, etc. The resin and the hardener should be stirred together rather than folded over, as this prevents air bubbles forming inside the mixture. The least possible amount should be spread on the inside of the bell cap and the abraded area of the stone. The bell cap should then be pressed firmly into position, any surplus adhesive removed with the point of a cocktail stick, and the stone stood upright in a tray of sand to set.

When the cap is securely fixed, any tiny particles of adhesive which have exuded can usually be picked off with the point of an orange stick, and a burnisher is then used to press down any edges which have not quite bedded onto the stone. A wipe over with methylated spirits will remove any finger marks, and the stone is ready to be hung on a chain.

A NECKLET FOR THE PENDANT

If, as has been suggested, chain is bought in bulk, the appropriate length is cut off, a jump ring fitted to one end and a bolt ring, attached by a second jump ring, to the other end. When fitting jump rings, they

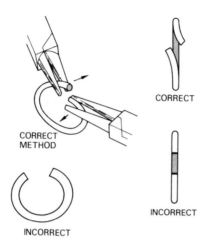

Fig. 34
Opening a jump ring

must always be opened sideways as this makes them easier to close without destroying their shape. A further jump ring of suitable size to accommodate the chain is then fixed to the bell cap, the chain passed through and the pendant is ready to wear.

BRACELETS

Bracelets can be made from tiny tumbled stones attached to chain in the same manner as in the popular charm bracelets, and bracelets consisting of a number of flat discs joined together can be bought from suppliers of findings. Children will derive considerable pleasure from sorting out stones of suitable shape, size, colour match or contrast, to include in these bracelets or on leaf spray brooches, pairs for cuff links and earrings and individual stones for mounting on ring shanks. The tasks will stimulate their interest and will inculcate a desire to progress to more advanced work.

ALTERNATIVE METHODS OF MOUNTING BAROQUES

Making a slot
The drilling of holes in tumbled stones is unsuitable for children, as, unless diamond-tipped drills are used, it is a tedious operation, but if a thin-bladed slitting saw is available, a tiny slot can be sawn at the top of the stone. The slot is then filled with epoxy resin adhesive and a jump ring pressed in, joint down. The surplus adhesive is then wiped off and when set, the resin is almost invisible and a strong neat job

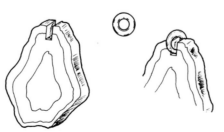

Fig. 35
Method of mounting
jump ring into saw cut

results. This is an excellent method for mounting pendant pieces when it is desirable, either because of shape or pattern, to ensure that one face of the stone should be presented to the front.

A wire cage

A slightly more difficult method of mounting baroque gems is to surround them in wire cages, and as $\frac{1}{32}$-in. diameter silver wire weighs approximately $\frac{1}{20}$ troy ounce per foot, the cost is quite reasonable.

An easy way for beginners to carry out an exercise of this type is for them to measure two suitable lengths of soft iron binding wire, which are then placed side by side and bent centrally over a piece of $\frac{3}{16}$-in. diameter bright rod. The wires are then gripped together with a pair of flat-nosed pliers and twisted together to form a loop with 4 "tails" which can now be shaped round the stone in such a manner that it could be permanently held.

*Fig. 36
Drawing down silver
wire with draw tongs*

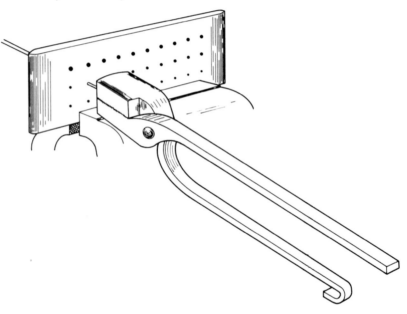

*Fig. 37
Method of mounting
baroque in wire cage*

The surplus is carefully measured and subtracted from the original lengths which will give the lengths of the silver wire needed to make the cage for the stone. These two pieces of silver wire can then be silver soldered into two separate loops, or better still, the four ends can be joined together each at 90° and after the joint has been cleaned, the cage should be thoroughly polished.

The stone is then placed in the centre of the cage with the joint at the base, the bright bar inserted between the stone and the wire, which is then tightened round the stone, forming a loop from which to suspend it from a necklet or bracelet.

This is a good introductory exercise into the use of silver, and although one or two failures can be expected at first, it will teach novices the basic techniques of silver soldering, namely, a tight, clean joint, adequately, but not too generously fluxed and the need to keep the flame moving.

Children can of course carry out the same exercise using annealed copper or brass wire and either soft or silver solder, but care should be taken to ensure that they appreciate that they are using gems.

With a plentiful supply of tumbled stones, children may become blasé, and every opportunity should be taken to bring to their notice the fact that many of the top jewelry designers of the world frequently introduce baroque gems in their designs. These usually involve specially designed claw settings or cages which are made up in such a manner as will enable the stone to be inserted after all the soldering has been carried out, although many modern jewelry designers incorporate castings into their creations.

In so doing, they are following one of the earliest known methods of working in metals, as the Bible tells how Aaron collected the golden earrings from the Israelites and made a "molten" calf and, more explicitly, Solomon had pillars of brass cast for the building of the Temple.

Fig. 38
Some suggested
designs for jewelry

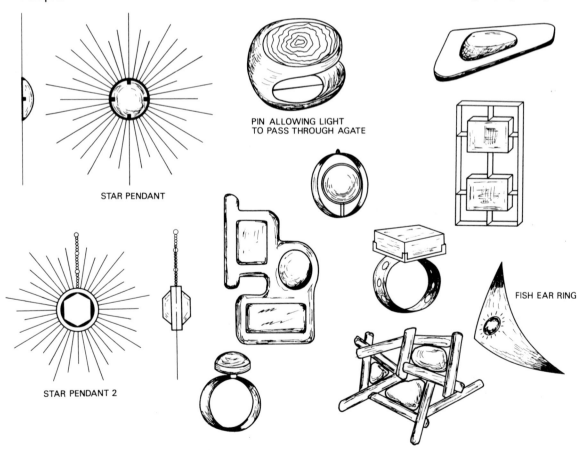

STAR PENDANT

PIN ALLOWING LIGHT
TO PASS THROUGH AGATE

STAR PENDANT 2

FISH EAR RING

CASTING MOUNTS   A more advanced technique

Although nowadays many substances, from rubber to concrete, are cast, so far as the jewelry maker is concerned, casting refers to the pouring of molten metal, usually gold or silver, into a mould. These castings can be made from patterns placed in an investment such as sand or plaster, or by pouring the molten metal directly into shapes cut into soft materials such as pumice stone, charcoal blocks or cuttlefish bone.

The art of casting, with its wide variety of methods, is the subject of many books and as, in this instance, we are only concerned with the mounting of baroque stones, only the most appropriate method will be considered.

This is the *cire perdue*, or lost wax process, in which the article to be created in metal is first made in wax, which, after being placed in a flask and surrounded by an investment, is burnt out, leaving a cavity of the desired shape to receive the molten metal.

Although practised from the beginning of civilisation and by many widely spread cultures, the process has its place in modern industry. Components for rocket and jet engines, made from ferrous alloys which are so hard that they can only be machined with considerable difficulty, are cast by this process to a 99·5 per cent degree of accuracy, the tolerance being 0·005 per inch.

In the type of jewelry which we are discussing, it is most probable that each stone to be set will require its own individual casting, and the wax pattern is best made from the types of waxes offered by firms dealing in dental equipment.

These waxes are mostly supplied in boxes of 40 sheets in various gauges, and are specially blended to ensure that they burn out without leaving any appreciable residue which would spoil the appearance of the casting.

Other properties possessed by these waxes are a relatively low melting point, and a range of differing degrees of hardness when cold combined with the property of being plastic when warm.

Making wax patterns

The wax is best worked with special wax knives, spatulas and carvers, obtainable from the same firms which supply the wax, but a friendly dentist is a blessing. The picks and probes which may be of no further use for dental purposes are ideal for modelling fine detail.

The tools are heated for use by holding them in a spirit lamp flame in such a position that it heats the tool about one inch from the tip, as by so doing, the heat travels towards the tip whilst the wax is being worked.

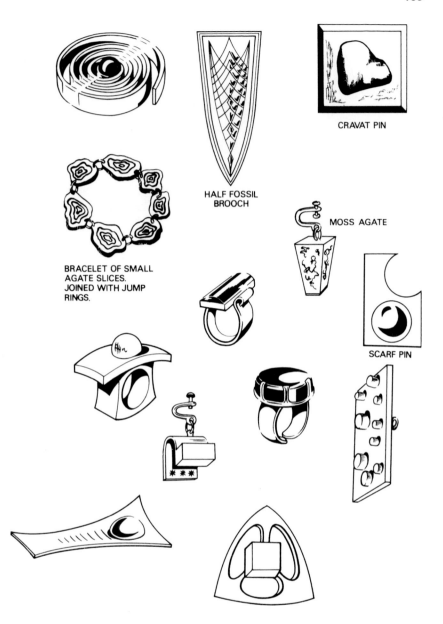

CRAVAT PIN

HALF FOSSIL
BROOCH

MOSS AGATE

BRACELET OF SMALL
AGATE SLICES.
JOINED WITH JUMP
RINGS.

SCARF PIN

Fig. 38a
Further designs
for jewelry

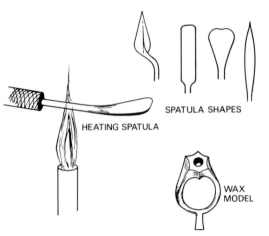

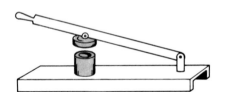

Fig. 39
*Process involved in
making and investing
wax patterns*

Fig. 40 (on left)
*Disposable plastic
hypodermic syringe for
making wax wires*

Fig. 41 (on right)
*School-made Solbrig
casting machine*

The pattern can be built up by the addition of wax from a heated
spatula, or wax wires which can be made by forcing hot wax through
a small hole in the end of a cylinder. A tool for this purpose is easily
contrived from an old oil gun, when differing nipples screwed onto the
end can be made to give a wide range of sizes of wires. Disposable
plastic hypodermic syringes can also be used for this purpose if the
needle is removed, providing the projection over which the needle
fits is not overheated. Care must be taken to avoid overheating the
tools as this will draw the temper, making the working portion soft
and more difficult to keep clean and highly polished. As with all tools,
picks, knives and spatulas must be kept clean and in good condition,
any surplus wax being wiped off before it sets.

Simple casting methods

Lost wax castings may be produced from the patterns by several
methods, all of which rely on some external force to ensure that the
molten metal enters every part of the mould, but only two methods
need to be considered here; steam pressure and centrifugal force.

The former is known as the *Solbrig* method. In this process, a
moistened pad of asbestos is forced down onto the top of the flask
immediately after the molten metal has been poured in.

The second method involves the use of a centrifugal casting machine,
and although many of these are in use in Colleges of Education and
Art Colleges, they may be too expensive for the average school or
amateur worker. A more simple method, yet one still favoured by
many dental mechanics, is the "chain and bucket" method, in which
a small bucket-shaped receptacle is attached to a strong chain and
handle. An old-fashioned "loo" chain is perfect, providing that it is
securely fixed to the wooden handle. The bucket forms the flask, and,
in use, is swung to and fro quickly before being swung round vertically
in a circle.

Plate 40
*Solbrig casting
machine in use*

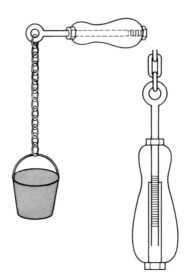

*Fig. 42
Chain and bucket for
lost wax casting*

*Plate 41
Casting with chain
and bucket*

The obvious precautions must be observed and a few dummy runs, first with the flask cold, then hot, carried out before a full-scale operation is attempted, as this will create confidence and ensure a good sharp swing.

Having made a wax pattern and decided on the method to be adopted, the pattern is mounted on a sprue or gate which is made to taper outwards to form a header which will receive the charge of molten metal, the whole exterior then being carefully painted over with a layer of investment plaster, mixed to a smooth slurry with water. This must be applied with a soft camel hair brush, taking care that no air bubbles are included. When it is dry, additional coatings can be given.

The pattern, now covered with a good surround of investment, is then held in the flask and a thicker mixture of investment plaster and water poured in, whilst the flask is tapped on the bench to prevent air being trapped.

After the investment has completely filled the flask, it must be allowed to set, preferably in a gentle heat to ensure that no moisture remains, and the next stage is to burn out the wax pattern.

Ideally, this should be done by supporting the flask, sprue down, on ceramic stilts resting on a small shallow Pyrex dish. This should be placed in a small kiln or muffle furnace, to ensure that the flask is heated evenly and the wax can run out into the dish. Reference to the Schools Council Project Technology Guidance Booklet No. 1, *Gas Fired Muffle Furnaces*, and the procedure suggested by Mr Ronald Rigby, will enable a suitable furnace to be made specifically for this purpose. We have not yet attempted the construction of a furnace as described in the Bulletin, but Mr Rigby assures me that the Mark IV Model would be ideal for this purpose, provided a very low flame is used.

If it is necessary to burn out the wax by heating with the blow torch, every effort must be made to heat the flask evenly all round, as uneven heating may cause parts of the investment to break down. When the wax has all been removed, the flask is brought to a red heat and the molten metal is poured in, then, depending on which method is used, the bucket is swung or the asbestos pad forced down.

Complete Solbrig outfits can be purchased if funds permit but the one illustrated, which was made by boys, functions quite satisfactorily. Irrespective of which method is used, the flask must be allowed to cool before finally quenching, to help in the removal of the casting from the investment, ready for cleaning up.

It will be appreciated by metalwork teachers that the techniques involved in lost wax casting differ from those usually employed in the normal gravity sand casting carried out in schools, and that only a brief introduction has been given to what is a rather specialised process.

A SURROUND FOR SLICES OR CABOCHONS

A very popular design of pendant, frequently made as a first job, is to mount a piece of stone which has been sliced and polished on both sides by surrounding it with a band of silver. To save time and the labour of sawing strips of silver from the sheet, it is best to buy the silver for this type of work as "slittings" of the width and gauge required; $\frac{3}{16}$ in. × 8's gauge, in length approximately 3 ft. 6 in. per oz. troy, has proved an excellent size to stock, as all that is required of the children is for them to saw off the appropriate length.

The circumference of regular shapes of slices and cabochons is easily and accurately obtained by means of a simple tool which can be quickly made by the following method.

A useful tool to make
Chuck a 4-in. length of $\frac{1}{4}$-in. A/F hexagonal brass in the lathe, turn a slight taper on the end, which should then be centred and drilled to a depth of about $\frac{3}{4}$ in. with a No. 54 drill. Remove from the lathe and drill two No. 60 drill holes on opposite flats, angled to break into the hole already drilled in the lathe and a blind $\frac{1}{8}$-in. diameter hole $1\frac{1}{2}$ in. from the end.

A $\frac{1}{8}$-in. brass rivet is then soldered into this hole and the tool is completed, ready for use as follows. Take a piece of thin, soft iron binding wire some 6 in. longer than the estimated circumference of the stone, bend it slightly, so that when it is pushed through one of the holes in the flats, it passes into the central hole. The wire is then passed back through the central hole and out of the hole in the opposite flat, leaving a loop projecting, slightly larger than the circumference of the stone. Both ends of the wire must then be secured round the rivet.

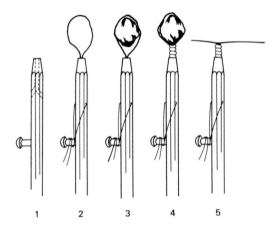

1 2 3 4 5

*Fig. 43
Use of tool for
obtaining
circumference of stone*

The stone is now laid on a flat surface, the loop passed over it and pressed down to the base of the stone with the fingers of one hand, whilst the other hand is used to twist the tool so that the wire tightens round the stone. When the wire is tight enough to hold the stone, it is slipped off, cut with snips or wire cutters and both ends pulled at right angles to the end of the twist, giving the exact length of silver to be cut off.

Both ends of the strip are then filed square with the sides, but with a very slight chamfer of only a few thousandths of an inch so that when the strip is shaped into a rough circle, the ends meet but leave a very slight groove on the inside. This groove ensures a good silver soldered joint, invisible after the work has been cleaned up, and the metal is then shaped to fit the slice which should be slightly less in thickness than the width of the silver strip.

It is preferable, at this stage, that the surround should be slightly too small to fit the stone as it can be stretched by planishing, whereas if it is too large, it must be cut at the joint, filed and re-soldered.

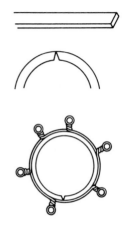

Fig. 44
Joining strip to form a surround or bezel (chamfer exaggerated for clarity)

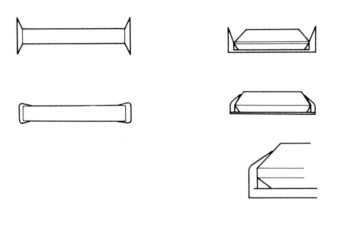

Fig. 45
Surrounds and bezels showing cutting back of edges

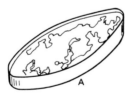
A

B

ENDS OVER FIRST

COMPLETE BURNISH

Children may not have the physical strength to burnish the edges over in order to retain the stone and a good tip is to cut back the inside edge with a three-cornered scraper so that the metal is brought to a sharp edge which does not offer so much resistance.

This cutting back of the edges of the surround also ensures a smooth, flush finish when burnished over, but before this final operation is carried out, some form of clip, loop or jump ring must be soldered on, to allow the pendant to be suspended from the necklace.

When mounting cabochons in closed settings for rings, cuff links or similar items of jewelry, this method of cutting back the edge allows a heavier gauge of metal to be used for the rim of the box in which the cabochon is to be set. The expert would most probably use a very thin gauge of silver, say 3's or 4's, but as the joint is the first of a series, hard solder is necessary, and novices tend to melt the thinner gauges. The amount of silver used in forming the rim is so small that the increase in cost is negligible, and if 6 or 8 gauge is used, the rate of failure will be considerably reduced.

The angle at which the scraper is held should be such that the metal tapers for as much of the depth of the rim as possible; this will enable the rim to be burnished very smoothly over the curved surface of the cabochon.

*Fig. 46
Holding ring in ring
clamp for burnishing
over the bezel*

An important point which must be observed when burnishing an oval or irregularly shaped cabochon is that the operation must always be started at the ends, because once these move, the sides follow much more easily, whereas if the longer curves are treated first, considerable difficulty may be experienced with the tighter curves.

MAKING YOUR OWN BURNISHER

Reference has been made to steel burnishers, which can readily be obtained from firms dealing in jeweler's tools. The ideal burnisher, however, is made from agate. Agate burnishers are difficult to obtain, but the lapidary worker can easily and quickly make one, which, with care, will last for more than a lifetime. In fact, a supply of agate burnishers of varying shapes should be available in any school which includes lapidary work and silversmithing as part of its curriculum.

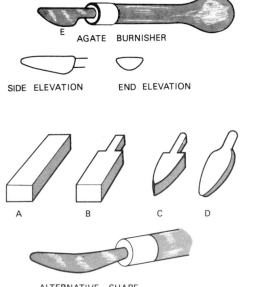

E   AGATE   BURNISHER

SIDE   ELEVATION   END ELEVATION

A   B   C   D

ALTERNATIVE   SHAPE
(SHAPES   VARY   ACCORDING   TO   INDIVIDUAL   PREFERENCE)

Fig. 47
Stages in making an agate burnisher

To make a burnisher, first cut a slice of agate approximately $\frac{5}{16}$ in. thick, $1\frac{1}{2}$ in. long and of the desired width, for example say $\frac{1}{2}$ in. Using the diamond saw, about half the length should be squared and then ground into a cylindrical shape, this rounded section then being mounted into a suitable wooden handle and secured with epoxy resin adhesive.

The projecting portion is then ground to the required size and shape, ensuring that all corners are smooth and rounded, then sanded and polished in the same manner as when making a cabochon.

From what has been said so far in this chapter, it will be appreciated that lapidary work opens up quite a new approach to the creation of jewelry in schools. Only a brief outline of the techniques of silver-smithing has been given and if this aspect of metalwork has not been previously attempted, reference should be made to some of the excellent and more specialised books listed in the bibliography.

DRILLING HOLES IN GEMSTONES

I feel that the chapter would not be complete without looking at the methods by which holes can be drilled in gemstones, as this is one of the most frequently asked questions by teachers intending to introduce lapidary work into their schools.

Quite frankly in my opinion, this is a process best left alone as far as children are concerned, as the expense of diamond-tipped drills or the time taken when using tube drills does not justify the end product.

The main reason for wishing to drill gemstones is to pass a wire or jump ring through, and it virtually only gives the same effect as sawing a slit as previously described.

Even though one may not wish to drill holes as a regular procedure, there may be occasions when the design of a particular piece of work makes it essential, and for the benefit of those who are placed in this situation, let us see how drilling holes can be accomplished.

Making and using a tube drill
The cheapest method is to use a tube drill, made from thin walled steel, copper or brass tube. The tube should first be squared off at the end, which is then belled out slightly to give clearance, otherwise there is a tendency for the drill to bind in the hole.

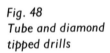

Fig. 48
Tube and diamond
tipped drills

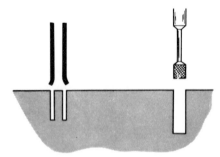

Prepare the stone for drilling by making a wall of Plasticine round the position of the hole. Having fixed the tube in the chuck of the drilling machine, partly fill the well formed by the Plasticine with a mixture of very light machine oil or turpentine and 100 silicon carbide grit.

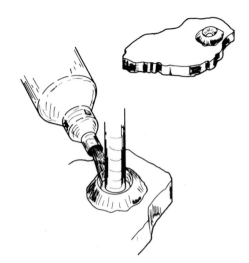

*Fig. 49
Drilling with tube drill*

High spindle speeds are not necessary in this type of drilling, as this is similar to the method used by the very early lapidarists who had only hand or foot driven drills.

*Plate 42
Tube and diamond
tipped drills*

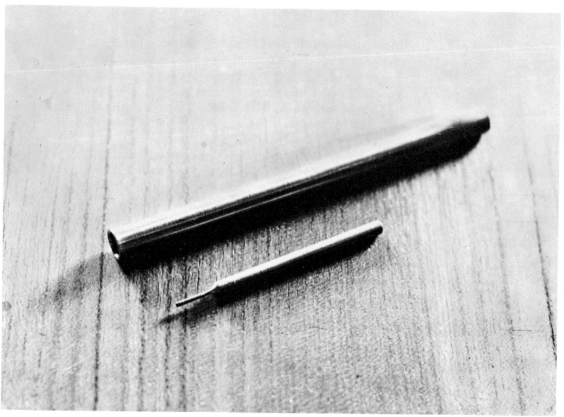

Only very light initial pressure should be used, and after an impression has been made, the drill must be frequently raised and lowered to remove the swarf and present fresh grit to the base of the hole.

On comparatively hard materials such as varieties of agate, progress will be slow and fresh supplies of grit must be added as necessary. The operator will feel when the cutting action ceases, and this is the time to add more grit and oil. Care must be taken when the hole is nearly through, as there is always the possibility that the edge will be chipped and ragged if undue pressure is exerted.

Quite large holes can be drilled by this method, and there is no reason why a hole saw of the Enox type could not be used with abrasive grits, providing the Morse twist drill is retracted. But for very small diameters difficulty will be experienced. The reason is, of course, the fact that the core projects into the tube and consequently tends to block the inside.

Other methods of drilling

Softer stones present very little difficulty, as these can be drilled at speeds of around 4000 r.p.m. using dentist's burrs tipped with tungsten carbide. In fact I was assured by a representative that these burrs would easily drill agate if a sufficiently high speed was obtained, but on visiting the firm he represented, 100,000 r.p.m. produced no visible effect on the slices I had taken with me.

Diamond core drills, which are only recommended for use in machines in which the spindle runs true, and is capable of giving a rate of cut over 40 feet per minute, can be obtained at prices ranging from £5 for $\frac{1}{4}$-in. diameter to £15 for $\frac{3}{4}$-in. diameter. These are very thin-walled tubes and are very easily damaged as the slightest degree of play in the spindle will soon render the drill useless.

Recently, one of the children in school was particularly anxious to make a pair of earrings, and produced a nice design which involved the drilling of a tiny hole in each of two pieces of Brazilian agate.

Agate is one of the difficult stones where drilling is concerned, but not wishing to discourage the youngster, I ordered two diamond-coated drills at 50p each from a firm supplying lapidary materials.

These are made from $\frac{1}{8}$-in. diameter tool steel, 2 in. overall length, $\frac{1}{2}$ being reduced to 0·031 in. to form the shank of the drill. At the tip, $\frac{1}{8}$ in. is coated with tiny particles of diamond to a depth of 0·007 in., giving an overall diameter of 0·045 in. and they are termed $\frac{1}{16}$ in. drills, this being the approximate diameter of the hole produced.

When fixed in the drilling machine, a $\frac{1}{8}$-in.-thick slice of agate can be drilled in about 4 minutes, by using the top speed, 4000 r.p.m., and keeping the tip well lubricated with turpentine, although a light machine oil would probably be just as effective.

The greatest care must be taken when starting to drill and the stone has to be firmly held to prevent the drill skidding across the surface, as this would mark the stone to such an extent that it would need to be re-ground and polished.

It's rather like drilling for wing mirrors on a brand new car, and the usual dodges of sticking a tiny piece of insulation tape or Sellotape to help pick up the centre have not been successful with our stones. The most satisfactory method discovered so far is to cement the stone to a flat piece of wood with dopping wax and, in the case of cabochons, packing up so that the position of the hole to be drilled is "square" to the drill tip.

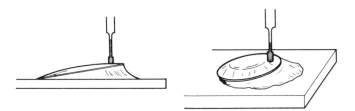

Fig. 50
Drilling cabochon with diamond tipped drill. Method of supporting cabochon

Plate 43
Drilling cabochon with diamond tipped drill

An absolute feather-light touch is necessary to begin with, and even when started, the feed must be as gentle as possible, about 4 minutes being taken to drill a hole through $\frac{1}{8}$-in.-thick agate.

So far more than a dozen holes have been drilled without casualty and the drill is still functioning efficiently, so that the cost has been only a few pence per hole drilled and the children have had the satisfaction of learning that the drilling of holes in gemstones is a very delicate operation.

Lapidary links with science subjects

There seems to be almost no limit to the extent to which lapidary work can be extended into other school subjects and, no doubt, practising teachers will increase the amount of correlation which has been suggested so far. Fresh avenues to be explored are frequently discovered, sometimes as a result of a casual enquiry, and recently, whilst conducting a course for teachers, I was asked where red Tiger's Eye came from. I explained that it was simply Golden Tiger's Eye which had been heat treated, and this led to a demonstration, following which a discussion arose on how other stones would react to specific degrees of heat.

Fortunately, the course was held in the school at which Mr Rigby was Head of the Craft Department, and consequently it was well equipped with furnaces, complete with pyrometers, and so an experiment was made.

HEAT TREATMENT

A slice of Brazilian agate was cut and halved, one being retained as a control, the other being placed in fine dry sand, encased in a piece of 2-in. diameter steel tube. This was placed in an electrically heated tube furnace and the temperature held at 150° Centigrade for 2 hours, after which it was raised to 300° Centigrade for a further hour.

The furnace was then switched off and when everything had cooled, we extracted the stone from the sand to find that a remarkable colour change had taken place. The specimens had been cut from a nodule some 3 in. in diameter, and in its rough state, the interior was pale grey with darker grey rings towards the outside and an outer casing of brown. The specimen which had been heat treated was now pale pink with darker pink radial markings, and towards the outer edge, a black band was sandwiched between two bands of pale orange whilst the outer edge was carnelian red in colour.

The children at my own school were intensely fascinated by the colour change and inevitably one boy asked could he undertake a similar experiment? Permission being granted, he chose to place a piece of Rose Quartz and a small piece of Brazilian Agate in sand, again in a 2-in. diameter steel tube.

Having no furnace, he spent a large part of his lunch-time heating the tube on the brazing hearth, and being somewhat over-enthusiastic, heated the tube to a good red heat, at a rough estimate around 750° Centigrade! The results were interesting but, to the boy, slightly disappointing. The Rose Quartz had changed from a lovely deep pink to a dirty white, whilst the agate, although it had undergone a remarkable colour change, had lost its translucence and had become opaque.

It is obvious that because of their chemical constituents, the colour of some gemstones can be changed. The scientific reasons governing the effects of heat on these chemical constituents and the atomic structure of minerals could form the basis for a considerable amount of research by science teachers.

Not all stones will undergo a colour change by this treatment, and it must be strongly emphasised that some gems are extremely susceptible to heat and will disintegrate or decompose. Opal, for example, must never be subjected to more than a very moderate degree of heat, no matter how carefully this is applied, otherwise it will shatter.

The method of heating must also be carefully considered. Most gemstones must be heated uniformly because uneven heating will cause uneven expansion and consequent breakage. Generally speaking, by metalworkers' standards, high temperatures are not required and about 375 to 400° C should be regarded as the maximum for any experiment carried out in the school workshop or science laboratory.

THE ARTIFICAL COLOURING OF GEMSTONES

The gem cutters of Idar Oberstein, the home of the German agate industry, have practised the colouring of agates for more than 100 years and they obtain strikingly beautiful results, vivid reds, blues, browns, greens and intense black being common. The method which they use is to introduce metallic salts into the pores of the agates by soaking them in various solutions and in some cases, subsequent heating.

From our experiments we have found that heating alone is sufficient to produce reddish colours in some varieties of agate. Good reds can be best obtained by soaking the stone in warm iron nitrate for periods of from a week to a month, the length of time being dependent on the thickness of the slice.

Differing shades of blue are the result of treatment with yellow or red prussiate of potassium and iron sulphate, greens by soaking in nickel nitrate, chromic acid, ammonium bichromate or potassium bichromate, but the simplest colour to obtain is a good black. To do this, the agate is soaked in a solution of sugar and water, in the ratio of 1 lb. of sugar to a pint of water, for about a fortnight, after which it is placed in sulphuric acid. The acid is slowly brought to boiling point and then allowed to cool, when the agate, which will be black and shining, can be removed and washed.

The degree of penetration into the surface of the agate is dependent on many factors, and if colour changes are effected for decorative, rather than experimental reasons, the slice or cabochon should be in its finished state before being treated.

Teachers will be aware of the safety precautions necessary when using the chemicals and processes mentioned.

This brief outline of methods of changing the colour of stones has been included in an effort to show how aspects of lapidary work can be extended beyond the craft room.

FLUORESCENCE

Many of our native minerals, which may not be suitable for inclusion in jewelry, become fluorescent when exposed to ultraviolet light and can be used to make a most unusual display. The cabinet in which the display is normally housed can also be used for identifying several varieties of gem material and mineral specimens, and will be a valuable teaching aid for use in many science, geography and geology lessons.

Most children will have learned about Sir Isaac Newton's experiments which prove that white light is composed from the colours of the spectrum, and will have possibly heard of ultraviolet light, sometimes called black, invisible or cold light, but will be totally unaware of the fact that it causes many substances to fluoresce.

Before proceeding further, let us discuss what exactly is meant by fluorescence as children may fail to appreciate the connection between fluorescent lights, paints, garments and minerals.

Light waves are measured in Angstrom Units, and whilst visible light ranges from approximately 4000 to 8000 AU the range of the invisible ultraviolet light is from 500 AU to 4000 AU. These invisible rays cause certain substances to emit visible light by supplying energy to the molecules.

The light which is emitted is very striking and was termed fluorescent light over 100 years ago by Sir George Stokes, the physicist who established the true nature of fluorescence. He created the term from the mineral fluorite, most varieties of which display this effect, although strangely enough, the best known variety, Blue John or Fluorspar from Castleton in Derbyshire, does not fluoresce.

With some substances, the fluorescent glow continues even after the ultra-violet light has been switched off, and in some instances, this afterglow, known as phosphorescence, is of a different colour.

SOME OF THE MINERALS WHICH FLUORESCE

Most varieties of fluorite give off a beautiful deep violet light, and other native minerals suitable for a fluorescent display are:

Calcite
Widely distributed throughout the country, usually white or clear, although may be stained by other minerals. Specimens obtained from Somerset, the Pennines and Shropshire assume shades varying from peach colour to deep rose red when subjected to U.V. light.

Autunite
This is a uranium mineral, occurring as thin layers on rocks found on Dartmoor. Fluoresces bright green.

Witherite
From Durham and the Northern Pennines. Varies in colour from greyish white to dark beige, but under the lamp shows a range of colour from bright yellow to deep orange.

Willemite
A silicate of zinc from widely spread locations with considerable variation in colour, but all varieties fluoresce brilliant green.

Amber
Although not a mineral, amber will fluoresce white, yellow, green or blue.

Apatite
Usually pale green colour which is greatly intensified to brilliant fluorescent green.

In addition, many varieties of marble, agates, alabaster and fossils will react, and a selection will make an interesting display if housed in a suitable cabinet which can either be purpose built or, as a novelty, adapted from an old T.V. cabinet.

ULTRA-VIOLET LIGHT

Ultra-violet rays are produced by the sun, but due to what could be termed atmospheric filtration, those which reach us are in the region of the range between 2900 to 4000 AU. These have a beneficial rather than a harmful effect on the human body, and this particular range, termed long-wave U.V., is most suitable for school use as all the minerals previously listed will react to it.

Short-wave U.V. radiation, although it causes a far wider range of specimens to fluoresce, is not to be recommended for use in schools unless the teacher is fully conversant with its effects.

It is sub-divided into two overlapping bands:

1 The wavelength between 2200 and 3100, known as the Germicidal
   radiation band, and
2 The Erythemal radiation band, from 2900 to 3100. Both these
   portions of the spectrum can be harmful, causing what amounts to
   sunburn, and even more painful, irritation of the eye.

This latter effect is most insidious as the damage only becomes
apparent some hours later. Anyone who has been sufficiently ignorant
or careless as to look directly at an electric welding arc, without
protective glasses, and has later suffered the intense pain from the
condition known as "arc eyes", will appreciate the reason why
short-wave U.V. should be treated with respect.

There are many methods by which the effects of long-wave ultra-
violet light can be observed, and the simplest is to pass a powerful
beam of light through a flask containing a strong solution of copper
sulphate. An excellent light source is a film strip projector, and if a
litre flask is filled with the copper sulphate solution, this will serve as
a light filter and a condensing lens. All light below the yellow wavelength is absorbed, and the blue visible light which passes through
will be invisible if viewed through a red filter.

If a mineral, being placed in the beam of blue light, and not illuminated
in any other way, is seen to glow when observed through a red filter,
it must be that the mineral is changing the blue light to light of a
longer wavelength by absorbing energy from it, in other words it is
fluorescing.

MAKING A U.V. DISPLAY CABINET

Our first display cabinet was constructed from an old T.V. cabinet into
which I installed a 125-watt Mazda Mercury Vapour U.V. lamp, similar
in appearance to an ordinary electric light bulb except for the fact
that the glass is almost black in colour.

The illumination is produced inside the lamp by a mercury arc and a
suitable choke and capacitor have to be included in the wiring circuit.
To prevent the lamp being inserted into an ordinary lamp holder, the
bayonet cap has 3 prongs instead of the usual 2, hence a special holder
is necessary.

The glass from which the lamp is made is known as Wood's Glass,
which only allows the long-wave light to pass through, although, due
to the thinness of the glass, a proportion of visible violet light passes
through.

Our latest cabinet was purpose built to the dimensions shown in
Figure 51 to accommodate a Philip's T.L.20.W 108 bi-pin U.V. tube,

L

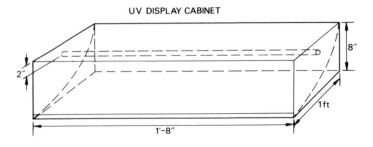

UV DISPLAY CABINET

Fig. 51
U.V. cabinet and
wiring diagrams

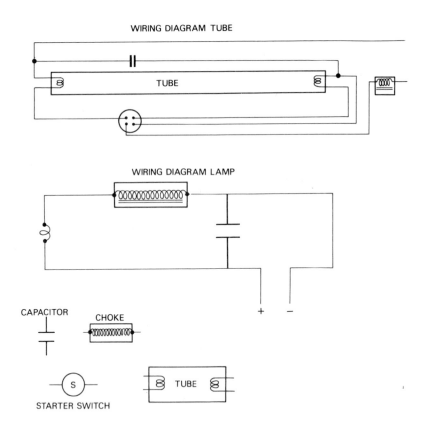

WIRING DIAGRAM TUBE

TUBE

WIRING DIAGRAM LAMP

CAPACITOR

CHOKE

+   −

STARTER SWITCH

TUBE

which is 18 in. long and consumes only 15 watts. This gives a more
even spread of light, resulting in a more spectacular permanent
display. Our original cabinet is now used for testing specimens rather
than displaying them.

To make a similar cabinet, construct an open-fronted box, 1 ft. 9 in.
by 1 ft. by 8 in. deep, from plywood or hardboard, and insert a piece
of 2 mm plywood across the full length of the inside, forming a gentle
curve from the base at the front to the top at the rear. This will

support the specimens and serve to mask the choke, starter, capacitor and wiring, whilst a 2-in. strip fastened across the top edge of the open front will mask the tube.

The interior must be given two or three coats of a suitable matt black paint (blackboard renovating paint is ideal) and the job is then completed, possibly for little more than the cost of the tube. The control gear, i.e. the choke, capacitor and starter, are identical with those used in many advertising display units which, when they have served their original purpose, or the lamp has been broken or burned out, are frequently discarded. Electrical contractors, if approached, are often quite willing to give them to a school.

A remote but possible source of danger could occur when some long-wave lamps are used. If the glass bulb is cracked, the lamp may continue to burn, as the light is created in a quartz glass tube, which may still be undamaged and emitting short-wave ultra-violet light, which could escape through the cracked bulb. Ordinary glass is a reasonably good protection against the more dangerous short-waves, and to be 100 per cent safe a glass front could be incorporated in the cabinet.

When fluorescing specimens are inspected under the influence of U.V. light, a peculiar haze effect is apparent to some viewers, and this is actually due to certain pigments in the eye itself fluorescing. This is in no way harmful, and ceases immediately the viewer looks away from the light, but this haze effect can be overcome if the specimens are viewed through sodium yellow glass.

If a pair of Nighthawk Night Driving Glasses are worn, the clarity of the specimens is greatly improved, and an added refinement to a viewing box could be the inclusion of peep-holes covered by pieces of this type of glass.

The phenomenon of fluorescence has many applications in art, medicine, industry, criminology and many branches of science. Writings which have been erased or altered can often be read under ultra-violet light, and many substances, which look exactly alike to the eye in natural light, differ considerably when caused to fluoresce. Mixtures of various types of flour can be detected, as also can margarine in butter, chicory in coffee, blood stains on red ink or paint. Although these applications have no connection with lapidary work as such, they are typical of the manner in which this fascinating craft can lead into new fields of interest.

Cutting and polishing techniques for specific gemstones

Although by no means comprehensive, the following materials have proved satisfactory for use in school; generally speaking, they are all comparatively cheap to buy and easy to work.

AGATES   Hardness 7.   Sp. Gr. 2·64

The wide range of varieties of this member of the quartz family is too vast to deal with in detail, but the differing colours and patterns revealed when an agate is sliced, are a constant source of anticipation to the lapidarist.

Every agate is unique in colour, pattern, shape or design; two identical agates have never been found and although many precious stones can be synthesised, a synthetic agate has yet to be produced.

Agate, or chalcedony to give it its correct name, is a translucent crypto-crystalline quartz, with inclusions of other minerals which form layers, spots or dendrites (fern-like) in a great variety of colours.

Although it has many commercial uses, for example pestles and mortars, fishing-rod eyes, burnishers and in chemical balances, etc., its main use since the days of Ancient Greece has been in jewelry. Found in every continent, agates vary greatly in size from tiny nodules weighing only a fraction of an ounce to boulders of several hundred-weight. The manner in which they were formed has been the basis for research by experts in many countries over a period of several years.

The most simple explanation is that steam cavities in lava became filled with colloidal silica which percolated through the rock, depositing particles on the wall of the cavity. In turn, other mineral-bearing solutions passed through the silica layer, forming the coloured bands which are a feature of so many varieties of agate.

In some cases, solutions which react to form crystals have resulted in the beautiful hollow geodes, many of which are lined with crystals of calcite, amethyst or other quartz crystals.

Dealers usually list agate according to place of origin, Brazilian, Mexican, Queensland, Rhodesian, Scottish, etc., and American dealers usually specify the state or district, hence Montana, Wyoming, etc., but basically, the main types are:

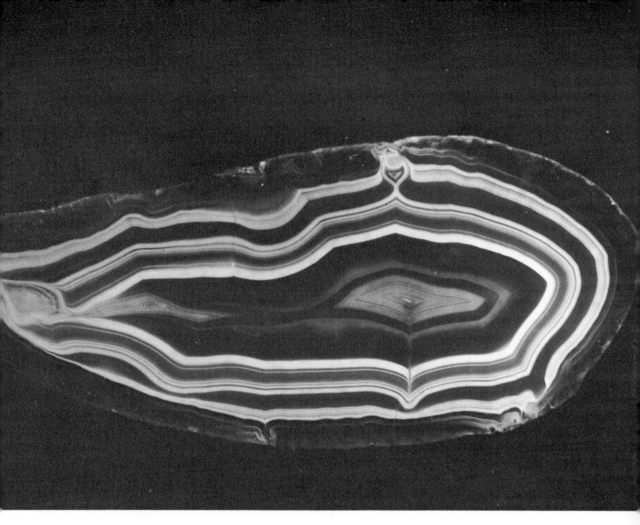

Plate 44
Brazilian agate full size. Property of Mr. K. Parkinson

Fortification Agate
In which the colours form bands which, when the stone is cut, show a marked similarity to the plan view of an Iron Age camp or fortress, as the bands are irregular and sharply angled.

Moss Agate or Mocha Stone
Fern or moss-like inclusions in clear agate, due to the colloidal precipitation of manganese dioxide in the silica, give the appearance of plants or feathers enclosed within the stone, and some varieties are termed Plume Agate and Flower Agate.

Banded Agate
The layers of colour, sometimes quite contrasting, are fairly even and concentric.

Most varieties of agate are extremely tough and may be considered insensitive to the heat of dopping or grinding, and providing the slice is free from flaws, good cabochons are easily produced. Remember to examine the slice in front of a good light before marking out, as I have found that flaws have a tendency to creep across the slice in the same manner as does a crack in a sheet of glass. Consequently, it is best to break the slice along the crack before marking out to avoid disappointment and waste of time.

Care should be taken in the early stages of grinding to prevent edges chipping.

Agates polish extremely well with cerium oxide on a leather or felt buff.

*Plate 45
Moss agate reputed to be the finest specimen in the world. Sold by Mr. K. Parkinson, F.G.A., to Mr. Floyd Beattie of San Francisco for $600 in 1969*

ALABASTER   Hardness 2.   Sp. Gr. 2·3

A compact form of gypsum, very soft and easy to cut but takes a high
polish. Grinding must be carried out on a true wheel, using plenty of
water, and when sanding, watch your mark very carefully, as even the
smoothest of discs will remove the material quite speedily. Polish with
tin oxide on soft damp leather.

AMAZONITE   Hardness 6.   Sp. Gr. 2·55

Massive microcline feldspar. The best quality is an attractive green
colour with occasional white flecks. Very popular with children as it
cuts and polishes easily with tin oxide on felt. All the varieties of
feldspar have strong cleavage planes and beginners should avoid
shallow cabochons. Not heat sensitive. When removing from the dop
stick, it is best to melt the wax rather than remove cold, to avoid
breakage.

AMBER   Hardness 2·5.   Sp. Gr. 1·04–1·10

One of the few gem materials which are of vegetable origin, being a
fossilised resin; good specimens are frequently found on the East Coast
beaches. The best amber comes from the Baltic and varies in colour
from very pale to brownish yellow. Darker colours, in varying shades,
from pale to reddish browns, are common in amber found in Sicily,
Rumania and Burma. Not always transparent, it may be cloudy due to
the inclusion of tiny air bubbles.

Very heat sensitive, it becomes soft at about 165° C. and melts above
250° C.

In view of its softness, can be easily cut with a jeweler's saw, shaped
with files and sanded with a plentiful supply of water to ensure that it
is kept cool. Final polish is best obtained on well-soaked soft leather
and cerium oxide, using very light pressure.

AMETHYST   (Quartz)

Crystalline quartz, varying in colour from almost colourless to deep
purple. Price increases with depth of colour. Look for flaws before
cutting rough material. Facets well, cut and polish as for agate.

APATITE   Hardness 5.   Sp. Gr. 3·2

Most common variety is transparent yellow green. Attractive
appearance but disappointing as the crystals usually contain many
flaws, are quite brittle and heat sensitive. Flawless pieces can be made
into very attractive faceted gems, but shellac should be used for
dopping, as the heat of dopping wax may cause damage. Very careful
sawing, grinding and sanding should be observed, finishing off with
very worn 600 grit discs and cerium oxide on soft leather.

ARAGONITE   Hardness 3·5.   Sp. Gr. 2·9

White or colourless orthorhombic crystalline mineral, chemically
similar to calcite. Good specimens can be found in this country.
Similar in working qualities to apatite and the same precautions should
apply.

AVENTURINE QUARTZ

Another member of the quartz family, available in varying shades of
green and blue, inclusions of mica causing a glittering effect. Excellent
for cabochons and tumbling, it has, however, a tendency to undercut,
and cabochons should be sanded at a fast speed using plenty of water.

AXINITE   Hardness 6·5.   Sp. Gr. 3·28

So named because the shape of the crystals resembles the blade of an
axe. Colour varies from yellow to brown, varying according to the
angle from which it is viewed. Cuts easily but has a directional
resistance, easier "with the grain". Not sensitive to normal heating.
Polish with cerium oxide on felt or hard leather.

AZURITE   Hardness 3·5.   Sp. Gr. 3·8

A lovely blue massive material which is rather soft for inclusion in
jewelry but makes lovely cabinet specimens. Very easily cut and
ground. Sanding must be carefully carried out, the final polish being
obtained from chrome oxide on wet soft leather using a very slow
speed. It is a copper bearing mineral and is found in many parts of
England where copper has been mined.

BARITE   Hardness 3.   Sp. Gr. 4·5

Soft and massive, and found in many areas of this country, varying in
colour from almost white to very dark brown. Several varieties when
cut and polished reveal a grain similar to wood, ranging from
sycamore to very old oak.

It is sensitive to heat, brittle and cleaves unexpectedly. Cut and polish
as for apatite.

BERYL   Hardness 7·5 to 8.   Sp. Gr. 2·65 to 2·85

Beginners may be confused by this mineral, an aluminium silicate,
which occurs in some igneous and some metamorphic rocks. Although
it crystallizes in the hexagonal system and crystals weighing many tons
have been found, these are usually massive and opaque. Gem varieties
of beryl are Emerald, pale to deepest green, Heliodor or Golden
Beryl, yellow, Morganite, pink, Aquamarine, pale sea green or blue,
but these, even in the rough state, are quite costly to buy. Some good
specimens have been found in Scotland.

Plates 4, 5, 6 & 7 are examples of jewelry by children and students.

Plate 4
Indian beggar beads from purchased agates.

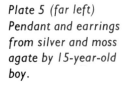

Plate 5 (far left)
Pendant and earrings from silver and moss agate by 15-year-old boy.

Plate 6 (left)
Silver and amethyst pendant.

Plate 7
Some unfinished pieces by 14-year-old girls.

In these plates each stone has been photographed twice— (a) in ordinary light and (b) in fluorescent light.

Plate 8a & b
Calcite (Shropshire)

Plate 9a & b
Scapolite

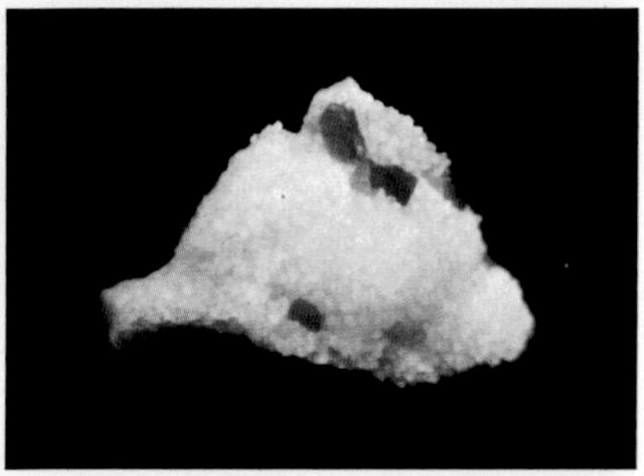

Plate 10a & b
Aragonite and sulphur

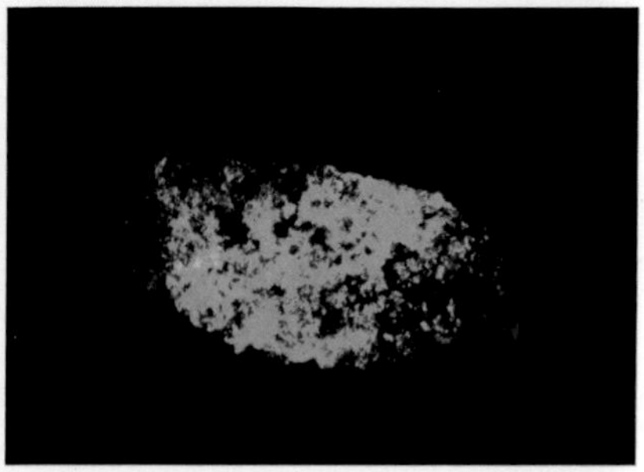

Plate 11a & b
Autunite (Devon)

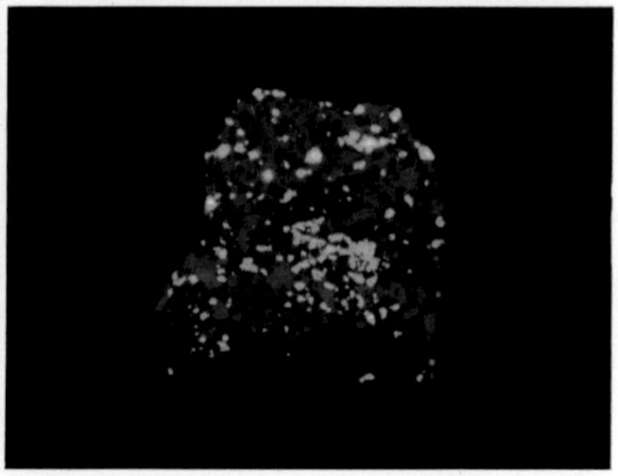

Plate 12a & b
Franklinite Witherite (green), Calcite (pink)

Plate 13a & b
Fluorite (Yorkshire)

Plate 14a & b
Witherite (Yorkshire)

Plate 15a & b
Hackmanite

Plate 16
Brazilian agate
On the right in its
natural state, on the
left when it has been
heat-treated.

Plate 17
Brazilian agate slice

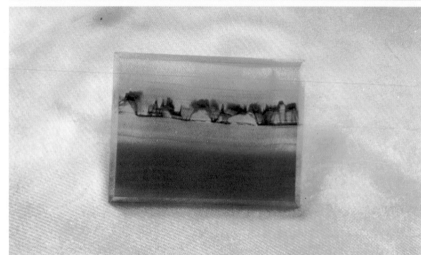

Plate 18
Scenic agate
An example of
Montana Dendritic.

Plate 19
Derbyshire Oak Stone
(Barite)

Ordinary beryl, which is more likely to be found, is opaque and coloured blue-grey, blue, yellow, white or banded. It has the appearance of quartz, but can readily be distinguished by the fact that beryl nearly always has grooves parallel to the length of the crystals.

All varieties are tough, heat resistant and take a high polish, in addition to producing excellent tumbled stones. Treat as for quartz.

BLUE JOHN   Hardness 4.   Sp. Gr. 3·18

This variety of fluorite is found only in Castleton, Derbyshire, where it is still mined commercially, and a visit to the mines is well worth while. It varies in colour from blue-black through varying shades of violet to deep purple and even orange and red.

Semi-transparent, brittle and heat sensitive, it breaks easily along strong cleavage planes and is extremely difficult to work in its natural state, but if soaked in hot shellac or gold size and allowed to cool, it can be worked with care. Grinding should never be carried out on a coarse wheel because it is fairly soft; sanding should be carried out on fine worn discs and the final polish from a soft leather disc with cerium oxide and water.

CAIRNGORM   (Quartz)

This smoky yellow to smoky brown variety of crystalline quartz takes its name from the Cairngorm Mountains and has been used for centuries in traditional Scottish jewelry, although a considerable quantity is imported from Brazil, when it is termed Smoky Quartz.

Cuts, polishes and facets well if procedure as for agate is adopted.

CALCITE   Hardness 3.   Sp. Gr. 2·71

Varies in colour and appearance from colourless transparent to opaque grey, yellow, brown, blue and red. I have collected a rather pleasant pink variety in the Malvern Hills and this has cut and polished well, adopting the same technique as for its close relation, alabaster. All the marbles are varieties of calcite and respond to similar treatment, whilst the transparent variety, of optical quality, is Iceland Spar, with its peculiar property of double refraction.

CARNELIAN OR CORNELIAN   (Quartz)

Orange to red variety of chalcedony, translucent, is very occasionally found in Scotland, but most supplies come from South America. Produces lovely tumbled stones and cabochons, and being a crypto-crystalline quartz, poses no cutting or polishing problems.

CASSITERITE   Hardness 6 to 7.   Sp. Gr. 7

The main source of tin, cassiterite is found in many parts of Cornwall and frequently found as pebbles in the beds of streams and on the beaches. Recognisable in the first instance by its heaviness, it varies in colour from yellow to brown or black. Very tough and heat resistant, it is difficult to cut and polish, the resultant gem hardly being worth the effort, especially when working with children.

CELESTITE   Hardness 3.   Sp. Gr. 3·97

This very soft and delicate mineral is heat sensitive and has strong cleavage planes. If found when prospecting in the West Country, samples are best retained unworked as cabinet specimens.

CHRYSOCOLLA   Hardness 2 to 4.   Sp. Gr. 2·2

The variety of this stone found in England is an uncrystallised copper silicate, green to greenish blue in colour and is too soft for inclusion in jewelry.

For cabinet display, specimens can be polished on one face if grinding and sanding is carefully carried out. Will accept a high polish from a very wet felt buff with cerium oxide.

CHRYSOPRASE   (Quartz)

This material, one of the rarest and most expensive members of the quartz family, is notable for its brilliant shades of green and must not be confused with the quartz variety, prase, which is dull and uninteresting. Australia is the best source of this material, and as prices range up to £5 per ounce, care must be taken when cutting and polishing, especially as it tends to undercut. Sharp new discs, plenty of water and a higher speed should be used when sanding, the final polish being obtained with cerium oxide on damp leather.

CITRINE   (Quartz)

Bright transparent, varying from pale yellow to orange red in colour, sometimes having a smoky tinge, this stone was once used extensively as a substitute for topaz, under the names Scottish Topaz, Occidental Topaz, etc.

Found in various parts of Great Britain, it is an excellent material for all round use, faceting, cabochon cutting or tumbling and does not present any problems.

FELDSPAR   Hardness 6 to 6·5.   Sp. Gr. 2·54 to 2·72

One of the most abundant of rock-forming minerals, varieties of feldspar are contained in most igneous and many metamorphic rocks. Many interesting specimens can easily be found in North-west Scotland although the more usually accepted gemstone varieties come from overseas, these being Amazonite, Labradorite, Moonstone and Sunstone.

A feature of the majority of feldspars is the strong cleavage planes, often at right angles, which means that great care must be taken to avoid breakage.

The Scottish rocks with which we have worked in school have, however, been more accommodating, due no doubt, to the inclusions of other minerals, and have polished quite well with cerium oxide on felt.

GARNET   Hardness 6·5 to 7·5.   Sp. Gr. 3·41 to 4·2

Most beginners think of garnet as a dark red stone, popular in Victorian jewelry, whereas in fact it is the name of a whole family of minerals, some of which are used as abrasives (garnet paper for example has superseded sand paper and glass paper in most school woodwork rooms).

It occurs in both crystalline and massive forms, the main varieties being:

Grossularite (calcium/aluminium garnet)
Green to greenish yellow, yellow brown to reddish orange, mainly translucent and very tough.

Almandine (iron/aluminium garnet)
Sometimes termed precious garnet, varying in colour from transparent deep red to brownish red.

Pyrope (magnesium/aluminium garnet)
Perhaps the best for gemstones, it is of a deep crimson colour, the variety found in South Africa sometimes being called the "Cape Ruby".

Spessartite (manganese/aluminium garnet)
A rarer variety, deep hyacinth colour to brilliant orange and red.

Andradite (calcium iron garnet)
The best varieties of this lovely transparent garnet come from Russia, the predominating colour being varying shades of green.

Most garnets are fairly brittle but cut and polish quite well. Care must be taken to prevent chipped edges, from the early stages of grinding right up to the setting of the finished gem. Nice cabochons or faceted stones can be produced by finally sanding with a very well worn fine grit disc before polishing on leather with chrome or cerium oxide.

GRANITES

Whilst most people regard these igneous rocks, composed mainly of quartz, feldspar and mica, as building materials, many of them can be quite attractive when cut and polished for inclusion in jewelry. They are excellent for "first attempts", as small pieces can usually be obtained from monumental masons.

Because of the many inclusions in its granular structure, care must be taken when sawing and grinding to ensure that tiny particles are not dislodged causing pit holes. A fine rate of feed when sawing, careful sanding and a final polish with cerium oxide on hard leather should produce nice cabochons.

HEMATITE   Hardness 5·5 to 6·5.   Sp. Gr. 4·9 to 5·3

One of the world's best-known sources of this oxide of iron is Cumberland. It is easily identified because irrespective of its external appearance, it produces a red streak when scratched or crushed, hence its name.

Sometimes found in botryoidal form (kidney stone) or massive; grey to blue grey in colour, although freshly broken pieces may exhibit the typical redness.

At one time used extensively for seals in signet rings, it is very messy to work with, staining the hands with the powder produced by cutting and grinding, this being virtually jeweler's rouge.

Finished stones have a metallic lustrous black colour and may be cabochon or facet cut. It is tough and heat resistance presents no problems in sawing or grinding (apart from the mess). Pre-polish by sanding with a well worn fine disc and finish with tin oxide on felt.

JET   Hardness 3·5.   Sp. Gr. 1·24

Beloved of Victorians for "mourning jewelry", the best quality in the world is that obtained from Whitby, and archaeologists have discovered that it has been used in this country since pre-historic times.

One of the few gems of vegetable origin, it is easily recognisable by its colour, light weight, and the fact that it does not soil the hands. Like amber, which it closely resembles in many ways, it becomes electrically charged when rubbed on wool. If a lighted match is applied to it, it will give off a bituminous smell.

Jet is best worked with hand tools as in the case of amber, and in fact, sanding could be carried out with ordinary wet and dry paper and the final polish obtained by hand with tin oxide on chamois leather.

LABRADORITE (Feldspar, q.v.)

On first sight, the rough appears most uninteresting, having the appearance of a slightly glossy blue grey slate. If cut correctly, the finished gem shows a beautiful display of colour, combinations of peacock blue, deep greens, yellows, orange and red appearing, dependent upon the angle from which it is viewed.

To ascertain the angle at which the slice must be cut, a good tip is to thoroughly wet the surface of the stone, which should then be held under a strong light and slowly rotated in all directions until the play of colour is seen. If the rough is sliced parallel to the side which exhibits the "labradorescence", as it is termed, the finished slice is said to be correctly oriented.

When orienting labradorite, the best effect is seen when the stone is viewed from the same angle as the light source, and if the worker stands immediately beneath the light bulb, the shadow of his forehead should almost touch the stone.

If the slice is not cut correctly, it will be necessary to tilt it to see the colour play, and the error should be corrected by making a fresh cut.

Labradorite makes superb pendant cabochons and is best worked using the same technique and precautions as for Amazonite.

LAPIS LAZULI   Hardness 5·5.   Sp. Gr. 2·75 to 2·9

The best quality of this rock (it is composed of lazurite, calcite and pyrite) is obtained from Afghanistan and Persia, when it is of a deep blue colour, whilst that from South America is usually a lighter blue.

Despite its softness, it is quite tough and not heat sensitive, but care must be observed when grinding and sanding so as not to cut below the mark.

Can be difficult to polish, and we have found that whilst cerium oxide on felt gives an inferior result, cerium oxide on moist leather gives a good polish, but the best results are obtained from Linde A on leather.

MALACHITE   Hardness 3·5.   Sp. Gr. 3·75 to 3·95

Easily recognisable by its brilliant green colour, this copper ore is widespread in this country, although the best gem material comes from the Congo and the South African copper belt, and is comparatively expensive for such a soft gem material. However, its beautiful appearance, sometimes with alternating bands of light and dark greens, makes it an attractive material with which to work.

Another soft stone which needs care to prevent over-grinding, it must also be carefully sanded with fine worn discs and a plentiful supply of water. Rather brittle, it is best cut as fairly high cabochons to prevent thin edges which are likely to break. Best polish is obtained from Linde A on leather.

MARBLE

A form of calcite, all the varieties of marble respond to the same treatment as given for alabaster and a wide range of varieties are found in the British Isles. Connemara and Iona marble is a lovely light to mid-green. The varieties which I have found in North-west Scotland are not so bright, and as previously stated, the landscape marbles of the Midlands are in varying shades of grey. Working procedure as for alabaster.

MOONSTONE

Another variety of feldspar, again fairly uninteresting in the rough; cleaves easily, but when polished looks extremely attractive with its blueish silvery sheen. Work as for amazonite and other feldspars.

OPAL   Hardness 5 to 6·5.   Sp. Gr. 1·95 to 2·2

A silica gel, or non-crystalline form of quartz, opal is far more wide-spread than the average person realises, but unfortunately, most of it is not worth using as gem material. However, the varieties which are used, known as precious opal, cannot be surpassed for their beauty, with vivid orange, reds, blues and greens, of extreme purity, appearing to float beneath the surface of the stone. The chief gem varieties are:

Black Opal
Displays range of brilliant colours on a black ground.

White (or Milk) Opal
Pearly white background with good play of colour.

Fire Opal
Semi-transparent reddish orange, sometimes with slight opalescence.

Jelly Opal
Transparent, with generally a green background, strong reds, greens, blues and orange showing throughout the stone.

Queensland Boulder Opal
Occurs as thin veins of opal in the usual brilliant colours in nodules of ironstone, sometimes of very large size, which are found in sandstone.

Prase Opal

Sometimes termed Moss Opal. It is transparent green in colour, sometimes with black and white inclusions. Although only infrequently appearing in dealers' lists, it is an unusual and attractive stone.

Dendritic Opal

Found in fairly large pieces of an opaque yellow colour with greeny brown dendritic markings.

For centuries, most opal came from Hungary or Czechoslovakia, but about 1875 boulder opal was discovered in Queensland and seam opal in New South Wales in 1890. Black opal was first mined in 1903 at Lightning Ridge, New South Wales, but the mines, virtually the only source of this lovely gem, are now completely worked out as are most of the other opal fields in that State.

The main Australian sources of opal are now located in South Australia. Andamooka (discovered in 1930) and Coober Pedy, which first produced in 1950, are the main mining areas, but Mexico and Honduras both produce a fair amount of first-class gem quality opal.

A large proportion of precious opal is found in thin seams, and due to its formation, the play of colour is often in very thin layers. Consequently, great care is needed to ensure that the colour is not ground away. As it is quite sensitive to heat, a plentiful supply of water must be maintained during sawing, grinding and polishing.

Opal, the most expensive stone which we use in school, is always cut with a specially thin blade, although sometimes the pieces are thin enough to rough out on the grinding wheel. If sawn, however, water is used instead of the usual cutting oil, because, containing as it does anything from 3 to 10 per cent water in its make-up, opal is slightly absorbent and the oil would cause discoloration.

Incidentally, our opal is always stored in glycerine or water, and finished stones should never be allowed to come into contact with oil, grease or greasy water, but it is beneficial to occasionally give them "a drink" of clean cold water.

If the precautions against overheating are observed, opal presents no problems in working and an excellent polish is obtained from cerium oxide on felt or leather, providing they are kept wet and the speed low.

Opal Doublets

Because of the fact that the best colour is found in very thin seams, opal is often made into "doublets" by grinding away the matrix (or potch as it is termed) and obtaining an absolutely flat surface by lapping.

A similar flat surface is then created, preferably on a black stone, such as obsidian, Wyoming jade or even black glass, and the two flats cemented together with an extremely thin coating of epoxy resin, care being taken to exclude any air bubbles. When the adhesive has set, the doublet is now ground as a cabochon, the black base being first ground down as thin as possible before the opal portion is domed. This is accepted commercial practice and many expensive black opals are doublets.

PETALITE   Hardness 6.   Sp. Gr. 2·39 to 2·46

This massive translucent material varies in colour according to location, but the variety obtained from South-west Africa is pale to deep pink. Fairly tough, it is not heat sensitive and polishes well with cerium oxide on leather.

RHODONITE   Hardness 6·5.   Sp. Gr. 3·6

This massive form of manganese silicate is very tough but cuts well and takes a good polish from cerium oxide on leather, providing very light pressure is used. Sanding should be carefully carried out with sharp new discs, finishing on well-worn fine grit discs, using plenty of water because of its tendency to undercut.

The main source of this lovely pink stone with its black dendritic markings of manganese is Australia, but some very nice specimens have been found in Cornwall.

SERPENTINE   Hardness 2·5 to 4·0.   Sp. Gr. 2·5 to 2·65

Always found in massive form, it is easily worked and is obtainable in a range of different colours from many parts of the world.

Our most common varieties are obtained from Cornwall (The Lizard) and Portsoy in Scotland; the latter is sometimes termed "precious serpentine" and is rich green or translucent yellow green in colour. Cornish serpentine is often mottled green, but varies from reddish brown to dark green and almost black.

To prevent undercutting, use plenty of water when sanding and polish with cerium oxide on damp leather.

SUNSTONE

Although the generally accepted main source of this oligoclase feldspar, with its golden flashes and pinky orange base colour, is Norway, pieces of Indian origin which we have used have been found to be superior. Although the pieces are smaller, they appear to be more homogeneous without very strong cleavage planes, and consequently have been easier for the children to work by normal "feldspar techniques".

TIGER EYE

The most popular member of the quartz family as far as my children are concerned, this is a most interesting stone to work. It is a crystallised quartz, derived from crocidolite, an asbestos mineral which has oxidised to a golden brown colour and has then been replaced by silica, so that when polished it exhibits pronounced chatoyancy, appearing to change colour in bands of pale gold to dark brown, which ripple across the surface of the stone.

Although golden tiger eye is best known, combinations of blue green and gold may be obtained, and as stated earlier, if subjected to heat treatment, golden tiger eye becomes a deep brick red.

Almost the only known source of this fascinating stone is South Africa, and it is unfortunate that in May 1968, the South African Ministry of Mines announced that exports of rough tiger eye would be restricted and would in fact cease on 1st June 1971. Naturally, this has resulted in a sharp rise in the price of this raw material and the upward trend will undoubtedly continue as dealers' stocks are reduced.

To work tiger eye, first ascertain the plane of chatoyance by wetting, as described for orienting labradorite, and saw the slice parallel to the plane in order to obtain the best effect. Grinding is more rapid than with the majority of other types of quartz and can often be completely carried out on a 220 grit wheel, but if coarser wheels are used, they should be very true.

The quality of tiger eye varies, and although we normally experience no difficulty when sanding and polishing, occasionally a piece will reveal a tendency to undercut. A sharp disc, increased speed and copious water should then be used and providing the stone has been well sanded, an excellent polish is obtained from cerium oxide on hard felt. Should undercutting persist, it may sometimes be overcome by sanding across the grain rather than by rotating the stone.

TOPAZ   Hardness 8.   Sp. Gr. 3·5 to 3·6

Most topaz comes from Brazil, and although the most generally accepted colour is yellow to yellow brown, it can be colourless or in varying shades of blue. Usually found in crystalline form, it is also found as pebbles and is usually faceted. Unaffected by moderate heat, it is tough but easily worked, final polish obtained with cerium oxide on leather or, for a special occasion, Linde A on leather.

TOURMALINE   Hardness 7 to 7·5.   Sp. Gr. 3·1

This must be the gem with the widest variety of colours, from colourless to black, white, red, yellow, blue, green, brown, pink, violet and even parti-coloured, some crystals being a different colour

M

at each end, whilst others may have a centre core of any of these colours with a different colour outside. The black variety is quite common in Devon, but varying colours are found in Scotland.

Common in almost all granite localities, it can easily be recognised by the striations along the length of the crystals. It is susceptible to heat so that careful dopping is necessary; preferably shellac should be used.

As it is fairly brittle, grinding wheels must be true, otherwise it may chip. Best polish obtained from Linde A, but tin oxide on leather usually produces acceptable results.

WOLLESTONITE   Hardness 4·5 to 5·0.   Sp. Gr. 2·85

This white or pale yellow stone is not often used but is included because it may be found on expeditions to the West Country, although the main commercial sources are Finland and Mexico. Having a hardness of 5 or less, it is similar to apatite in its working qualities.

In compiling this list of stones, I have listed them by their more usual names as I feel that the beginner would be more inclined to think of, say, moonstone, as such rather than "Feldspar-Orthoclase, var. Moonstone". The quartz varieties are even more numerous and I have only dealt with the more popular varieties or those which may pose cutting and polishing problems, as most of them are easy to work.

Regarding this family of gemstones, I am convinced that it cannot be surpassed for its wide variety of colour, and yet it is so reasonable in price. The agates and jaspers offer the widest range, with their diversity of markings and designs, ranging from plain and banded varieties to the wonderful scenic and dendritic types. I am indebted to Ken Parkinson for the following list of names by which some of the quartz varieties are commonly known.

Rock Crystal
Rutilated Quartz
Tourmalinated Quartz
Sagenitic Quartz
Thetis Hair Stone
Fleches D'Amour
Love Stone
Cupid's Darts
Venus Hair Stone
Ghost Quartz
Iris Quartz
Skeletal Quartz
Dendritic Quartz
Stalagtitic Quartz
Smoky Quartz
Milky Quartz
Ferruginous Quartz
Ferrous Quartz
Morion
Citrine
Cairngorm
Prase
Agate
Seaweed Agate
Landscape Agate
Scenic Agate
Ribbon Agate
Ribband Agate
Banded Agate
Fortification Agate
Ruin Agate
Dot Agate
Polka Dot Agate
Fire Agate
Fern Agate
Tree Agate
Mocha Stone
Moss Agate

Quartz Topaz
Scottish Topaz
Madeira Topaz
Madeira Stone
Spanish Topaz
Topaz Quartz
Madagascar Citrine
Spanish Citrine
Rose Quartz
Star Quartz
Quartz Cat's Eye
Schiller Quartz
Occidental Cat's Eye
Hungarian Cat's Eye
Crocidolite
Falcon Eye
Hawk Eye
Tiger Eye
Tigerite
Jasper
Scenic Jasper
Jasp Agate
Rainbow Agate
Eyed Agate
Owl Eyed Agate
Ox Eyed Agate
Iris Agate
Cloudy Agate
White Moss Agate
Wood Agate
Scotch Pebble
Plume Agate
Chalcedony
Chalcedony Moonstone
Mohave Moonstone
White Cornelian
Cornelian

Zebra Jasper
Orbicular Jasper
Blood Jasper
Ribbon Jasper
Riband Jasper
Swiss Lapis
German Lapis
Petrified Wood
Woodstone
Agatised Wood
Bloodstone
Heliotrope
St Stephen's Stone
Aventurine
Potato Stone
Drusy Quartz
Gold Quartz
Flint
Chert
Hornstone
Black Chalcedony
Sard
Sardstone
Black Onyx
Onyx
Sardonyx
Siderite
Chrysoprase
Nicolo
Amethyst
Bishop's Stone
Lavendine
Cacoxenite
Amethyst Quartz
Occidental Amethyst

Rock hunting

Whilst discovering lapidary work we will be led by our own particular inclinations to various methods of using rocks and minerals. The Americanism "Rockhound" is most applicable, as it refers to all who are interested in anything connected with the many offshoots of the craft. Personally, I do not like the term; even less do I like the term "Pebble Pups" which, in some American magazines, is applied to beginners, but in the absence of a more appropriate generic noun I am forced to use it.

Rockhounds, then, usually fall into two basic types, one of which is solely devoted to either buying or collecting samples for the joy of appreciating their natural beauty, using their lapidary skills to cut away unwanted portions, or maybe polish one particular face of a specimen. The other type places most emphasis on working with the basic materials, to cut and polish them, producing finished gems, not always to be mounted into jewelry, as many workers regard the finished stone as an end in itself.

When first I became interested in the craft, I was envious of all American workers, because when reading their magazines, I visualised that they all had easy access to vast supplies of raw materials, just awaiting collection, whereas we in the British Isles had very little. I was wrong on both counts. Some American workers would need to travel more than a thousand miles to collect specific items, whereas I have found jasper and varieties of feldspar in my own garden, once I had acquired the ability to recognise them. These are not indigenous rocks but the result of glaciation, and the educational implications were borne home to me quite recently, as the following story will show.

Twin boys in one of my second-year classes are keen on collecting pebbles, whilst walking their dog along an un-made road within the city of Worcester's boundary. Specimens which show hardness or colour are frequently brought to the craft room for cutting and polishing to add to their collection.

Whilst on holiday in the north of Scotland, I had collected a quantity of various rocks suitable for beginners to practise on, including several large pieces of Feldspar with inclusions of Hornblende. When cut and polished, attractive cabochons, deep orange red, specked with black, were made by several of the children in the twins' form. They were amazed when they discovered that one of their pebbles, which they had picked up in Worcester, was identical with the large piece of rock which I had collected in Wester Ross. They themselves had obtained concrete proof of something which, for them, had only been regarded as "something out of the geography books".

I find that my own early misapprehensions are prevalent among many beginners. They are surprised to learn of the possibilities which will enable them to start cutting and polishing at little or no cost for basic materials.

With the ever-increasing construction of new roads, motorways and housing estates, countless acres of our countryside are being excavated, with the result that rocks and pebbles which have been underground for thousands of years are exposed to view. Ballast for filling in is frequently transported from different parts of the country and may contain unusual samples of minerals. Only recently, a friend showed me a superb piece of botryoidal hematite, larger than a man's clenched fist, which had been picked from a load of road ballast. He has it polished as a cabinet specimen, whereas I can visualise a whole series of lovely cabochons which could be cut from it.

An article in the *Radio Times* last year stated that the well-known T.V. artist, Mr Rolf Harris, was a keen collector of agates, and that he had found one of his choicest specimens near Hyde Park Corner, dug out of one of those "holes in the road" which abound in all our cities.

A teacher in Shropshire, during one of my talks, produced a superb piece of amethyst quartz, picked up in a lay-by near Inverness; a fellow member in the Kingston Lapidary Society, only a few weeks before I wrote this, found a piece of amber containing parts of an insect, on a Yorkshire beach. More personal, there was the lovely white quartz pebble, lined with tiny amethyst crystals, picked up by my wife from my feet on a Scottish beach, whilst I was exulting over what proved to be a rather inferior piece of pink banded agate which I had just picked up.

Wherever Rockhounds meet, similar stories will be told, treasures exhibited, and frequently, woebegone expressions will accompany the tale of "the one I just missed". However, the collector is eternally optimistic, so let us take a quick look around Great Britain and see what may be found.

Our beaches abound with a wide variety of sea-washed pebbles, agate, amber, amethyst, citrine, carnelian, chalcedony, jet and fossils, and the beachcombing enthusiast should first read Clarence Ellis's *Pebbles on the Beach* in which he deals with all aspects of pebbles and their collection.

Quarries, a complete list of which can be found in *Sources of Road Aggregate in Great Britain*, are wonderful sources of supply for specimens of all types of rocks and minerals. Permission should be sought from the company's offices before a visit is made. Very rarely is this refused, providing the applicant is willing to sign a form indemnifying the company against any claim for injury which may be sustained during the visit. A guide is usually provided and he will invariably assist by pointing out exact locations from which the best specimens may be safely collected.

The spoil heaps of disused mines can prove to be treasure houses for the collector, and enquiries in the neighbourhood usually reveal a local inhabitant who will be only too pleased to give information. Remember, these sites are usually off the beaten track, often in areas of great scenic beauty, far removed from large towns, and many collectors spend their holidays in pursuit of specimens.

Most collectors have a favourite area, and as my personal preference is North of the Border, let us start at the top and work down.

SCOTLAND

Without delving too deeply into a geological survey of what has frequently been termed "The Geologist's Paradise", we know that although Scotland is geologically composed of four main faulted blocks, three of them make up the area north of a line drawn from approximately Stonehaven on the east coast, extending in a south-westerly direction to Helensburgh, on the Firth of Clyde. This area, with the exception of a strip extending south from Thurso to the Moray Firth, is mostly composed of the most ancient of rocks, the Pre-Cambrian, which include metamorphosed and unmetamorphosed rocks.

These rocks are composed of tiny particles of minerals, one of the most common being feldspar, which occurs in several different guises, as will be seen in the chapter on cutting and polishing specific materials. Feldspar, together with quartz and mica, form granite, varieties of which abound in this area, and although it cannot really be classed as a gemstone, it is an excellent material for youngsters' first attempts. In addition to the feldspar contained in the granites, massive feldspar, in combination with other minerals, provides a source of cabochons in varying shades of pink, green and mottled reds, black and white.

The green "Assynt Marble" found in west Sutherland, although not so colourful as the well-known Iona marble, is easily cut and polished. Incidentally, although Iona is well worth a visit, do not expect to return loaded with this lovely green stone. On my last visit, a Brother who guided us round the monastery assured me that the quarry had not been worked for twenty years. However, pebbles can be found on the western beaches if one has the time and energy to search for them, as the best pebbles are found on the west coast of the island.

The more generally accepted gemstones, garnet, tourmaline, topaz, cairngorm, amethyst, sapphire, beryl, etc., have usually been formed by crystallisation in the rocks in which they are found. Frequently, this process of crystallisation occurs in druses or geodes and the gems line the inner wall of the cavity, so that one never knows what will be found until the druse is cut or broken open.

Due to the natural processes of weathering over countless centuries, druses become dislodged from the parent rock, broken and crumbled by a natural tumbling process in the swift-running rivers and streams, releasing their contents into the river and subsequently the beach gravels. Consequently, the burns and lochs of the Highlands are happy hunting grounds for the collector, and in Sutherland, zircon, cairn-gorm, tourmaline, topaz and serpentine have been found south of Tongue near Ben Loyal and Ben Hope.

In Rossshire, zircon, precious garnet and serpentine are found in several localities, whilst tourmaline and amethyst have been found near Loch Luichart and Loch Fannich.

Over to the east, the counties of Aberdeenshire and Banffshire are areas of great interest to the collector, as a wide range of gems have been found, including varieties of beryl, cairngorm, topaz, tourmaline, varieties of garnet, amethyst and serpentines, including the well-known Portsoy marble.

Invernessshire is also a good collecting area where the famous Scottish mineralogist, Professor M. Foster Heddle, collected many of his specimens, including a yellow-green beryl, 3 in. long, zircon, tourmaline and precious garnet near Struy Bridge, delicate pink amethyst by Loch Morar and precious serpentine in Glen Falloch.

Continuing our tour southwards into Argyllshire, let us first go to Oban and cross to Mull, which I always think of as the Pink Isle, because of its beautifully coloured rocky outcrops and beaches. Although it is sparsely populated (there are more deer than people on the island) one will not have to wait long before seeing a kindred spirit tapping the rocks with a hammer, searching for sapphire, blue kyanite, tourmaline and chalcedony.

Back on the mainland, Argyllshire and its neighbouring county, Perthshire, are to me the end of the Highlands but still full of interest. We are approaching the agate country, and carnelian, cairngorm, agates, bloodstone and heliotrope, all varieties of chalcedony, are found, mostly at the southern tip of the peninsula of Kintyre. Amethyst is also found in this area, tourmaline in Glen Finart, zircon and garnet near the village of Strontian in the north of the county on the A861 at the head of Loch Sunart. It was this village which gave its name to the element strontium when it was discovered in 1792.

One would obviously expect to find agate at Agate Knowe, the local name given to one of the Sidlaw Hills near to the Perthshire village of Abernyte, but a neighbouring hill with the delightful name of Tinkletop is not so obvious.

Abernyte is best approached by leaving the A94, Coupar Angus to Perth road, at Balbeggie and taking the B953, passing en route the

Iron Age hill fort of Dunsinane, "Macbeth's Castle", from which Shakespeare's Birnam Wood may be seen.

This area, Strathmore, was the centre of the ancient kingdom of the Picts and is notable for many interesting relics of the Dark Ages, which have been left by early workers in stone. Most notable is "King Malcolm's Gravestone", 9 feet high and beautifully carved with the Cross, a salmon, warriors and horsemen, which stands in the grounds of the Manse at Glamis, whilst the museum at Meigle is full of similar relics.

Other agate localities in the county are Pittrodie, east of Perth, just off the A85; Inchture and Ballindean (where milk opal may be found), about 5 miles farther along the same road, in the Ochil Hills, north-east of Dunblane, Rossi Ochil and Path of Condie which can be approached along a quiet road running south off the B935 near Forteviot.

In Glen Falloch and also near Dunkeld, tourmaline has been found, and in the north of the county, east of Ben Chuallaich (B847), fine specimens of blue kyanite have been collected.

The east coast, south from Montrose to the Firth of Tay, is also excellent agate country. Geodes up to 12 in. in diameter can be seen in the rock at Mains of Usan. Fishtown of Usan, Boddin Point, Ferryden and the district south of Scurdie Ness all provide good sites for the agate hunter, as also does the south bank of the River Tay from Wormit to Newburgh, where, in addition to agate, amethyst collecting is possible.

South of the Tay, the A914 passes through country which is interesting to the gem hunter, as the district around Luthrie is a source of amethyst, cairngorm, blue, moss and banded agates. Between Luthrie and Fernie, many of the fields have heaps of stones piled against the walls, and these heaps repay inspection, as many geodes have been found in them – a speedy method of acquiring specimens, most of the work having been done by the farmer's plough.

The north coast of the Firth of Forth, around Elie, is also worth a visit before leaving the area, as zircon and pyrope garnet have been found; local people call this latter stone the Elie ruby.

To the geologist, the area to the south of the Highland Boundary Fault, down to a line drawn from Dunbar in the east, to Girvan on the west coast, is known as the Central Rift Valley. It contains the industrial heart of Scotland, dominated by the great conurbation of Glasgow.

Although one cannot set out with the intention of prospecting in the streets of a town, I am certain that "holes in the road", the excavations of building sites and road works would repay inspection, as cairngorm, amethyst and many varieties of agate are recorded from widely scattered places throughout the area.

Fossils also abound, and the Fossil Grove, in Victoria Park, Glasgow, is worth a visit, if only to see the tree stumps and roots which have been exposed by removing the sedimentary rocks in which they lay buried for millions of years.

Over on the west coast, the beach at Dunure is one of my favourite haunts because of its great variety of pebbles, among which one is almost certain to find agates, whilst the shipping in the Firth of Clyde furnishes a constant excuse to straighten an aching back.

The Southern Uplands, an area of ancient sedimentary rocks, although lacking the scenic grandeur of the Highlands, possess a beauty of their own and provide many gem and mineral locations, one of the most interesting being Wanlockhead and Leadhills. To reach this area, take the B797, which joins the A76 some 3 miles south of Sanquhar, and travel for some 8 miles to Wanlockhead. Gold was mined here from 1125 until comparatively recent years, and documents in the British Museum contain records of large quantities of gold washed from the burns in the district and mined at Crawford, a few miles to the north-west. In the hall of the Hopetown Arms Hotel, Leadhills, is a photograph of the ring, made from local gold and presented to Princess Victoria Mary of Teck on her marriage in 1893 to the Duke of York, later King George V. Whilst on the subject of gold, which has also been found in gravel washings from the River Tweed, about 12 miles from its source, readers are reminded that gold mining rights are vested in the Crown, so that in addition to permission from the land-owner and the river authority, a Crown Estate Permit (£10 plus £1·28 Office Charges and Stamp Duty) is legally required.

Perhaps we had best quietly look for the mineral specimens of galena, pyrites, rock crystal and malachite, to mention but a few of the minerals, many of them extremely rare, which can be found around the district, before going over the Border into the Lake District.

THE LAKE DISTRICT

Millions of years ago, a dome of ancient sedimentary and metamorphic rocks, penetrated by flows of lava and masses of granite and covered with carboniferous limestone, developed a radiating pattern of streams, which cut through the limestone. Subsequent glacial erosion created the lakes which give the district its name.

Considering its small area, the Lake District abounds in minerals, many of which are suitable for inclusion in jewelry. Travelling south, the first stop is Roughtongill, in the Caldbeck Fells, some $3\frac{1}{2}$ miles south-west of Caldbeck village.

The B5299 from Carlisle is pleasant to drive along and after passing through the village, an unclassified road leads to Bassenthwaite. Study of the Ordnance Survey Maps will show the sites of many old lead mines. Copper was also mined in this area as long ago as the sixteenth century, and the old dumps contain specimens of calcite, barite, malachite and other minerals, whilst tourmaline, pale green apatite and schulite, which fluoresces so beautifully, are also reported as having been found.

Two miles south of Keswick and overlooking Derwentwater stands Wallow Crag, and in the lava which forms its summit epidote, agate, jasper and carnelian may possibly be found. Falcon Crag, a mile to the south, is a reputable source of epidote in many shades of green and brown, also calcite, quartz and garnet. Hematite is fairly common over to the south and west in Eskdale and Langdale and in the mining areas around the coast.

A more popular route south from Scotland is, of course, along the A6, passing through the village of Shap, where the quarrymen are mainly concerned with the excavation of the famous Shap granite. If a request is made, permission is usually granted to have a look around the quarry and collect a few specimens of some of the lovely varieties of feldspar-bearing rocks, pyrites or fool's gold and possibly vugs lined with crystals in varying colours from lilac to pale green.

THE NORTH-EAST AND THE EAST COAST

To my mind, a more pleasant route south is to cross Carter Bar and down to Hexham, then taking the B6305 which leads towards Weardale. Near the quiet village of St John's Chapel are more lead mines which were worked in bygone years and are now disused. As was usual, the old miners concentrated on the excavation of the lead ores and the spoil heaps contain lovely specimens of fluorite in a great variety of colours, quartz in many forms, chalcedony and hematite, to mention only a few.

This route could lead towards Wharfedale and Ingleton, a district containing innumerable caves, or south-east to the caves of the North York Moors, most of which can be approached by roads leading off the A170 between Thirsk and Pickering. Caves are nearly always worth prospecting, providing one takes adequate safety precautions, but if cave exploring seems undesirable, the east coast is only a few miles away.

Beachcombers on the east coast from Whitby, source of the finest jet in the world, down to the beaches of Essex and Kent are likely to find pebbles of varieties of quartz, agate, colourful and possibly fossil-bearing flints, carnelian, chalcedony, jet, jasper and, if fortunate, amber.

THE MIDLANDS

The northern edge of the Midlands, between the High Peak and
Ashbourne, is another area of caves, quarries and disused mines,
abounding in a variety of minerals, many of them suitable for
cabochons, one of the loveliest being the variety of fluorspar known as
Blue John, still mined commercially at Castleton, Derbyshire. I can
remember, as a boy, large pieces of Blue John used as doorstops by the
residents of this Peakland village, but now it is becoming quite rare,
although samples can still be found in the caves on the slopes of the
Winnats Pass, which leads off the A625 to the B6061. The disused lead
mines at Dirtlow Rake and Bradwell Moor should yield samples of
fluorite, lead zinc ores, calcite and barite, but the best specimens of
this latter mineral which I have seen came from Arbor Low, the site
of a prehistoric stone circle, approximately two miles south from the
village of Monyash. Known locally as Oak Stone, it has the appearance
of very old, dark brown wood, and although rather soft, cuts and
polishes well with a high gloss. Even if one is unsuccessful in finding
this particular variety, many other types of barite and minerals can be
picked up from the dumps of several disused mines within a two-mile
radius of the village.

Alderley Edge, Cheshire, can hardly be classed as being in the
Midlands, but is close enough to be dealt with at this stage, and is the
highest place in the Cheshire Plain. From the A34 in the centre of the
town, a minor road leads towards Macclesfield and climbs towards the
Wizard Inn and the Wizard's Well, the wizard presumably being
Merlin, as the hill behind is one of the many reputed resting places of
King Arthur and his knights. We may not be particularly interested in
the folk-lore of the area, but the nearby copper mines, blocked up
since I explored them some 40 years ago, once produced considerable
quantities of copper. Green and blue azurite and malachite, together
with galena or cerussite, may still be found.

The county of Nottinghamshire is popular with collectors of mineral
specimens rather than lapidarists, because of the variety of calcareous
rocks which are worked at several places. Satinspar, glittering silver
white, is quarried around Newark, mainly for the manufacture of
plaster of Paris, whilst alabaster is fairly common in several parts of the
county. Both are very soft and brittle but polish quite well and can be
used with advantage as bases for small metal sculptures, trophies and
other forms of decorative metalwork.

Over to the west, in the Welsh border county of Shropshire, are
several disused mines, the spoil heaps of which have furnished me with
many excellent fluorescent specimens, the calcites revealing shades
from pale to very deep pinks under the lamp. Most of these mines are
concentrated in an area about 10 to 12 miles south-west of Shrewsbury,
perhaps the best known being the Snailbeach Mine which was worked
for lead in Roman times and finally closed in 1913. It is recorded that

over 230,000 tons of lead ore were produced by these mines between 1845 and 1913 in addition to quantities of barites, zinc and copper ores.

Witherite, a white, translucent mineral, often faceted, quartz, pyrites and fluorspar have also been found in the vicinity, which is best approached by the A488 from Shrewsbury to Minsterley. The mines at Snailbeach, Shelve, Habberley, Westcott and several others all lie along unclassified roads leading east off the main road.

Crossing the border into Wales, we can again find scores of disused mines where lead, zinc and copper ores have been worked, but I regret that I have not been able to explore these personally. Recently, a colleague gave me some very fine dark green magnetite, which he had collected from Anglesey and when polished it had the appearance of Wyoming Jade, but unfortunately he could not give me the exact location. The area around Dolgellau and Trawsfynydd is, of course, well known for its gold-bearing potentialities and one can still speak to old men who worked in the gold mines which, it is reported, are soon to be re-opened.

THE WEST COUNTRY

My good friend, Bob Jones of Ross-on-Wye, a Fellow of the Gemmological Association and a keen amateur collector, often says, "Give me the West Country and you can keep the rest." When I inspect his superb collection, I can see his point of view, as the variety of rocks and minerals which abound in the counties of Gloucester, Somerset, Devon and Cornwall, are, in my opinion, second only to those found in Scotland, but I admit that I am prejudiced.

Travelling from the North and the Midlands, the most direct route is along the A38, and when some 3 miles south of Tewkesbury, take the B4213, signposted Ledbury, for about $1\frac{1}{2}$ miles to the tiny village of Apperley when a narrow rough road leads to the banks of the River Severn. Along this stretch, fossils have been picked up and I have collected some very nice inter-penetrated cubes of pyrite or fool's gold.

Returning back to the A38 again, south of Gloucester the road leads past the Severn Wild Fowl Trust at Slimbridge, a few miles south-west of which is the magnificent Berkeley Castle, both suitable places for a break from rock-hunting before tackling the next three sites. The first of these is Aust Rock, just north of the new bridge which carries the M4 across the Severn. Good specimens of gypsum can quite easily be found.

The next two sites are quarries which are still worked, one near Tytherington, the other near Wickwar, and as these are rather off the beaten track the map references are 658888 and 715898, respectively,

on the I-inch Ordnance Survey Sheet No. 156. Lovely specimens of
calcite varieties and pyrite may be found before heading almost due
south to map reference 706859, where permission should be sought
from the quarry owners to prospect for blue, white and pink celestite
crystals. At the nearby village of Goose Green, map reference 710837,
a crushing mill specialises in producing supplies for pyrotechnics, pink
petalite, serpentine and Italian marbles, in addition to other imported
minerals, being used.

To do full justice to the neighbouring county of Somerset would
demand a chapter in itself, as from Bristol the A38 leads over the
Mendip Hills where, in addition to the commercialised caves, many
other caves of greater interest to the prospector abound. The
Quantock Hills are also a good prospecting area and if one tires of the
hills, the pebble-strewn beaches around Porlock Bay and Clevedon
contain interesting specimens, including agates which have broken out
of the old red sandstone.

Obtained from the area around Bristol, Landscape Marble, with its
lovely dark grey tree patterns and paler grey background, is an
excellent rock for use in schools. A form of calcite, it is quite soft,
easily cut and shaped but takes quite a good polish and can be used
to make ash trays, bases for trophies, ink stands and similar articles.

In other parts of the county are found Potato Stones, nodules usually
about 2 or 3 inches in diameter. Although their rough reddish exterior
is very unprepossessing, when sawn across they present quite a
different appearance. Some are solid quartz in varying shades of pink
and white, whilst others are hollow, lined with crystals of quartz or
calcite.

It will be appreciated that it is not possible to give locations where all
the minerals of Somerset may be found, but enthusiastic rockhounds
are likely to find some of the following:

White crystalline aragonite, many varieties of grey, white or pink
barite; white, brown and grey calcite, lustrous crystalline cerussite,
galena, black to brown goethite, rock crystal, brown to white siderite
and purple massive bornite or "Peacock ore". Whilst some of these
are of purely geological interest, others can be included in jewelry
although most of them lack the hardness of true gemstones.

DEVON AND CORNWALL

If Somerset would merit a whole chapter, then surely the counties of
Devon and Cornwall would take a whole book to do full justice to
their great variety of rocks and minerals, as may be judged from the
following list which names but a few of them. Agate in many varieties,
amethyst, apatite, axinite, azurite, barite (varieties), cairngorm,

calcite (varieties), carnelian, cassiterite, chalcedony (varieties), chrysocolla, citrine, feldspar (varieties), fluorite, garnet, jasper, malachite, opal, prase, rhodonite, rock crystal, serpentine (varieties), topaz and tourmaline.

One point I am forced to concede when supporting Scotland against the West Country is the fact that, in Devon and Cornwall, the collecting area is much more concentrated. A few diversions off the last hundred miles of the A30 from east of Exeter to Land's End, will cover most of the best sites, so let us pick up the A30 some 4 miles east of Okehampton, near the village of South Zeal to look for varieties of garnet, axinite and actinolite.

About 3 miles past Okehampton a side road leads to Meldon, where two quarries provide a wealth of a wide variety of specimens, before taking the A386 to cross the edge of Dartmoor which, being virtually solid granite, is a great collecting area, particularly around gravel pits and in the beds of streams. One mineral which is a "must" for anyone interested in fluorescence is autunite, a hydrous calcium uranium phosphate, usually found as thin light yellow, or greenish yellow, plates on the surface of the granitic rocks which abound. This will always fluoresce with a vivid yellow green colour and is the only important uranium bearing mineral which does so.

A good locality where autunite may be picked up is in the area of Merivale, 5 miles east of Tavistock. A word of warning, however, regarding "The Moor". If you prospect this area, please do be careful not to get involved in army exercises as did a party of members of my lapidary society, when searching for tourmalines, as this could be embarrassing as well as dangerous.

South-west of Tavistock on the A390, the area between Gunnislake and Callington contains a number of old mines where the dumps may be picked over for specimens of malachite, chrysocolla, azurite and other copper minerals, in addition to various colours of fluorite, barite, chalcedony and galena. These, and several other minerals are quite likely to be found around a lead mine near Menheniot, a small village which can be approached by a minor road which leads south off the main road, 4 miles beyond Callington.

From the village, another minor road leads to the A38 for Liskeard and Bodmin. Between Bodmin and St Austell is yet another area abounding in sites where, plus many of the minerals mentioned, turquoise, white beryl, garnet and apatite have also been reported.

Before tackling the chief mining area of Cornwall, the beginner would be well advised to make the next port of call Truro, where the County Museum has exhibits of what one hopes to collect. Whilst on the subject of museums in this area, the Geological Museums at Penzance and the world-renowned School of Mines at Camborne are well worth visiting.

Between Redruth and Land's End, there must be as many mines and quarries as there are saints in the Cornish calendar. Many are disused, but even as I write these words, my morning paper carries a photograph of construction work being carried out at Wheal Jane tin mine, and the accompanying article states that this mine alone will supply some 7 per cent of our tin in 1971.

The range of specimens found is nearly as wide as the number of mines, and as a natural consequence, the pebbles on the beaches display a similar variety, the beach at Marazion being one of the most prolific in its range of varied pebbles.

One should not leave Cornwall without visiting the Lizard peninsula, which as most visitors to Cornwall realise, is famous for its serpentine. A quick scrutiny of the local gift shops will give an indication of the varieties which abound in the area.

We have travelled the length of Great Britain and whilst I appreciate that many areas have been missed, I have only dealt with those which have been visited either by me personally or by my friends. My main intention in including this chapter is to dispel the idea that we have very little in this country to interest the lapidarist. In conclusion, I would like to make the following suggestions.

1. Always be careful to observe the laws of trespass, as all sites are owned by someone: the State, local authorities, companies or individuals; and technically, the removal of samples is larceny. Consequently, and especially if taking a school party, permission should be obtained before prospecting begins. A courteous request is rarely refused.

2. Although rock hunting is no more dangerous than any other out-door activity, care must be taken when exploring caves, quarries, old mines, rock faces and cliff paths, and normal safety precautions should be observed.

3. Equipment needed is fairly simple. For the lone prospector a geological hammer, a builder's bolster chisel plus a small cold chisel for tiny specimens, a rucksack and a magnifying glass are essentials. Remember that rock splinters sometimes fly, and goggles, sun glasses or government surplus plastic anti-gas goggles will afford some measure of protection.

4. On expeditions, take careful notes of exact locations from where specimens are obtained. My own system is to number and keep them in individual boxes or plastic bags, together with the map reference of the site.

5. Increase your knowledge by visiting museums, joining, or even forming a club and taking part in organised field trips. The Central

Council for Physical Recreation usually organises a gem hunting course, based on Aviemore, in July each year. The British Young Naturalists Association, Newton House Field Centre, Littlebeck, near Whitby, Yorks, arranges courses in Geology, Fossil Collecting and similar subjects for parties of school children.

6. Observe the Country Code regarding gates, fences and litter. Never try to extract specimens from walls and don't take more than you need.

7. Finally, don't expect to make your fortune; most of our gem materials cannot compare with those found in recognised sources. Our sapphires and emeralds are very small, our malachite cannot be compared with that from the Congo, and so on, but whether for jewelry-making or geological purposes, it is well worth having a go. Good hunting.

Historical aspects of the craft

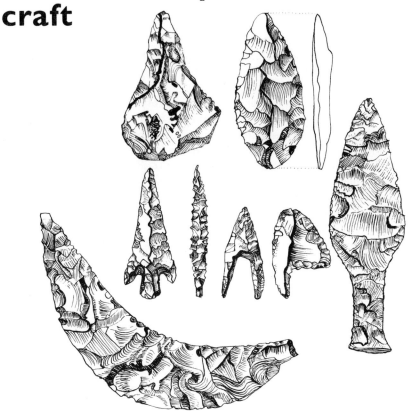

Fig. 52
Some primitive stone instruments

One definition of the word lapidary (from the Latin *Lapidorius*) is "One engaged in the cutting and polishing of stone" and the original lapidarist was surely the first of our primitive ancestors to discover that his piece of rock, if broken with a sharp edge, was more efficient as a tool or weapon than a "blunt instrument".

It was this early mastery of the cruder techniques of working with stone which raised man above the level of the animal, for he soon discovered that his stone club or axe gave him an advantage when faced with an enemy or wild animal, whilst his sling, and later his stone-tipped arrows, enabled him for the first time to be able to kill from a distance. His stone axe enabled him to cut and trim small trees and saplings to provide materials for his bows, arrows and spears, his first crude habitation other than a tree or cave, and last but not least, his fire. Although it can never be proved how man first discovered fire, it can be safely assumed that he soon learned, whilst shaping a weapon, that sparks were given off when certain rocks were struck sharply together, and that these sparks could be made to ignite kindling.

N

To keep his fire within bounds, he would most probably have surrounded it with stones, and the Stone Age ended with the birth of the Bronze Age, when man discovered that the substance which had flowed out of the rocks surrounding his fireplace had cooled into a residue which was no longer stone but was, in fact, a new material, softer and more malleable, which he could hammer into shape, using his stone hammer and his stone anvil.

The next step up the ladder of man's progress was when he discovered differing characteristics in the residues of certain rocks, and that iron tools were more efficient than those made of bronze, and so he became more discriminating in his choice of stone. No longer was it necessary for him to discover flints, now his efforts were devoted to the finding of suitable ores for specific purposes, the progenitor of the modern prospector with his Geiger counter, searching for uranium. Thus it can be claimed that stone is the basis of human civilisation.

We must not presume to think that primitive man was devoid of a sense of aesthetic appreciation and that all his lapidary work was solely functional; indeed, the highly developed pictorial art exemplified in the drawings and wall paintings, executed by Paleolithic man and still to be seen in the caves in France and Spain, prove that as long ago as 35,000 B.C. man was susceptible to both form and colour.

Our earliest ancestors have left traces of their inhabitation in many parts of the world, and as ancient burial grounds are excavated, carvings and pieces of primitive jewelry are unearthed. It can safely be assumed that colourful pieces of rock or pebbles would be treasured and used as some form of personal adornment, in the same manner as the twentieth-century Stone Age men, the savage tribesmen of Papua and New Guinea, when they decorate themselves with the plumage of exotic birds.

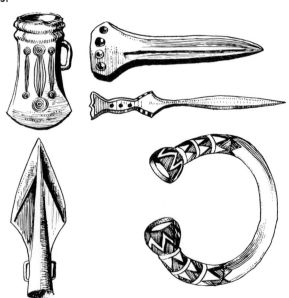

Fig. 53
Primitive metal
tools and ornaments
decorated with
gemstones.

With the growth of the early civilisation the work of the lapidary
became of increasing importance and man became more selective in
his choice of material, prizing some above others because of certain
characteristics, either of colour, durability or scarcity. It is recorded
that in ancient China jade was worshipped, perhaps because of its
appearance and toughness. Whatever the reason, jade carvings
automatically incline one's thoughts to the Far East, despite the fact
that there are many deposits of fine types of jade in America.

Although the New World cannot compare with the Old World in its
relics of ancient civilisations, carvings in jade and basalt, together with
mosaics of serpentine, have been excavated from sites in Mexico. One
such mosaic is estimated to have involved the use of some 5,000 tons
of this green stone, which must have been transported about 350
miles by water, and dates from about 800 B.C.

Comparatively few examples of jewelry or work in precious stones
have been unearthed in America, but such examples as remain, for
example the Aztec sacrificial knife depicted bears witness to the early
stone workers' art and skill. Who knows, perhaps such examples as
remained at the time were part of the booty acquired by Cortez and
his successors?

Fig. 54
Aztec knife

The love of working in stone, born of man's necessity, was stimulated
by his inherent desire to utilise his creative powers by working with
the materials to hand, and progressed concurrently, but quite
independently, in every civilisation. The durability of gemstones has
made it possible for examples of work, executed thousands of years
ago in all parts of the world, to be displayed in museums today.

THE BIBLE AND LAPIDARY WORK

From beginning to end, the Bible contains many references to gemstones, the first being in the second chapter of Genesis and the last in
the penultimate chapter of the Book of Revelations. The study of these
Biblical references is fascinating, but extremely complex, and some of
the world's greatest experts are in complete disagreement on many
points, particularly in the nomenclature of various stones.

The first reference, Genesis 2, verse 12, referring to the Garden of
Eden is "And the gold of that land is good, there is bdellium and the
onyx stone." Now the Oxford Dictionary states that bdellium is "A
balsam-bearing tree or its resin; Latin from the Greek translation of
the Hebrew *b'dolakh* of uncertain meaning (carbuncle or crystal or
pearl)." We know that amber is not stone but fossilised resin, so it
could be argued that this is what the early writer intended, especially
as amber is used in Ezekiel on three occasions as a synonym for the
brightness of a fire.

Many authorities regard amber as the material referred to by the

Hebrew word *leshem*, which is translated into ligurion, a corruption of the Greek *lyncurion* (*linkos*-lynx, *oron*-urine) from the belief that amber was the petrified urine of the lynx.

Theophrastus, who lived about 350 B.C. and who wrote a history of stones, says that "Lyncurion will attract leaves, straw and thin plates of copper and iron when rubbed, also it is dug out of the ground in Liguria." This is, of course, a well-known property of amber. Liguria is now a district in France, near Marseilles, where amber is still occasionally found and although the Ancient Greeks referred to amber as *electron*, the Septuagint translates *leshem* as ligure. The late Sir W. M. Flinders Petrie states that *leshem* could most likely be yellow quartz, whilst Young's Concordance to the Bible gives *leshem-ligure* as the opal or Jacinth. Petrie, in his article, assures us that jacinth is zircon, unknown in early Egyptian work, so it may be that the word could be translated as opal, especially in view of the fact opal is not mentioned in the Bible although it must have been known in biblical times.

Some authorities assure us that diamonds and sapphires were used in biblical times, whilst Petrie says, "It is obviously useless to attempt to identify gems which were unknown before the Roman Age with any of the earlier names and hence the diamond and sapphire are outside of the question." One biblical reference which we can be sure has been mistranslated is Revelations 21, verse 11, which reads: "And her light as like unto a stone most precious, even like jasper stone, clear as crystal." We know that jasper is always opaque.

It is interesting to note that scholars and lapidarists have for centuries attempted to determine the names, as we know them, of the gemstones mentioned in both the Old and New Testaments and most of this research is connected with three main lists of stones, namely, those used in the making of Aaron's Breastplate (Exodus 28), the Breastplate of the King of Tyre (Ezekiel 28) and the foundations of the walls of the holy city, described in the Book of Revelations.

Because of the many translations, from the Aramaic, Ancient Hebrew, Latin and Greek, the complexity of this research can readily be appreciated and as Aramaic and Hebrew are read from right to left, transpositions may have occurred. An additional complication is created by the fact that the words used to describe certain stones makes it impossible to arrive at any decision as to what is meant.

A modern reproduction of a Biblical ornament
Aaron's breastplate comprised 12 gemstones, each inscribed with the name of one of the 12 tribes of Israel, and in 1955, Mr A. Paul Davis, an American whose hobby was lapidary work, conceived the idea of creating a replica of this jewel. The necessary research, the acquiring, cutting and engraving of the appropriate stones, together with the goldsmithing, took four years devoted labour, the project being

completed at the end of 1959. An account of this superb example of the lapidary's craft appeared in *The Lapidary Journal* of June 1960 and was subsequently reprinted in the issue of February 1969, together with the results of a brilliant piece of research on the same subject by Mr E. L. Gilmore of Tulsa, Oklahoma.

Mr Gilmore consulted no fewer than 217 books of reference, spanning more than 2,000 years, before arriving at his conclusions regarding the actual stones used by the Israelites, and his findings do not always coincide with those of his fellow countryman.

The late Sir W. M. Flinders Petrie, the famous Egyptologist, also carried out considerable research on the same subject and his findings were not conclusive as he gave two lists which he terms "early" and "late".

The results of these many years of research may be summarised as follows:

Name of Tribe	Hebrew word for appropriate gem	Findings of A. P. Davis	Findings of E. L. Gilmore	Findings of Sir W. M. Flinders Petrie	
				Early	Late
Reuben	Odem	Red Jasper	Sard	Red Jasper	Sard
Simeon	Pitdah	Golden Citrine	Peridot	Yellow/Green Serpentine	Peridot
Levi	Bareketh	Emerald	Malachite	Quartz Crystal	Emerald
Judah	Nophek	Ruby	Garnet	Garnet or Yellow Jasper	Garnet or Topaz
Issachar	Sappir	Amethyst	Lapis Lazuli	Lapis Lazuli	Lapis Lazuli
Zebulon	Yahalom	Yellow Jasper	Corundum	Onyx	Onyx
Joseph	Leshem	Golden Beryl	Amber	Yellow Agate	Yellow Agate
Benjamin	Shebo	Chrysoprase	Agate	Agate, Red Carnelian or Feldspar	Black and White Agate
Dan	Ablamah	Lapis Lazuli	Amethyst	Amethyst	Amethyst
Napthali	Tarshish	Rock Crystal	Beryl	Yellow Jasper or Garnet	Topaz or Garnet
Gad	Shoham	Golden Sapphire	Onyx	Green Feldspar	Beryl
Asher	Yashepheh	Blue Sapphire	Jasper	Dark Green Jasper	Dark Green Jasper

THEOPHILUS – CRAFTSMAN OF A BYGONE ERA

One of the earliest accounts on lapidary work is contained in *The Treatise on Divers Arts* by Theophilus, who is identified by some scholars as a Benedictine monk who lived in Cologne in the middle of the tenth century. Others assert that he was Roger of Helmershausen, whose skill is exemplified by a bejewelled book cover, still to be seen in Nuremburg, and two portable altars which are preserved in Paderborn and which date from about A.D. 1100.

His treatise, which has been translated from the original Latin by many scholars, consists of three books which cover respectively, painting, glass and metalwork. A study of the treatise will amply repay any craftworker for the time spent in reading it, as many of the processes and techniques which he outlines so clearly are applicable today. Although much of the context of the treatise falls outside the scope of this book, his section on polishing gems covers the basic processes which we still must carry out before producing a finished stone.

As may be expected in any medieval work a certain amount of superstition and misapprehension is included, one example being his statement that Rock Crystal is water turned into ice, which age has hardened into stone.

Theophilus' method of polishing gems

It is cut and polished in this manner. "Cement the crystal with chaser's pitch onto a long piece of wood and when cold rub it with both hands on a piece of hard sandstone, adding water until it assumes the required shape. Next, rub it on another stone of the same kind, but finer and smoother, until it becomes completely smooth. Now take a lead plate, flat and smooth, and on it put a moistened tile (which has been abraded to dust with saliva on a hand hone) and polish the crystal on it until it becomes brilliant. Lastly, put some tile dust moistened with saliva on an untanned goat skin which has been stretched onto a piece of wood and fastened on the underside with nails. Rub the crystal on this until it is completely clear."

This procedure is basically identical with that carried out today, simply, the use of suitable abrasives of diminishing degrees of coarseness being used to shape and polish the stone. The substitution of silicon carbide wheels or powders for sandstone and tile dust, plus an electric motor instead of hand rotation, means, however, that the time spent on producing a gem from the rough will take only minutes instead of months.

A primitive method of drilling gems

From what has been previously written, it will be appreciated that the drilling of gem material is the most difficult basic lapidary process, even when using modern techniques. Theophilus, however, had an answer even for this operation.

Apparently, Bishops' staves were surmounted by a knop, frequently made from a gemstone, and his instructions for making a knop are as follows:

"Make yourself two hammers as thick as your little finger, almost a span long, very slender and well steeled at each end. Set the knop in a hollow in a piece of wood so that it lies in half-way and fix it in firmly with wax. Now take one of the small hammers and strike gently in one place in the middle of the knop until you make a small hole. Then enlarge the hole by striking in the middle and by carefully chipping around.

"Keep working in this way until you reach the mid-point of the knop; then turn it over and do the same on the other side until you have pierced it through. Then hammer a copper rod, a foot or so long, so that it can go through the hole, take some sharp sand mixed with water, put it in the hole and file with the copper rod. When you have widened the hole a little, hammer out another thicker copper rod and file with it in the same way. If need be, use a third copper rod, still thicker.

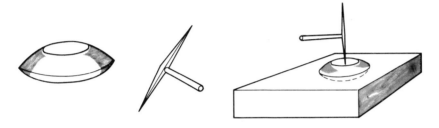

Fig. 55
Drilling gemstones as
outlined by Theophilus

"After enlarging the hole as much as you want, crush some sand stone very finely, put it in the hole and file with a new copper rod until it becomes smooth. Then take some lead, similarly round, add tile dust with saliva and polish the inside and outside of the knop as above."

This procedure may seem to be impracticable, but I can distinctly remember as a child in the North of England, how the slaters when fixing slates and stone roofing slabs, rapidly drilled holes with amazing facility, by repeated blows of the long sharp spikes of their hammers.

Sawing without a diamond saw
In most cases, the first operation in creating a gemstone from a piece of rough is to cut a slice and the instructions outlined in the treatise are fundamentally the same as have been practised by lapidarists all over the world until comparatively recent years. In fact, many American amateurs still use a machine which they term the "mud saw" for cutting very large specimens, sometimes too large to move, in situ, perhaps in the deserts of Arizona, Utah, Nevada or any of the many areas of the U.S.A. where "cuttable rocks" are to be found.

This appliance is simply a large disc of soft steel, often running in simple wooden bearings and driven by a petrol engine or power take-off from a vehicle. The saw rotates in a trough filled with a slurry of grit and water, or alternatively, the slurry may be fed through a drip feed onto the blade at the point of cut and there are many variations of these home-made machines. With this type of saw, the speed of rotation must be slow and only slight pressure exerted, which necessarily means that considerable time is taken to slice through a rock. However, this is a faster process than that described by Theophilus, who writes:

"If you want to cut up a piece of crystal, fix four wooden pegs on a bench so that the crystal lies firmly between them. They should be spaced so that each of the pairs is so closely fitted above and below so that a saw can just be drawn between them and cannot be deflected anywhere.

*Fig. 56
Cutting rock crystal by
primitive method –
Theophilus*

"Then insert an iron saw and throw on sharp sand mixed with water. Have two men standing there to draw the saw and to throw on sand mixed with water unceasingly. This should be continued until the crystal is cut into two parts; then rub and polish them as previously described.

"Hyacinth, which is harder, is polished in the following way. There is a stone called emery, which is crushed until it is like sand, then placed on a smooth copper plate and mixed with water and the hyacinth is shaped by rubbing on this. The washings which run off should be carefully collected in a basin and be allowed to stand overnight. On the following day, the water should be entirely removed and the powder dried. Afterwards, put it on a smooth flat limewood board, wet with saliva, and polish the hyacinth on it."

This procedure is almost identical with present-day practice, as many of the harder gemstones are finished on suitably impregnated copper or wooden laps.

Emery is, of course, another name for corundum, forms of which include both ruby and sapphire, and is second in degree of hardness to diamond, whilst hyacinth or jacinth as it is sometimes termed is another stone whose modern name is debatable. Some authorities assert that it was sapphire whilst others state that it was zircon, but in either case, the method of using the residue from the polishing on the copper lap as a final polish on the limewood lap is sound basic practice.

An ancient superstition
One cannot leave Theophilus without strongly disagreeing with his method of carving rock crystal. It most definitely cannot be recommended as a general classroom practice!

He states, "If you want to carve a piece of rock crystal, take a two- or three-year-old goat and bind its feet together and cut a hole between its breast and stomach, in the place where its heart is, and put the crystal in there, so that it lies in its blood until it is hot. At once, take it out and engrave whatever you want on it, while this heat lasts."

According to the instructions, as the stone cooled, it hardened and the gory process had to be repeated continually until the stone was ready for its final polish, ". . . with a woollen cloth, soaked in the goat's blood!"

It must be concluded that Theophilus was not a lapidarist and was not writing from experience, as this is one of only three deviations from sound workshop practice in the whole of the treatise. With the exception of the final short chapter on the drilling of pearls, the working of stone is mentioned in only one of the ninety-six chapters of which the treatise is comprised.

Although time was of little concern to him, he designed many tools and simple machines, including crude types of lathe and circular saw. Therefore it is reasonable to conclude that, had he ventured into the field of lapidary work, he would have constructed a machine capable of providing rotary motion for his cutting and polishing.

Throughout the ages the craft of the lapidary has been a closely guarded secret, techniques being passed on from father to son, and such information as is recorded in medieval books on the craft is frequently misleading. This may have been done deliberately in order to enhance the esteem in which the craftsman was held by his influential patron, who was usually a member of the nobility or a prince of the Church. It is impossible to estimate the time which must have been taken to grind and polish some of the world's most famous gems, for example the Black Prince's Ruby (which, incidentally, is not a ruby but is, in fact, a spinel) or the Koh-I-Noor diamond, both of which can be seen in the Tower of London.

Both these stones are of great antiquity, the "ruby" being part of the spoils of war at Crecy in 1315 whilst the history of the Koh-I-Noor diamond has been traced to the Rajah of Malwa in 1304, although some reports state that it was owned by Sultan Alu-ad-Din who reigned from 1288 to 1321. When presented to Queen Victoria in 1849, it weighed 186 carats and was subsequently re-cut to improve its brilliance and now weighs 109 carats.

The necessity for re-cutting arose because the original worker did not appreciate the scientific principles which must be observed when faceting a gemstone. Even in very recent years the first consideration of most Eastern cutters was to produce the largest possible finished stone from the rough, rather than considering beauty, shape, form and faceting angles.

Some still carry out their operations either by laboriously rubbing diamond against diamond by hand, emphasising the natural crystal faces, or by using simple machines, operated by hand or foot, the only change which has taken place over many centuries being the use of modern abrasives.

Having taken up the craft as a hobby, there is no reason why we cannot equal, if not surpass, the efforts of these hand workers. It may be said that they have more time at their disposal, but we are more than adequately compensated by the fact that our machines, however simple they may be, are much more speedy than their manual processes.

Glossary of terms

Angstrom Units   The units used to express the wavelengths of light, ultra-violet radiations and X-rays. Abbreviated to AU = 0·0000001 millimetre. Named after the Swedish physicist A. J. Angstrom.

A/F   Engineers' abbreviation to denote the distance across the flats of hexagonal bars of metal.

Anneal(ed)   To heat metal to such a degree that work stresses are relieved enabling it to be worked cold without cracking.

Arbor   A shaft upon which a rotatable part is mounted.

Bails   Open flat metal loops, the ends of which overlap, enabling a pendant to be attached to a chain.

Baroque   Of an indefinite or irregular shape.

Bell Caps   Metal claws which may be manipulated to conform to the shape of a portion of a baroque stone, enabling it to be suspended.

Bolt Ring   A tubular ring of metal, having a slit which is normally closed by a spring-loaded bolt, usually fixed to a chain by a jump ring (q.v.).

Boring Table   A lathe accessary which enables a piece of work to be machined by means of a tool mounted in the chuck.

Botryoidal   Term applied to minerals when their surfaces form spherical protuberances.

Brazing Spelter   Alloy, usually of copper and zinc, used for joining metal together by fusion.

Capacitor   A piece of electrical apparatus, previously known as a condenser, which reduces the current taken from the mains supply when used in a fluorescent lighting circuit.

Chaser   A lathe tool which enables screw threads to be accurately finished.

Chaser's Pitch   A mixture of Burgundy pitch, tallow and plaster of Paris, used to support metal which is being decorated by means of a hammer and punches.

Chatoyancy   The "cat's eye" effect, due to the reflection of light from fibres or channels within a stone. This effect is best seen when stones are cut *en cabochon*.

Choke   A piece of electrical apparatus in a fluorescent lighting circuit, serving two purposes: (a) It provides the initial high voltage to initiate the discharge in the lamp, and (b) it limits the current in the circuit once the discharge has taken place.

Chuck   Device attached to the spindle of a machine tool to grip either the work or a tool.

Chuck, To   To secure a piece of work in position in a chuck.

Cleavage Plane   Layers parallel to the crystal faces of a mineral along which it has a tendency to split.

Colloidal   A state of matter wherein extremely minute particles of one substance are diffused through another.

Continuous Rated   An electric motor which gives its rated output continuously without suffering ill-effects or specified temperature-rise.

Crypto-Crystalline   The term used to define minerals in which the crystals of which it is formed are sub-microscopic.

Crystal   A solid body whose atoms are arranged in a definite pattern. The faces of a terminated crystal are an outward expression of the regular arrangement of the atoms.

Crystal Axes   Lines of reference which intersect at the centre of a crystal. The axes, by their relative lengths and attitudes, determine the system to which a crystal belongs.

Crystallographer   An expert in the study of the properties, structure and forms of crystals.

Culet   The point at which the pavilion facets of a brilliant cut stone meet. Frequently made flat and parallel to the table facet, hence – Culet facet.

Dendritic   Tree-like markings, frequently consisting of oxide of manganese or iron, which occur in rocks.

Dexion   Commercial form of steel angle, having perforations which enable the rapid construction of frames, structures and supports.

Druse   A crust of crystals lining a cavity or a cavity containing crystals. (*See* Geodes.)

Eureka Can   A container, said to have been designed by Archimedes, having a spout which facilitates the measuring of the volume of an irregular object.

Feed   The rate at which a cutting tool is advanced.

Fettling   The process of cleaning the surface and chipping away projections on a casting.

Flameproof   Electrical apparatus so designed that an explosion of inflammable gas within the apparatus will not ignite inflammable gas outside.

Gate   The channel in a mould through which the molten metal is led from the runner to the moulding cavity.

Gel   Apparently solid material of jelly-like appearance formed from a colloidal solution.

Geode   Large cavities in rocks, lined with crystals which have been free to grow inwards. Frequently lined with agate.

Glazed   Term used to denote the condition of a grinding wheel when the spaces between the grits of the cutting face become clogged.

Header   The hollow portion of a mould for lost wax casting which receives the charge of molten metal before it is forced into the moulding cavity.

Igneous   Rock masses formed by the solidification of molten materials injected into the earth's crust.

Investment (Plaster)   A special form of heat-resistant plaster used to make the moulds for lost wax casting.

Jump Ring   Wire ring which can be opened and subsequently closed to encompass a link on a chain. Used to suspend pendants or to accommodate a bolt ring to form chain into necklet or bracelet.

Mandrel   (1) The headstock of a lathe. (2) An accurately turned shaft upon which work already bored can be mounted. (3) Ring mandrel, a tapered cylindrical rod used for shaping rings.

Massive   Minerals which have no definite crystal form or are composed of masses of small crystals.

Matrix   (1) Disc of mild steel around the periphery of which are inserted segments of sintered diamond to form a diamond saw.
(2) The mass of rock in which minerals and crystals are found.

Metamorphosed   Rocks derived from pre-existing rocks by processes operating in the earth's crust.

Microcline (Feldspar)   A silicate of potassium and aluminium which crystallises in the triclinic system forming Amazonite.

Milling Machine   A machine tool in which a horizontal arbor or vertical spindle operates a rotating multi-toothed cutter, the work being supported on a horizontal power-fed table.

Nibs   Projections on the edge of a slice of rock, caused by the slice breaking before being completely sawn through.

Nodules   Occur in sediments. Caused by a nucleus of some mineral grain or fossil which encourages precipitation. Agates and flints are frequently found in nodular form.

Oligoclase (Feldspar)   Consisting of Albite (ideally silicate of sodium and aluminium, but commonly contains small quantities of potash and lime in addition), and Anorthite (silicate of calcium and aluminium) molecules combined in the ratio 9:1 or 7:3. Forms Sunstone or Labradorite.

Orthoclase (Feldspar)   A silicate of potassium and aluminium which crystallises in the monoclinic system to form Moonstone.

Petrologist   A student of rocks with special reference to their mode of origin, chemical and mineral compositions, present conditions, their alteration and decay.

Plagioclase (Feldspar)   An isomorphous series of Albite and Anorthite in all proportions. Triclinic.

Planishing   A hammering process used to finish and harden a surface. Small facets are formed which reflect the play of light and enhance the appearance of the finished work.

Plummer Blocks   Journal bearings for line shafting, etc., consisting of a box form casting enclosing bearing brasses.

Rutiles   Needle-like inclusions of copper-coloured and golden rutile fibres in colourless or pale smoky quartz.

Slocombe Drill   A special drill with a 60° taper end, used for centring bars for turning between centres in a lathe.

Slurry   A thin paste made by mixing plaster or grits with water.

Spectroscope   An instrument which analyses a ray of light into the colours of the spectrum. The light is made parallel by a collimating lens and, falling onto a prism or diffracting grating, is dispersed when the spectrum becomes visible through other lenses.

Sprue In lost wax casting, a tapered wax support for the pattern to be cast. On burning out, the space left becomes the hole through which the metal enters the moulding cavity.

Starter In a fluorescent lighting circuit, the starter is an automatic switch which causes the lamp to be pre-heated by breaking the inductive circuit of the choke (q.v.), thus applying a high voltage across the lamp.

Swarf Material removed by cutting tools during machining operations.

Synthetic Gemstones produced in the laboratory which have the same chemical composition, physical properties and crystal structure as the natural minerals which they represent.

Terminated Crystals Complete crystals which usually have grown to such a size that the crystal faces are obvious, giving them the appearance of having been faceted or polished.

Tolerance The permissible limits of error which may be allowed on a piece of finished work. It is usually shown on drawing alongside the dimension figure, e.g. $0.5'' \pm 0.001$. This shows a tolerance of $\frac{2}{1000}$ inch.

Torque The turning force exerted by a tangential force acting at a distance from the axis of rotation. Expressed in lb/ft.

Tribotechnology The science and technology of interacting surfaces in relative motion.

Tripoli A fine earth used for polishing metals. Frequently bonded into a soap-like bar for use on a buffing machine.

Vugs A cavity in a lode, usually lined with well-formed crystals.

Wasters Foundryman's term for castings which are unsatisfactory.

Useful tables and data

APPENDIX I

Troy weight   Used for precious metals.

$$24 \text{ grains} = 1 \text{ pennyweight} = 7{\cdot}77 \text{ carats}$$
$$20 \text{ pennyweights} = 1 \text{ ounce troy} = 155{\cdot}54 \text{ carats}$$
$$12 \text{ ounces troy} = 1 \text{ troy pound (no longer used)}$$
$$= \tfrac{14}{17} \text{ pound avoirdupois}$$

In this country, since 1920 precious stones must be weighed by the troy ounce (480 grains) divided decimally, or as is more usual, by the metric carat.

$$1 \text{ carat (metric)} = \tfrac{1}{5} \text{ gramme (200 milligrammes)} = 3\tfrac{1}{16} \text{ grains}$$
$$= 0{\cdot}007 \text{ ounce avoirdupois}$$

Avoirdupois

$$16 \text{ drachms} = 1 \text{ ounce} = 437\tfrac{1}{2} \text{ grains} = 141{\cdot}76 \text{ carats}$$
$$= 0{\cdot}91146 \text{ oz. troy} = 28{\cdot}35 \text{ grammes}$$

$$1 \text{ lb.} = 16 \text{ oz.} = 14{\cdot}58 \text{ oz. troy} = 453{\cdot}6 \text{ grammes} = 7000 \text{ grains}$$

Note: The avoirdupois and troy grain are equivalent in weight.

The terms grain and carat may need some clarification to the beginner. The metric and avoirdupois grains are equal weights but the term grain is also used for weighing pearls when it is equal to $\tfrac{1}{4}$ carat.

When applied to precious metals, the term carat represents $\tfrac{1}{24}$ part, hence 18 carat gold is $\tfrac{18}{24}$ pure gold.

APPENDIX 2

Tables of Conversions
Weight
To convert

Grains to Grammes	multiply by		0·0647989
Pennyweights to Grammes	,,	,,	1·55518
Ounces Troy to Grammes	,,	,,	31·1035
Ounces Troy to Metric Carats	,,	,,	155·517
Ounces Avoirdupois to Grammes	,,	,,	28·3495
Ounces Avoirdupois to Metric Carats	,,	,,	141·7475
Ounces Avoirdupois to Grains	,,	,,	437·5
Ounces Troy to Grains	,,	,,	480·0
Ounces Troy to Ounces Avoirdupois	,,	,,	1·09714
Ounces Troy to Pounds Avoirdupois	,,	,,	0·06857
Pounds Avoirdupois to Ounces Troy	,,	,,	14·583328
Pounds Avoirdupois to Grains	,,	,,	7000·0
Grains to Pounds Avoirdupois	,,	,,	0·0001428
Grammes to Grains	,,	,,	15·4324
Grammes to Pennyweights	,,	,,	0·64301
Grammes to Ounces Troy	,,	,,	0·0321507
Grammes to Ounces Avoirdupois	,,	,,	0·035274
Grains to Ounces Avoirdupois	,,	,,	0·0022857
Grains to Ounces Troy	,,	,,	0·0020833
Ounces Avoirdupois to Ounces Troy	,,	,,	0·911458
Pounds Avoirdupois to Kilogrammes	,,	,,	0·4535924
Kilogrammes to Pounds Avoirdupois	,,	,,	2·20462
Kilogrammes to Ounces Troy	,,	,,	32·1507
Kilogrammes to Ounces Avoirdupois	,,	,,	35·274

Length, Area and Volume

Millimetres into Inches	,,	,,	0·03937
Inches into Millimetres	,,	,,	25·4
Square Millimetres into Square Inches	,,	,,	0·00155
Square Inches into Square Millimetres	,,	,,	645·16
Cubic Centimetres into Cubic Inches	,,	,,	0·061024
Cubic Inches into Cubic Centimetres	,,	,,	16·3871

APPENDIX 3

Circumferences useful in calculating pulley combinations, cutting, grinding or polishing speeds

Diameter in inches	Circumference in inches	Diameter in inches	Circumference in inches
1·5	4·71	7	21·99
2	6·28	7·5	23·56
2·5	7·85	8	25·13
3	9·42	8·5	26·7
3·5	10·99	9	28·27
4	12·56	9·5	29·84
4·5	14·13	10	31·41
5	15·7	10·5	32·98
5·5	17·27	11	34·55
6	18·84	11·5	36·12
6·5	20·42	12	37·69

APPENDIX 4

Speed in revs. per minute given by various pulley combinations

Motor pulley at 1450 r.p.m.	Shaft pulley sizes							
	2″	2·5″	3″	3·5″	4″	4·5″	5″	6″
2″	1450	1160	966	828	725	644	580	483
2·5″	1812	1450	1208	1035	906	805	725	604
3″	2175	1740	1450	1243	1087	966	870	725
3·5″	2537	2030	1694	1450	1268	1127	1015	846
4″	2900	2320	1933	1657	1450	1288	1160	966
4·5″	3262	2610	2175	1864	1631	1450	1305	1087
5″	3625	2900	2416	2071	1812	1611	1450	1208
6″	4350	3480	2900	2485	2175	1933	1740	1450

APPENDIX 5

Surface feet per minute of saw blades

Arbor speed of rotation	Diameter of saw, etc.					
	4″	5″	6″	8″	10″	12″
100	105	131	157	209	262	314
250	262	327	392	523	654	785
500	523	654	785	1047	1309	1571
750	785	981	1177	1570	1963	2356
1000	1046	1308	1570	2094	2617	3142
1250	1308	1635	1962	2618	3272	3927
1500	1569	1962	2355	3141	3926	4712
1750	1831	2289	2748	3665	4580	5498
2000	2092	2616	3140	4188	5235	6284
2250	2354	2943	3532	4712	5889	7069
2500	2616	3270	3925	5235	6544	7854
2750	2878	3597	4317	5758	7188	8641
3000	3138	3924	4710	6282	7852	9426

APPENDIX 6

Decimal and metric equivalents of common fractions

Fractions of an inch	Decimals of an inch	Equivalent in millimetres	Fractions of an inch	Decimals of an inch	Equivalent in millimetres
$\frac{1}{64}$	0·01562	0·397	$\frac{33}{64}$	0·51562	13·097
$\frac{1}{32}$	0·03125	0·794	$\frac{17}{32}$	0·53125	13·494
$\frac{3}{64}$	0·04687	1·191	$\frac{35}{64}$	0·54687	13·891
$\frac{1}{16}$	0·0625	1·588	$\frac{9}{16}$	0·5625	14·288
$\frac{5}{64}$	0·07812	1·984	$\frac{37}{64}$	0·57812	14·684
$\frac{3}{32}$	0·09375	2·381	$\frac{19}{32}$	0·59375	15·081
$\frac{7}{64}$	0·10937	2·778	$\frac{39}{64}$	0·60937	15·478
$\frac{1}{8}$	0·1250	3·175	$\frac{5}{8}$	0·625	15·875
$\frac{9}{64}$	0·14062	3·572	$\frac{41}{64}$	0·64062	16·272
$\frac{5}{32}$	0·15625	3·969	$\frac{21}{32}$	0·65625	16·669
$\frac{11}{64}$	0·17187	4·366	$\frac{43}{64}$	0·67187	17·066
$\frac{3}{16}$	0·1875	4·763	$\frac{11}{16}$	0·6875	17·463
$\frac{13}{64}$	0·20312	5·159	$\frac{45}{64}$	0·70312	17·859
$\frac{7}{32}$	0·21875	5·556	$\frac{23}{32}$	0·71875	18·256
$\frac{15}{64}$	0·23437	5·953	$\frac{47}{64}$	0·73437	18·653
$\frac{1}{4}$	0·2500	6·350	$\frac{3}{4}$	0·75	19·050
$\frac{17}{64}$	0·26562	6·747	$\frac{49}{64}$	0·76562	19·447
$\frac{9}{32}$	0·28125	7·144	$\frac{25}{32}$	0·78125	19·844
$\frac{19}{64}$	0·29687	7·541	$\frac{51}{64}$	0·79687	20·241
$\frac{5}{16}$	0·3125	7·938	$\frac{13}{16}$	0·8125	20·638
$\frac{21}{64}$	0·32812	8·334	$\frac{53}{64}$	0·82812	21·034
$\frac{11}{32}$	0·34375	8·731	$\frac{27}{32}$	0·84375	21·431
$\frac{23}{64}$	0·35937	9·128	$\frac{55}{64}$	0·85937	21·828
$\frac{3}{8}$	0·3750	9·525	$\frac{7}{8}$	0·875	22·225
$\frac{25}{64}$	0·39062	9·922	$\frac{57}{64}$	0·89062	22·622
$\frac{13}{32}$	0·40625	10·319	$\frac{29}{32}$	0·90625	23·019
$\frac{27}{64}$	0·42187	10·716	$\frac{59}{64}$	0·92187	23·416
$\frac{7}{16}$	0·4375	11·113	$\frac{15}{16}$	0·9375	23·813
$\frac{29}{64}$	0·45312	11·509	$\frac{61}{64}$	0·95312	24·209
$\frac{15}{32}$	0·46875	11·906	$\frac{31}{32}$	0·96875	24·606
$\frac{31}{64}$	0·48437	12·303	$\frac{63}{64}$	0·98437	25·003
$\frac{1}{2}$	0·5	12·700	1	1·000	25·400

APPENDIX 7

Ring sizes

British Standard Ring Sizes begin at Size A, the smallest, and increase by $\frac{1}{2}$ sizes (A, A$\frac{1}{2}$, B, B$\frac{1}{2}$) to Size Z$\frac{1}{2}$, which is the largest standard size, hence there are 52 different sizes in this range.

Size A is 0·475 in. inside diameter whilst Z$\frac{1}{2}$ is 0·870 in. and the increase between each half size is generally about 0·007 to 0·008 in.

American Sizes, of which there are 25, covering approximately the same range, are numbered 1 (0·486 in. inside diameter) by half sizes to 13 (0·875 in.), the increase between half sizes being mostly 0·016 in.

Continental Sizes, 32 in number, begin with the smallest, numbered 38, which is between the British A and A$\frac{1}{2}$ but smaller than American size 1, being 0·4762 in. inside diameter. Progression is by increases between sizes of 0·0125 or 0·0126 to the largest, No. 69, which is 0·8647 in. inside diameter.

This means that it is possible to obtain 104 different sizes of rings as in five cases sizes coincide.

APPENDIX 8

Gauge comparisons

It is most important for anyone working in precious metals for the first time to become familiar with the method of ordering. In this country, sheet and wire is measured in units of the Birmingham Metal Gague or Shakespeare's Gauge in which the gauge numbers vary in reverse to the British Standard Wire Gauge Numbers, No. 1's Birmingham Gauge being the thinnest whereas in the British Standard Wire Gauge, No. 1 is the thickest.

Beginners may be further confused when reading American publications as in the U.S.A., the Brown and Sharpe Gauge is used, and as in the British Standard Wire Gauge, No. 1 is the thickest size.

Gauge comparisons and approximate weights of sterling silver

Inches	Millimetre	Birmingham Metal Gauge	British Standard Wire Gauge	Brown and Sharpe Gauge	Approximate Weight per square inch in oz. Troy
0·0084	0·213	—	35	—	0·047
0·0085	0·216	1	—	—	0·048
0·0089	0·228	—	—	31	0·049
0·0092	0·234	—	34	—	0·050
0·0095	0·241	2	—	—	0·053
0·010	0·254	—	33	30	0·055
0·0105	0·267	3	—	—	0·059
0·0108	0·274	—	32	—	0·060
0·0112	0·286	—	—	29	0·062
0·0116	0·298	—	31	—	0·064
0·012	0·305	4	—	28	0·068
0·0124	0·315	—	30	—	0·069
0·0136	0·345	—	29	—	0·074
0·014	0·356	5	—	—	0·079
0·0142	0·362	—	—	27	0·081
0·0148	0·376	—	28	—	0·087
0·0159	0·405	—	—	26	0·089
0·016	0·406	6	—	—	0·090
0·0164	0·417	—	27	—	0·094
0·0179	0·455	—	—	25	0·098
0·018	0·457	—	26	—	0·101
0·019	0·483	7	—	—	0·107
0·020	0·508	—	25	24	0·110
0·0215	0·546	8	—	—	0·121
0·022	0·559	—	24	23	0·125
0·024	0·610	9	23	—	0·136
0·0253	0·645	—	—	22	0·139
0·028	0·711	10	22	21	0·158
0·032	0·813	11	21	20	0·181
0·035	0·889	12	—	—	0·198
0·036	0·914	—	20	19	0·202
0·038	0·965	13	—	—	0·215
0·040	1·016	—	19	18	0·221
0·043	1·092	14	—	—	0·243
0·045	1·146	—	—	17	0·248
0·048	1·219	15	18	—	0·272
0·051	1·295	16	—	—	0·289
0·055	1·397	17	—	—	0·311
0·056	1·422	—	17	—	0·312
0·057	1·447	—	—	15	0·313
0·059	1·499	18	—	—	0·334
0·062	1·575	19	—	—	0·351
0·064	1·626	—	16	14	0·361

0·065	1·651	20	—	—	0·368
0·069	1·753	21	—	—	0·387
0·072	1·829	—	15	13	0·395
0·073	1·854	22	—	—	0·416
0·077	1·956	23	—	—	0·435
0·080	2·032	—	14	12	0·443
0·082	2·083	24	—	—	0·458
0·090	2·286	25	—	11	0·515
0·092	2·337	—	13	—	0·529
0·100	2·54	26	—	—	0·578
0·102	2·591	—	—	10	0·597
0·104	2·642	—	12	—	0·608
0·112	2·845	27	—	—	0·634
0·114	2·907	—	—	9	0·658
0·116	2·946	—	11	—	0·682
0·124	3·150	28	—	—	0·702
0·128	3·251	—	10	8	0·749
0·136	3·454	29	—	—	0·770
0·144	3·658	—	9	7	0·816
0·150	3·810	30	—	—	0·867
0·160	4·064	—	8	—	0·891
0·162	4·115	—	—	6	0·899
0·166	4·216	31	—	—	0·928
0·176	4·470	—	7	—	0·992
0·181	4·597	—	—	5	1·018
0·182	4·623	32	—	—	1·030
0·192	4·577	—	6	—	1·089
0·200	5·080	33	—	—	1·134
0·204	5·181	—	—	4	1·156
0·212	5·385	—	5	—	1·201
0·216	5·486	34	—	—	1·224
0·229	5·816	—	—	3	1·314
0·232	5·893	—	4	—	1·331
0·238	6·045	35	—	—	1·348
0·250	6·35	36	—	—	1·412
0·252	6·404	—	3	—	1·424
0·257	6·527	—	—	2	1·449
0·270	6·858	37	—	—	1·531
0·278	7·061	38	—	—	1·576
0·289	7·341	39	—	1	1·648
0·300	7·620	40	1	—	1·708

List of suppliers

Mr K. Parkinson, F.G.A., 11, Fitzroy Street, Hull. Tel. No. Hull 409585.
Finished gems of all types, tumbled stones, rough materials, display
specimens. Diamond saw blades, grinding wheels, grits and polishes.
Shafts, arbors, bearings and all types of discs and equipment for those
wishing to assemble their own machine.

For the specialist, Mr Parkinson supplies a wide range of gem testing
equipment and is always willing to assist with any gemmological or
lapidary problems.

P. & M. Roberts, Atholl Road, Pitlochry, Perthshire, Scotland.
Tel. No. Pitlochry 356.
Manufacturers of the P.M.R. range of lapidary machines, combination
units, saws, lapping machines and tumblers.

Wide range of discs, grits and polishes, templates, British and
American publications, findings in base metals and silver, rough
materials for cutting.

Crafts Unlimited, 21, Macklin Street, London, W.C.2.
Tel. No. 01 242 7053
School Contractors and Hobby Suppliers.

Stock an excellent variety of rough materials for cutting and tumbling,
grits, polishes, powders and resin bonded plastic backed sanding discs.
These discs have proved to have a much longer life than the cloth
backed type.

Agents for P.M.R. and Robilt machines, this firm also carries the
widest possible range of findings. They also cater for many other
crafts, having in stock enamelling kilns, enamels by different manufacturers, kits for kiln making, plastics and books on various crafts.

Hirsh Jacobson Merchandising Co. Ltd, 91, Marylebone High Street,
London, WIM 4AY. Tel. No. 01 935 4709.
Carries a varied range of rough gemstones, tumble-polished stones,
ready slabbed materials, findings in base metals and diamond saw
blades. Agent for Rytime-Robilt Ltd, Australian Lapidary Equipment
manufacturers.

R. F. D. Parkinson & Co. Ltd, Doulting, Shepton Mallet, Somerset.
Tel. No. Granmore 243.
Suppliers of geological specimens, fossils and equipment. Carry a wide
range of rocks and minerals for research, display and educational
purposes in addition to collections for specific purposes.
Rough gem and slabbing materials for lapidary work, including an
excellent stock of British materials.

Mr A. Bennett, Wacot, High Hill, Keswick, Cumberland.
Tel. No. Keswick 797.
Good supplies of selected gem and mineral specimens in boxes and
cases for display. A speciality is Mr Bennett's range of minerals and
fossils from Cumberland, in addition to imported rough materials for
the lapidarist. Tumbled stones and silver findings, books on minerals,
gems and lapidary work and agent for the American "Highland Park"
Lapidary Equipment Company.

Mr J. O. Yates, Wessex Gems, Ltd, "Gemini", Lanham Lane,
Winchester, Hants.
Agent for the P.M.R. range in addition to Australian and American
machines and accessories. Diamond saw blades and drills, grits,
polishes, templates, American publications, findings in base and
precious metals, rough materials for cutting and ready-sliced slabs.
Will also slice materials by arrangement.

Kernowcraft Rocks and Gems, Highertown, Truro, Cornwall.
Tel. No. Truro 2695.
Rough materials for cutting and tumbling, slabbed materials, ready
tumble-polished stones, very wide range of findings in silver, rolled
gold and base metals. Agent for Robilt machines; saw blades, grinding
wheels, polishing materials and templates.

Mr Daryl Roder, Box 77 The Post Office, The Opal Fields,
Andamooka, South Australia.
also c/o The Post Office,
Coober Pedy, South Australia.
Mr Roder buys opal from the diggers personally and will send parcels
to your requirements on approval. I have deliveries sent direct to
school and pay by personal cheque.

Gemrocks Ltd, 7/8, Holborn, London, E.C.1. Tel. No. 01 405 6786.
A wide range of all types of lapidary equipment and accessories, rough
materials for cutting, mineral specimens, findings and books on
lapidary work.

Charles Cooper (Hatton Garden) Ltd, 92/93, Hatton Garden,
London, E.C.1. Tel. No. Holborn 6083.
Comprehensive range of specialists' tools for jewelry work, in addition
to workshop equipment. Although a few findings in base metals are
stocked, the very varied range of findings offered are mostly in gold,
rolled gold and silver.

E. Gray & Son, Grayson House, 12/14/16, Clerkenwell Road,
London, E.C.1. Tel. No. Clerkenwell 1174.
Suppliers of specialists' tools for jewelers, workshop equipment and
tools for school metalwork shops.

Johnson Matthey & Co. Ltd, Vittoria Street, Birmingham, 1. Also
Hatton Garden, London, E.C.1.
Gold and silver in sheet, wire and tube form, solders and fluxes, great
variety of findings of all types in precious metals only.

Brydon, 18, Wordsworth Road, Colne, Lancs. Tel. No. Colne 3617.
Importers, wholesalers and retailers of minerals and gemstones.
Under the personal direction of the proprietor who guarantees
satisfaction.

A good range of materials is stocked, in addition to base metal
findings, books, machines and accessories. Has recently acquired the
sole agency for a superb faceting machine and also offers hand-made
silver findings, specially made to customers' own designs.

Gemstones, 44, Walmsley Street, Spring Bank, Hull, E. Yorks.
Tel. No. 0482 25722.
Manufacturers of a wide range of lapidary machines including saws,
grinders, combination units, lapping machines and tumblers. Also
furnish components for the Do-It-Yourself enthusiast who wishes to
construct his own machines.

An excellent range of findings in gold and silver, in addition to base
metals, is stocked, together with books and a good selection of all
materials.

A special point made by this firm is that they do not stock any dyed or
synthetic materials.

Owners of the famous Parkland Agate Collection, on display at their
premises, reputed to be the finest natural agate collection in the
British Isles.

*Griffin & George Ltd, Ealing Road, Alperton, Wembley,
Middlesex.* Tel. No. 01 997 3344.
Suppliers of a whole range of Technical Studies Kits which includes
one on lapidary work—The Griffin Gemstone Rock Collection.
Packed in stout container, this contains thirty gemstone minerals
suitable for preliminary investigations in cutting, grinding and
polishing as well as five copies of an instruction booklet.

Also suppliers of the "Gemtek" combination lapidary machine and
various other tools. Prices and further details are given in the Griffin
Technical Studies Brochure, available from the above address.

Whilst it is appreciated that there are many other suppliers of
materials and tools for lapidary work and jewelry making, I list these
because I have had personal contact with all of them and have always
received courtesy and satisfaction.

Bibliography

A Dictionary of the Bible. (T. & T. Clarke, 38, George Street, Edinburgh.)

Analytical Concordance to the Bible. R. Young, LL.D. (George Adam Young & Co., Edinburgh).

On Divers Arts, The Treatise of Theophilus. J. G. Hawthorne and C. S. Smith (University of Chicago Press Ltd).

Gem Cutting – A Lapidary's Manual. John Sinkankas (O. Van Nostrand Co., New York).

Van Nostrand's Standard Catalogue of Gems. John Sinkankas.

Tumbler's Guide. Ronald J. Balej (Minnesota Lapidary Supplies, Inc., Minneapolis).

The Art of the Lapidary. Francis J. Sperisen (Bruce Publishing Co., Milwaukee).

Gem Cutter's Guide. Ronald J. Balej (Minnesota Lapidary Supplies, Inc., Minneapolis).

The Art of Gem Cutting. Dr H. C. Dake (Gembooks, Mentone, California).

Gemcraft. L. Quick and H. Leiper (Chilton Company, Book Division, Philadelphia).

Gem Testing. B. W. Anderson (Temple Press, London).

Practical Gemmology. Robert Webster (N.A.G. Press, London).

Gemmologist's Compendium. Robert Webster (N.A.G. Press, London).

Australian Gemstones. R. and N. Perry (A. H. & A. W. Reed, Artarmon, New South Wales).

The Lapidary Journal. Published monthly (Lapidary Journal, Inc., San Diego, California).

Introduction to the Mineral Kingdom. Richard H. Pearl (Blandford Press, London).

Minerals and Rocks. J. F. Kirkcaldy (Blandford Press, London).

Pebbles on the Beach. Clarence Ellis (Faber & Faber, London).

Lakeland Geology. E. H. Shackleton (Dalesman Publishing Co., Clapham, Yorkshire).

Collector's Guide to Minerals, Rocks and Gemstones in Devon and Cornwall. Cedric Rogers (D. Bradford Barton, Truro, Cornwall).

Scottish Gemstones. W. J. McCallien (Rank Xerox).

Silverwork and Jewellery. H. Wilson (Sir Isaac Pitman & Sons, London).

Metalwork and Enamelling. H. Maryon (Chapman & Hall, London).

Modern Jewellery. Graham Hughes (Studio Books, London).

Design and Creation of Jewellery. Robert von Neumann (Sir Isaac Pitman, London).

Creative Casting. Sharr Choate.

Jewellery Making for the Amateur Craftsman. Klares Lewes.

Hand-made Jewellery. Louis Weiner (Van Nostrand Co., New York).

Sources of Road Aggregate in Great Britain. (H.M.S.O.)

Index